Contents

❖

Abbreviations Used in this Book

AAA	American Automobile Association
ABA	American Breeders Association
AKC	American Kennel Club
AARP	American Association of Retired Persons

Introduction

How many vacations have been dampened or cut short over the years because you either couldn't find an appropriate sitter for your beloved pets or you simply couldn't bear to leave them behind? If only you could bring your dog along to explore the scenic areas of the Mid-Atlantic and Chesapeake, chase gulls along a sandy beach, retire before a flagstone hearth...

You can. And Pets Welcome™ is here to show you how. We've done the leg-work for you.

Pets Welcome™ features a compilation of select three-, four- and five-paw hotels and motels, spas and bed-and-breakfast accommodations that welcome you and your pet, so nobody has to stay home.

This book caters to all kinds of budgets by offering an array of lodging options ranging from the luxurious and romantic to the quirky and rustic. Each location, selected for its ambiance, guest amenities and pet-friendliness, has been artfully described, complete with architectural renderings. The summaries provided on each property will enable you to select the ideal location to accommodate the particular travel needs of you and your "best friend." In addition, comprehensive listings of points of interest amenable to both you and your pet are highlighted throughout the guidebook.

Whether you and your pet are seasoned traveling companions or venturing out for the first time, you will be well served by the Humane Society's traveling tips regarding transportation, security and pet care while "on the road." These helpful hints provide insight into traveling by car, plane, boat or train, offering specialized guidance on crating animals, documentation and basic care. Being an informed pet owner will make your trip more enjoyable and comfortable for both you and your pet.

It is our hope and our experience that as you explore the Mid-Atlantic and Chesapeake areas, Pets Welcome™ will become your finest resource and your favorite traveling companion...well, maybe your second-favorite.

What People Are Saying About Our Books

"*Pets Welcome*™ is the definitive guide to traveling with your pet—
and the hotels, inns and resorts that welcome them."
– Pet Business News

"More than just a travel guide…this book selects only those
establishments that offer superior service and care
for pet owners traveling with their pets."
– Pet Age

"Discover the best places to lodge with Fido
by referring to *Pets Welcome*™."
– Dog World

"A perfect guidebook to hotels, inns and resorts."
– Los Angeles Times

As "cover girl," and officer manager of Bon Vivant Press

and owner of authors Kathleen and Robert Fish,

I would like to share the joys of our vacations and working

trips to produce our *Pets Welcome* series. Special thanks to

my bon vivant canine pal, Danny.

— *Dreamer Dawg*

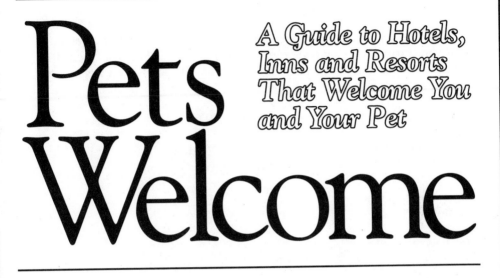

Pets Welcome

A Guide to Hotels, Inns and Resorts That Welcome You and Your Pet

KATHLEEN AND ROBERT FISH

BON
VIVANT

Library of Congress Cataloging-in-Publication Data

Pets Welcome™ Mid-Atlantic and Chesapeake Edition
A Guide to Hotels, Inns and Resorts That Welcome You and Your Pet

Fish, Kathleen DeVanna
Fish, Robert N.
99-071842
ISBN 1-883214-29-7
$15.95 softcover
Includes index

Cover photography by Robert N. Fish
Editorial direction by Judie Marks
Production management by Nadine Guarrera
Cover design by Smith Bowen Advertising, Inc.
Illustrations by Crockett Design Studio; Robin Brickman, Illustrator;
    Gopa Design; and Gerrica Connolly, Design Studio
Interior by Cimarron Design

Published by Bon Vivant Press
a division of The Millennium Publishing Group
P.O. Box 1994
Monterey, CA 93942

Printed in Canada by Friesens

Top Ten Travel Tips

1 Bring your pet's own food, dishes, litter and litter box, leash, collar with ID tags, a first aid kit and a bottle of water from home. This will make your pet more comfortable, prepare you for emergencies and decrease the chances of an upset stomach from a strange brand of food. Maintain the normal feeding and walking schedule as much as possible. Be sure to bring old bath towels or paper towels in case of an accident and plastic bags to dispose of your pet's waste. It is a good idea to bring a picture of your pet for identification purposes in case you and your pet become separated.

2 Bring your pet's vaccination records with you when traveling in state, and a health certificate when traveling out of state. If you plan on boarding him at anytime during your vacation, call the boarding kennel to reserve his space, see what they require you to bring and if they require a health certificate.

3 Bring your pet's favorite toys, leash, grooming supplies, medications and bedding. It is a good idea to bring an old sheet or blanket from home to place over the hotel's bedding, just in case your pet gets on the bed. It will also come in handy to protect your car seats from hair and dirty paws.

4 Tape the address of where you are staying on the back of your pet's ID tag or add a laminated card or new ID tag to your pet's collar, or add a second collar with a friend or family members phone number. This information is also good to have on your pet's collar in case of a natural disaster so that someone out of your area can be contacted if you and your pet become separated.

5 Do not leave your pets unattended in a hotel room. The surroundings are new and unfamiliar to your animal and may cause him to become upset and destroy property he normally would not or bark excessively and disturb your neighbors. You also run the risk of his escaping. If a maid should open the door to clean your room, the pet may see this as a chance to find you and escape, or worse, he may attack the maid out of fear.

6 Train your pet to use a crate. This will come in handy if you ever need to travel by plane. Make sure the crate has enough room for your pet to stand up comfortably and turn around inside. Be sure to trim your pet's nails so that they don't get caught in the crate door or ventilation holes. Crates come in handy in hotel rooms, too. If your pet is already used to being in a crate, he will not object if you leave him in one long enough for you to go out to breakfast. Never take your pet with you if you will have to leave him in the car. If it is 85 degrees outside, within minutes the inside of the car can reach over 160 degrees, even with the windows cracked, causing heat stroke and possible death. According to The Humane Society of the United States, the signs of heat stress are: heavy panting, glazed eyes, a rapid pulse, unsteadiness, a staggering gait, vomiting, or a deep red or purple tongue. If heat stroke does occur, the pet must be cooled by dousing him with water and applying ice packs to his head and neck. He should then be taken to a veterinarian immediately.

7 When your pet is confined to a crate, the best way to provide water for your pet is to freeze water in the cup that hooks onto the door of your pet's crate. This way they will get needed moisture without the water splashing all over the crate. Freezing water in your pet's regular water bowl also works well for car trips.

8 Be sure to put your pet's favorite toys and bedding in the crate. Label the crate with "LIVE ANIMAL" and "THIS END UP," plus the address and phone number of your destination, as well as your home address and phone number and the number of someone to contact in case of an emergency.

9 When traveling by plane, be sure to book the most direct flights possible. The less your pet has to be transferred from plane to plane, the less chance of your being separated. This is also important when traveling in hot or cold weather. You don't want your pet to have to wait in the cargo hold of a plane or be exposed to bad weather for any longer than necessary. Check with airlines for the type of crate they require and any additional requirements. They are very strict about the size and type of crate you may carry on board.

10 Do not feed your pet before traveling. This reduces the risk of an upset stomach or an accident in his crate or your car. When traveling by car, remember that your pet needs rest stops as often as you do. It is a good idea for everyone to stretch their legs from time to time. If your pet is unfamiliar with car travel, then get him use to the car gradually. Start a few weeks before your trip with short trips around town and extend the trips a little each time. Then he will become accustomed to the car before your trip and it will be more pleasant for all involved.

Traveling With Your Pet

Courtesy of The Humane Society of the United States (HSUS)
2100 "L" Street, N.W.
Washington, D.C. 20037

 f you are planning a trip and you share your life with a pet, you have a few decisions to make before you set off. The following are tips to help you plan a safer and smoother trip for both you and your pet.

SHOULD YOU TRAVEL WITH YOUR PET?

Some pets are not suited for travel because of temperament, illness or physical impairment. If you have any doubts about whether it is appropriate for your pet to travel, talk to your veterinarian.

If you decide that your pet should not travel with you, consider the alternatives: Have a responsible friend or relative look after your pet, board your pet at a kennel or hire a sitter to visit, feed and exercise your pet.

If a friend or relative is going to take care of your pet, ask if that person can take your pet into his or her home. Animals can get lonely when left at home alone. Be sure your pet is comfortable with his or her temporary caretaker and any pets that person has.

If you choose to board your pet, get references and inspect the kennel. Your veterinarian or local shelter can help you select a facility. If you are hiring a sitter, interview the candidates and check their references. (A pet sitter may be preferable if your pet is timid or elderly and needs the comfort of familiar surroundings during your absence.)

Whatever option you choose, there are a few things to remember. Your pet should be up-to-date on all vaccinations and in sound health. Whoever is caring for your pet should know the telephone number at which you can be reached, the name and telephone number of your veterinarian and your pet's medical or dietary needs. Be sure your pet is comfortable with the person you have chosen to take care of him or her.

If You Plan to Travel with Your Pet

THE PRE-TRIP VETERINARY EXAMINATION

Before any trip, have your veterinarian examine your pet to ensure that he or she is in good health. A veterinary examination is a requisite for obtaining legal documents required for many forms of travel.

In addition to the examination, your veterinarian should provide necessary vaccinations such as rabies, distemper, infectious hepatitis and leptospirosis. If your pet is already up-to-date on these, obtain written proof.

Your veterinarian may prescribe a tranquilizer for the pet who is a nervous traveler; however, such drugs should be considered only after discussion with your veterinarian. He or she may recommend a trial run in which your pet is given the prescribed dosage so you can observe the effects. Do not give your pet any drug not prescribed or given to you by your veterinarian.

LEGAL REQUIREMENTS

When traveling with your pet, it is always advisable to keep a health certificate (a document from your veterinarian certifying that your pet is in good health) and medical records close at hand. If you and your pet will be traveling across state lines, you must obtain from your veterinarian a certificate of rabies vaccination.

Although pets may travel freely throughout the United States as long as they have proper documentation, Hawaii requires a 120-day quarantine for all dogs and cats. Hawaii's quarantine regulations vary by species, so check prior to travel.

If you and your pet are traveling from the United States to Canada, you must carry a certificate issued by a veterinarian that clearly identifies the animal and certifies that the dog or cat has been vaccinated against rabies during the preceding 36-month period. Different Canadian provinces may have different requirements. Be sure to contact the government of the province you plan to visit.

If you and your pet are traveling to Mexico, you must carry a health certificate prepared by your veterinarian within two weeks of the day you cross the border. The certificate must include a description of your pet, the lot number of the rabies vaccine used, indication of distemper vaccination and a veterinarian's statement that the animal is free from infectious or contagious disease. This certificate must be stamped by an office of the U.S. Department of Agriculture (USDA). The fee for the stamp is $4.

Get Ready to Hit the Road

TRAVEL CARRIERS

Travel carriers are useful when your pet is traveling by car; they are mandatory when your pet is traveling by air. Your pet's carrier should be durable and smooth-edged with opaque sides, a grille door and several ventilation holes on each of the four sides. Choose a carrier with a secure door and latch. If you are traveling by air, the carrier should have food and water dishes. Pet carriers may be purchased from pet-supply stores or bought directly from domestic airlines. Select a carrier that has enough room to permit your animal to sit and lie down but is not large enough to allow your pet to be tossed about during travel. You can make the carrier more comfortable by lining the interior with shredded newspaper or a towel. (For air-travel requirements, see the "Traveling by Air" section.)

It is wise to acclimate your pet to the carrier in the months or weeks preceding your trip. Permit your pet to explore the carrier. Place your pet's food dish inside the carrier and confine him or her to the carrier for brief periods.

To introduce your pet to car travel in the carrier, confine him or her in the carrier and take short drives around the neighborhood. If properly introduced to car travel, most dogs and cats will quickly adjust to and even enjoy car trips.

CAREFUL PREPARATION IS KEY

When packing, don't forget your pet's food, food and water dishes, bedding, litter and litter box, leash, collar and tags, grooming supplies and a first aid kit and any necessary medications. Always have a container of drinking water with you.

Your pet should wear a sturdy collar with ID tags throughout the trip. The tags should have both your permanent address and telephone number and an address and telephone number where you or a contact can be reached during your travels.

Traveling can be upsetting to your pet's stomach. Take along ice cubes, which are easier on your pet than large amounts of water. You should keep feeding to a minimum during travel. (Provide a light meal for your pet two or three hours before you leave if you are traveling by car and four to six hours before departure if you are traveling by airplane.) Allow small amounts of water periodically in the hours before the trip.

On Your Way

TRAVELING BY CAR

Dogs who enjoy car travel need not be confined to a carrier if your car has a restraining harness (available at pet-supply stores) or if you are accompanied by a passenger who can restrain the dog. Because most cats are not as comfortable traveling in cars, for their own safety as well as yours, it is best to keep them in a carrier.

Dogs and cats should always be kept safely inside the car. Pets who are allowed to stick their heads out the window can be injured by particles of debris or become ill from having cold air forced into their lungs. Never transport a pet in the back of an open pickup truck.

Stop frequently to allow your pet to exercise and eliminate. Never permit your pet to leave the car without a collar, ID tag and leash.

Never leave your pet unattended in a parked car. On warm days, the temperature in your car can rise to 160 degrees in a matter of minutes, even with the windows opened slightly. Furthermore, an animal left alone in a car is an invitation to pet thieves.

TRAVELING BY AIR

Although thousands of pets fly every year without experiencing problems, there are still risks involved. The Humane Society recommends that you do not transport your pet by air unless absolutely necessary.

If you must transport your companion animal by air, call the airline to check health and immunization requirements for your pet.

If your pet is a cat or a small dog, take him or her on board with you. Be sure to contact airlines to find out the specific requirements for this option. If you pursue this option, you have two choices: Airlines will accept either hard-sided carriers or soft-sided carriers, which may be more comfortable for your pet. Only certain brands of soft sided carriers are acceptable to certain airlines, so call your airline to find out what carrier to use.

If your pet must travel in the cargo hole, you can increase the chances of a safe flight for your pet by following these tips:

- Use direct flights. You will avoid the mistakes that occur during airline transfers and possible delays in getting your pet off of the plane.

- Always travel on the same flight as your pet. Ask the airline if you can watch your pet being loaded and unloaded into the cargo hold.

- When you board the plane, notify the captain and at least one flight attendant that your pet is traveling in the cargo hold. If the captain knows that pets are on board, he or she may take special precautions.

- Do not ship pug-nosed dogs and cats such as Pekinese, Chow Chows and Persians in the cargo hold. These breeds have short nasal passages that leave them vulnerable to oxygen deprivation and heat stroke in cargo holds.

- If traveling during the summer or winter months, choose flights that will accommodate temperature extremes. Early morning or late evening flights are better in the summer; afternoon flights are better in the winter.

- Fit your pet with two pieces of identification—a permanent ID tag with your name and home address and telephone number and a temporary travel ID with the address and telephone number where you or a contact person can be reached.

- Affix a travel label to the carrier, stating your name, permanent address and telephone number and final destination. The label should clearly state where you or a contact person may be reached as soon as the flight arrives.

- Make sure your pet's nails have been clipped to protect against their hooking in the carrier's door, holes and other crevices.

- Give your pet at least a month before your flight to become familiar with the travel carrier. This will minimize his or her stress during travel.

- Your pet should not be given tranquilizers unless they are prescribed by your veterinarian. Make sure your veterinarian understands that this prescription is for air travel.

- Do not feed your pet for four to six hours prior to air travel. Small amounts of water can be given before the trip. If possible, put ice cubes in the water tray attached to the inside of your pet's kennel. A full water bowl will only spill and cause discomfort.

- Try not to fly with your pet during busy travel times such as holidays and summer. Your pet is more likely to undergo rough handling during hectic travel periods.

- Carry a current photo of your pet with you. If your pet is lost during the trip, a photograph will make it easier for airline employees to search effectively.

- When you arrive at your destination, open the carrier as soon as you are in a safe place and examine your pet. If anything seems wrong, take your pet to a veterinarian immediately. Get the results of the examination in writing, including the date and time.

Do not hesitate to complain if you witness the mishandling of an animal—either yours or someone else's—at any airport.

If you have a bad experience when shipping your animal by air, contact The HSUS, the U.S. Department of Agriculture (USDA) and the airline involved. To contact the USDA write to: USDA, Animal, Plant and Health Inspection Service (APHIS), Washington, D.C. 20250.

TRAVELING BY SHIP

With the exception of assistance dogs, only a few cruise lines accept pets—normally only on ocean crossings and frequently confined to kennels. Some lines permit pets in private cabins. Contact cruise lines in advance to find out their policies and which of their ships have kennel facilities. If you must use the ship's kennel, make sure it is protected from the elements.

Follow the general guidelines suggested for other modes of travel when planning a ship voyage.

TRAVELING BY TRAIN

Amtrak currently does not accept pets for transport unless they are assistance dogs. (There may be smaller U.S. railroad companies that permit animals on board their trains.) Many trains in European countries allow pets. Generally, it is the passengers' responsibility to feed and exercise their pets at station stops.

HOTEL ACCOMMODATIONS

There are approximately 8,000 hotel, motels and inns across the United States that accept guests with pets. Most hotels set their own policies, so it is important to call ahead and ask if pets are permitted and if there is a size limit.

IF YOUR PET IS LOST

Whenever you travel with your pet, there is a chance that you and your pet will become separated. It only takes a moment for an animal to stray and become lost. If your pet is missing, immediately canvas the area. Should your pet not be located within a few hours, take the following action:

- Contact the animal control departments and humane societies within a 60-mile radius of where your pet strayed. Check with them each day.

- Post signs at intersections and in store fronts throughout the area.

- Provide a description and a photograph of your missing pet to the police, letter carriers or delivery people.

- Advertise in newspapers and with radio stations. Be certain to list your hotel telephone number on all lost-pet advertisements.

A lost pet may become confused and wary of strangers. Therefore, it may be days, or even weeks, before the animal is retrieved by a Good Samaritan. If you must continue on your trip or return home, arrange for a hotel clerk or shelter employee to contact you if your pet is located.

DO YOUR PART TO MAKE PETS WELCOME GUESTS

Many hotels, restaurants and individuals will give your pet special consideration during your travels. It is important for you to do your part to ensure that dogs and cats will continue to be welcomed as traveling companions. Obey local animal-control ordinances, keep your animal under restraint and be thoughtful and courteous to other travelers.

If you have more specific questions or are traveling with a companion animal other than a dog or cat, contact the Companion Animals section of the HSUS.

HELPFUL HINTS

- To transport birds out of the United States, record the leg-band or tattoo number on the USDA certificate and get required permits from the U.S Fish and Wildlife Service.

- Carry a current photograph of your pet with you. If your pet is lost during a trip, a photograph will make it easier for others (airline employees, the police, shelter workers, etc.) to help find your pet.

- While thousands of pets fly without problems every year, there are risks involved. The HSUS recommends that you do not transport your pet by air unless absolutely necessary.

- Whenever you travel with your pet, there is a chance that you and your pet will be separated. If your pet is lost, immediately canvas the area and take appropriate action.

PETS WELCOME™
Delaware

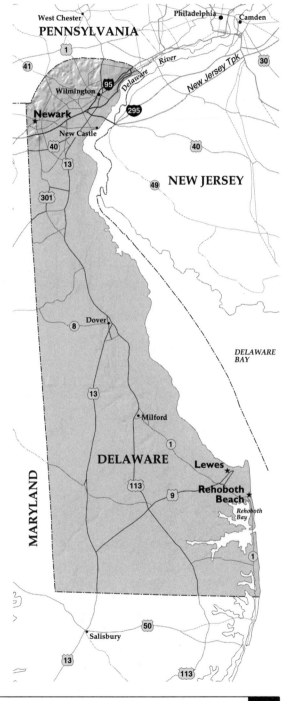

Kings Inn

Kings Inn
151 Kings Highway
Lewes, Delaware 19958
302-645-6438
E-mail: prockett@juno.com

Room Rates:	$65–$85, including full breakfast. Call for discounts.
Pet Charges or Deposits:	$5 per day. Credit card imprint required. Manager's prior approval required.
Rated: 3 Paws ❀❀❀	5 guest rooms.

Lewes, the "First Town in the First State," is full of small-town charm. Dating from 1631, it has an interesting and varied history, which can be savored on a walking tour of historical houses, churches and parks. The downtown area is replete with shops, boutiques and excellent restaurants, while maintaining a relaxed, tree-lined quietness. Lewes, centrally located for many tourists, is 2½ hours from Washington D.C., Philadelphia and Baltimore and 4 hours from New York City.

The Kings Inn, built in 1888, features a large period room with high ceilings and stained glass. Guest rooms are reached by an impressive staircase in the foyer or by the convenient back stair. Quiet, personal entertainment includes a Jacuzzi for two, videos, cable TV, and a stereo with classical, operatic and jazz collections. Bicycles are available for guest use. Swedish coffee and hot cinnamon bread with berries are served each morning in the plant-filled sunroom.

Residence Inn by Marriott

Residence Inn by Marriott
240 Chapman Road
Newark, Delaware 19702
800-331-3131 ▪ 302-453-9200
Web Site: www.residenceinn.com

Room Rates:	$83–$165, including continental breakfast and weekday evening reception. AAA, AARP, Entertainment and Quest discounts.
Pet Charges or Deposits:	$50 per day.
Rated: 3 Paws ❄❄❄	120 guest suites with fireplaces and kitchens. Pool, whirlpool, sports court and complimentary health club passes. Coin-operated laundry on premises.

Residence Inn offers a pool to keep cool, heated spa to melt tensions away, the popular Sport Court® to expend energy and a quiet suites where guests can relax in privacy with cable TV and free daily newspaper.

The versatile suites feature separate sleeping and living areas; fully equipped kitchens with refrigerator, microwave and coffeemaker; plenty of space for entertaining or meeting with colleagues and space to set up an office when you're on the road.

Corner Cupboard Inn

Corner Cupboard Inn
50 Park Avenue
Rehoboth Beach, Delaware 19971
302-227-8553
Web Site: www.dmv.com/business/ccinn
E-mail: ccinn@dmv.com

Room Rates:	$80–$250, including breakfast and dinner.
Pet Charges or Deposits:	$15 per day.
Rated: 3 Paws ❄❄❄	18 guest rooms.

A tradition in some families for generations, the Corner Cupboard Inn is a quiet oasis in this thriving resort town. A short walk will bring you into the hustle and bustle of downtown Rehoboth, with its many shops and boutiques. The ocean is so near, you can often hear the surf above the wind in the pine trees surrounding the Inn.

Air-conditioned guest rooms feature private baths with rooms in the main house, charming annex or cottage rooms with either private or shared patios.

The restaurant is open to the public from Memorial Day weekend through the middle of September. Rates for house guests include both breakfast and dinner. Dine on such local favorites as soft-shell crabs, lobster and prime rib. A selection of homemade desserts is always available.

WHERE TO TAKE YOUR PET IN

Delaware

Please Note: *Pets must be on a leash at all times and may be restricted to certain areas. For directions, use fees, pet charges and general information, contact the numbers listed below.*

Visitor Information

Delaware Tourism Office
99 Kings Highway
P.O. Box 1401
Dover, Delaware 19903
800-441-4271
302-739-4271

State Parks General Information

Delaware Division of Parks
  and Recreation
89 Kings Highway
P.O. Box 1401
Dover, Delaware 19903
302-739-4702

Delaware Division of Fish
  and Wildlife
89 Kings Highway
P.O. Box 1401
Dover, Delaware 19903
302-739-4431

State Parks

DAGSBORO

Holts Landing State Park encompasses 746 acres of parkland. It is located 9 miles northeast of Dagsboro, off State Route 26, on the south shore of the Indian River. Visitors to the park will enjoy picnic areas, hiking trails, boating, a boat ramp, fishing, game courts and horse trails.

DEWEY BEACH

Delaware Shore State Park, located 14 miles from Dewey Beach to the Indian River Inlet off State Route 1, is a 2,656-acre park offering camping, picnic areas, boating, a boat ramp, fishing, swimming, hiking trails, sailing and wind-surfing.

DOVER

Killens Pond State Park, 12 miles south of Dover, off U.S. Highway 13, is a historic 1,207-acre park offering camping, picnic areas, hiking and nature trails, canoeing, boating, a boat ramp, boat rentals, fishing and swimming.

FENWICK ISLAND

Fenwick Island State Park is a 442-acre park extending from South Bethany Beach to Fenwick Island off State Route 1. Visitors to the park will find picnic areas, boating, fishing and swimming.

LAUREL

Trap Pond State Park is a 2,517-acre park located 6 miles southeast of Laurel off State Route 24. It offers camping, picnic areas, hiking trails, horse and nature trails, boating, a boat ramp, boat rentals, fishing, swimming and a visitors' center.

LEWES

Cape Henlopen State Park, 1 mile east of Lewes on State Route 9, is a historic 4,013-acre park with camping, picnic areas, hiking and bicycle trails, fishing, swimming, game courts, nature trails and a visitors' center.

NEWARK

Lums Pond State Park is a historic 1,884-acre park located 10 miles south of Newark off State Route 71, offering camping, picnic areas, hiking trails, boating, a boat ramp, boat rentals, fishing, swimming, winter sports, horse and nature trails and a visitors' center.

White Clay Creek State Park, 3 miles north of Newark via State Route 896, consists of 1,862 acres of historic parkland with picnic areas, fishing, hiking and horse trails, winter sports and a visitors' center.

PEA PATCH ISLAND

Fort Delaware State Park, located on Pea Patch Island, encompasses 710 acres of historic parkland, with picnic areas, fishing, hiking and nature trails and a visitors' center. For more information, call 302-834-7941.

SOUTH BETHANY BEACH

Fenwick Island State Park is a 442-acre park extending from South Bethany Beach to Fenwick Island off State Route 1. Visitors to the park will find picnic areas, boating, fishing and swimming.

WILMINGTON

Bellevue State Park, located 4 miles northeast of Wilmington off Interstate 95, is a historic 506-acre park with picnic areas, hiking and bicycle trails, fishing, winter sports, game courts and horse trails.

Brandywine Creek State Park, 9 miles east of Wilmington at the junction of State Routes 92 and 100 and Adams Dam Road, is a 1,009-acre park offering picnic areas, hiking and bicycle trails, fishing, winter sports, horse trails and a visitors' center. For more information, call 302-571-7747.

Veterinary Care in Delaware

B

Lums Pond Animal Hospital
3052 Wrangle Hill Road
Bear, DE 19701
302-836-5585

Bridgeville Animal Hospital
Route 13
Bridgeville, DE 19933
302-337-7524

Four Paws Animal Hospital
Country Road 531
Bridgeville, DE 19933
302-629-7297

C

Claymont Animal Hospital
3315 Philadelphia Pike
Claymont, DE 19703
302-798-4368

D

Glasgow Veterinary Center
Peoples Plaza, #650
Delaware City, DE 19702
302-834-1118

Pet Medical Center
Route 13 North
Delmar, DE 19940
302-846-2869

Brenford Animal Hospital
2219 North Dupont Highway
Dover, DE 19901
302-678-9418

Dover Animal Hospital
1151 South Governors
 Avenue
Dover, DE 19904
302-674-1515

Governors Avenue Animal Hospital
1008 South Governors
 Avenue
Dover, DE 19904
302-734-5588

Jeters Animal Hospital
4564 North Dupont Highway
Dover, DE 19901
302-734-3240

G

Cokesbury Equine Clinic
Rural Route 2, Box 700
Georgetown, DE 19947
302-629-2782

Georgetown Animal Hospital
307 North Dupont Highway
Georgetown, DE 19947
302-856-2623

Selbyville Animal Hospital
307 North Dupont Highway
Georgetown, DE 19947
302-856-2623

H

Hockessin Animal Hospital
643 Yorklyn Road
Hockessin, DE 19707
302-239-4383

Lantana Veterinary Clinic
306 Lantana Drive
Hockessin, DE 19707
302-234-3275

Limestone Veterinary Clinic
6102 Limestone Road
Hockessin, DE 19707
302-239-5415

L

Eastern Shore Veterinary Hospital
Georgetown-Laurel Highway
Laurel, DE 19956
302-875-5941

Savannah Animal Hospital
Wescoats Corner Road
Lewes, DE 19958
302-645-8757

M

Atlantic Veterinary Center of Middletown
741 Broad Street
Middletown, DE 19709
302-376-7506

Middletown Veterinary Hospital
366 Warwick Road
Middletown, DE 19709
302-378-2342

Milford Animal Hospital
900 South Dupont Highway
Milford, DE 19963
302-422-3502

N

Red Lion Veterinary Hospital
1047 Red Lion Road
New Castle, DE 19720
302-834-2250

Kirkwood Animal Hospital
1501 Kirkwood Highway
Newark, DE 19711
302-737-1098

New London Veterinary Center
437 New London Road
Newark, DE 19711
302-738-5000

Pike Creek Animal Hospital
297 Polly Drummond Hill
 Road
Newark, DE 19711
302-454-7780

White Clay Creek Veterinary Hospital
107-A Albe Drive
Newark, DE 19702
302-738-9611

R

Rehoboth Animal Hospital
Route 1 and James A Street
Rehoboth Beach, DE 19971
302-227-2009

S

Seaford Animal Hospital
Atlanta Road
Seaford, DE 19973
302-629-9576

Avenue Veterinary Association
10 Artisan Drive
Smyrna, DE 19977
302-653-2300

Smyrna Animal Hospital
5121 Dupont Highway
Smyrna, DE 19977
302-653-9970

W

Brandywine Hundred Veterinary Hospital
806 Silverside Road
Wilmington, DE 19809
302-792-2777

Branmar Veterinary Hospital
2006 Marsh Road
Wilmington, DE 19810
302-475-5700

Centerville Veterinary Hospital
5804 Kennett Pike
Wilmington, DE 19807
302-655-3315

Circle Veterinary Clinic
1531 Maryland Avenue
Wilmington, DE 19805
302-652-6587

Colonial Dog and Cat Clinic
1919 West Fourth Street
Wilmington, DE 19805
302-655-1022

Concord Animal Hospital
3001 Concord Pike
Wilmington, DE 19803
302-478-0648

Kentmere Veterinary Hospital
1710 Lovering Avenue
Wilmington, DE 19806
302-655-6610

Suburban Animal Hospital
2102 Kirkwood Highway
Wilmington, DE 19805
302-994-2574

Windcrest Animal Hospital
3705 Lancaster Pike
Wilmington, DE 19805
302-998-2995

Wilmington Animal Hospital
828 Philadelphia Pike
Wilmington, DE 19809
302-762-2694

PETS WELCOME™
Washington, D.C.

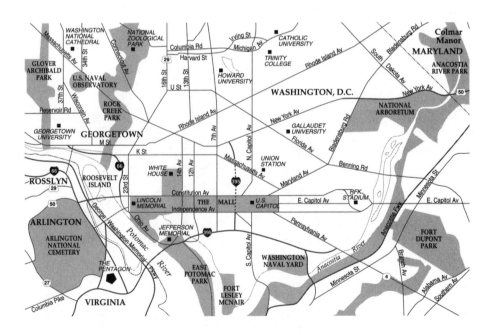

Capital Hilton Hotel

Capital Hilton Hotel
16th Street and K Street Northwest
Washington, D.C. 20036
800-HILTONS ▪ 202-393-1000
Web Site: www.capital.hilton.com

Room Rates:	$159–$359. AAA discount.
Pet Charges or Deposits:	Manager's prior approval required.
Rated: 4 Paws 🐾🐾🐾🐾	544 guest rooms including 34 suites. Health fitness center, restaurants and lounge.

L ocated in the center of downtown Washington, D.C., you are just two blocks from the White House and within walking distance of monuments, museums, shopping, the National Mall, local attractions, restaurants, the metro subway system and many other major points of interest in the city. Airline ticket offices and an airport terminal are located in the same city block.

Guest rooms are comfortably appointed and well designed with three telephones, dataport capabilities, two phone lines, voice mail messaging, two televisions and minibar refreshment center.

DoubleTree Guest Suites

DoubleTree Guest Suites
801 New Hampshire Avenue Northwest
Washington, D.C. 20037
800-222-8733 ▪ 202-785-2000
Web Site: www.doubletreehotels.com

Room Rates:	$119–$179, including continental breakfast on weekends. AAA and AARP discounts.
Pet Charges or Deposits:	$15 per day.
Rated:3 Paws ❀❀❀	101 guest suites. Rooftop pool.

Located amid stately brownstones in one of Washington's finest neighborhoods, Doubletree Guest Suites offers travelers all the comforts of home with easy access to the monuments and museums of the city. Rock Creek Park, a pet-friendly park, is a few blocks from the hotel.

Each of the spacious one- and two-bedroom suites is beautifully appointed with a separate living room and full kitchen. Enjoy the rooftop pool here, or, for a nominal fee, an indoor pool, saunas and fully equipped state-of-the-art health club is nearby.

The Foggy Bottom metro stop is a convenient half block from the hotel. Visit the Smithsonian, the National Gallery of Art, the White House, the U.S. Capitol and the Vietnam Memorial. Enjoy fantastic shopping in historic Georgetown and the Pentagon City Mall. The Kennedy Center is within walking distance of the hotel.

Georgetown Suites

Georgetown Suites
1111 30th Street Northwest
Washington, D.C. 20007
800-348-7203 ▪ 202-298-7800
Web Site: www.georgetownsuites.com

Room Rates:	$125–$300, including continental breakfast. AAA discount.
Pet Charges or Deposits:	$7 per day. $200 refundable deposit.
Rated: 3 Paws 🐾🐾🐾	216 guest suites and townhouses with fully equipped kitchens.

L ocated in the heart of Georgetown, Washington's most prestigious neighborhood, you'll love the tree-lined streets, lovely historic homes and tremendous views of the Potomac River, Washington Harbor, and the John F. Kennedy Center for the Performing Arts. This convenient location offers easy access to the Capitol, White House, monuments, museums and theaters.

Guest rooms are individually decorated, offering a sitting area or separate living room, fully equipped kitchen and free in-room movies.

A complimentary continental breakfast is served daily in the lobby lounge.

Hereford House Bed and Breakfast

Hereford House Bed and Breakfast
604 South Carolina Avenue Southeast
Washington, D.C. 20003
202-543-0102
E-mail: herefordhs@aol.com

Room Rates:	$45–$68, including full breakfast.
Pet Charges or Deposits:	$50 refundable deposit. Manager's prior approval required.
Rated: 3 Paws 🐾🐾🐾	4 guest rooms.

Hereford House Bed and Breakfast, now in its 12th year, is an early 1900s brick townhouse that has been converted into a private home, bed and breakfast and guest cottage on an attractive, quiet, residential avenue on Capitol Hill, one block from the underground subway train. This ideal location is a ten-minute walk to the U.S. Capitol, Supreme Court, Library of Congress and tourmobile for guided tours of the city. Easily reached on foot or by public transportation are the Mall, art galleries and Smithsonian museums.

Guest rooms are clean, well furnished and economical. Three blocks away from the Hereford House is the guest house—a two-bedroom, two-bath cottage with living room. A traditional full breakfast or a healthy continental breakfast is included in your room rates.

Hotel Sofitel

Hotel Sofitel
1419 Connecticut Avenue Northwest
Washington, D.C. 20009
800-424-2464 ▪ 202-797-2000
Web Site: www.sofitel.com

Room Rates:	$199–$259. AAA discount.
Pet Charges or Deposits:	$25 per stay. $25 nonrefundable deposit.
Rated: 3 Paws 🐾🐾🐾	144 guest rooms and 36 suites. A fitness center and sports complex is located across the street. Restaurant.

T he Sofitel Washington, D.C., is an elegant hotel with upscale European service and large, spacious rooms and suites. Located in the heart of the nation's capital, in the fashionable embassy district, this hotel is close to the U.S. Capitol, the White House and the Kennedy Center.

Situated only five miles from the airport, the hotel provides shuttle service for guests. Nearby attractions include Dupont Circle shopping, the K Street business district, the Textile Museum, the Phillips Collection, the House of President Woodrow Wilson and the Smithsonian Institution.

The menu at the Trocadero Café features French regional classics and traditional bistro favorites. A vast selection of French and California wines is available by the glass or bottle.

Hotel Washington

Hotel Washington
515 15th Street Northwest
Washington, D.C. 20004
800-424-9540 ▪ 202-638-5900
Web Site: www.hotelwashington.com
E-mail: sales@hotelwashington.com

Room Rates:	$174–$680. Call for discounts.
Pet Charges or Deposits:	Manager's prior approval required. Sorry, no cats.
Rated: 4 Paws 🐾🐾🐾🐾	350 guest rooms and 16 suites. Restaurants and lounge.

R ecognized as Washington's most prestigious address, at the corner of 15th Street and Pennsylvania Avenue is the Hotel Washington. The hotel overlooks the White House and is at the center of Washington's national landmarks and corporate and federal offices. Unquestionably the consummate location is worthy of a hotel that has hosted virtually every president and vice president of the United States since 1918.

Designed by noted New York architects, the Hotel Washington was created in the European style inspired by the Italian Renaissance. Deep-toned woods and exquisite fabrics inspire a gracious flourish of hues that delight your visual senses.

Madison Hotel

Madison Hotel
15th and M Streets Northwest
Washington, D.C. 20005
800-424-8577 ▪ 202-862-1600

Room Rates:	$225–$425. AAA discount.
Pet Charges or Deposits:	$30 per day.
Rated: 4 Paws 🐾🐾🐾🐾	318 guest rooms and 35 suites with refrigerators, mini-bars, 24-room service. Health Club. Restaurants and lounge.

This prestigious landmark hotel provides a high standard of personalized service in an atmosphere of Old World elegance. The public areas are graced by original paintings and antiques from the owner's private collection.

Set in the heart of the business and government district, the Madison Hotel is within walking distance of the White House, Capitol, museums and Georgetown.

Attractive European-style guest rooms and suites offer magnificent city views, some with balconies. A state-of-the-art Health Club includes a gym, massage room, steam shower, exercise equipment and aerobics.

Swiss Inn

Swiss Inn
1204 Massachusetts Avenue Northwest
Washington, D.C. 20005
800-955-7947 ▪ 202-371-1816
Web Site: www.theswissinn.com
E-mail: Swissinndc@aol.com

Room Rates:	$59–$108. AAA, AARP, AKC and ABA discounts.
Pet Charges or Deposits:	Manager's prior approval required.
Rated: 3 Paws 🐾🐾🐾	7 guest rooms with kitchens.

The Swiss Inn has the distinction of being the smallest hotel in downtown Washington. Family-owned and operated for over a decade, the hotel is a renovated turn-of-the-century, four-level brownstone with high ceilings and bay windows.

Each room has individual heating and air conditioning, a television, a fully equipped kitchenette, a telephone and a private bath. The Inn is surrounded by a well-tended flower garden and offers adjacent parking, free on weekends.

Conveniently located on Massachusetts Avenue, in the heart of Washington, you are within walking distance of the White House, the Smithsonian Museums, Embassy Row, the Washington Convention Center, Chinatown, the monuments and across the street from historic St. Agnes Church.

Swissôtel Washington–The Watergate

Swissôtel Washington–The Watergate
2650 Virginia Avenue Northwest
Washington, D.C. 20037
202-965-2300
Web Site: www.swissotel.com

Room Rates:	$225–$475.
Suite Rates:	$525–$1,950.
Pet Charges or Deposits:	Manager's prior approval required. Small pets only.
Rated: 4 Paws 🐾🐾🐾🐾	100 guest rooms and 150 suites. Health club, sauna and indoor pool. Restaurant and lounge.

Situated on the banks of the Potomac River in the nation's capital, Swissôtel Washington–The Watergate is within walking distance of national monuments, museums and the White House. Adjacent to the Kennedy Center for the Performing Arts, this legendary hotel is part of the fashionable shopping district of Georgetown.

Guest rooms are beautifully appointed and feature two-line phones with voice mail, fax modems and refreshment centers.

Enjoy the pleasures of fine dining at Aquarelle, an exquisite blend of European and American cuisine. The Potomac Lounge features daily afternoon tea and cocktails.

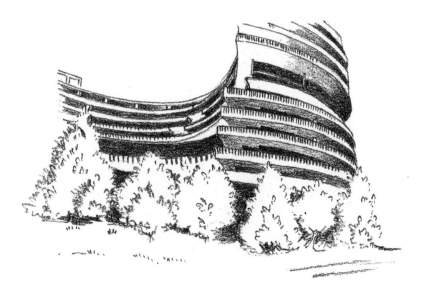

Washington Monarch Hotel

Washington Monarch Hotel
2401 M Street Northwest
Washington, D.C. 20037
888-222-2266 ▪ 202-429-2400
Web Site: www.washingtonmonarch.com

Room Rates: $289–$1,700.
Pet Charges or Deposits: Small pets only.
Rated: 4 Paws 🐾🐾🐾🐾 405 guest rooms and 10 suites. Fitness center with lap pool and mini-spa. Restaurant and lounge with 24-hour room service.

From the open, elegant lobby, sun-drenched loggia and classical garden courtyard to the luxurious accommodations, the Monarch Hotel is an exceptional property for the business or leisure traveler. With a fully staffed Business Center and Fitness Center, you are never far from the desired amenities. Guest rooms feature over-sized writing desks, spacious seating areas, three telephones, mini-bars with refrigerators and a variety of luxurious personal comforts. The 17,000-square-foot health club offers a complete exercise facility, including a lap pool, squash and racquetball courts, fully equipped exercise and weight rooms, massage, sauna and steam room, tanning booths, whirlpool and aerobics classes.

Ideally located downtown in the fashionable West End, the Washington Monarch Hotel is just minutes from museums, monuments, dining options and world-class theater, including the Kennedy Center.

Willard Inter-Continental

Willard Inter-Continental
1401 Pennsylvania Avenue Northwest
Washington, D.C. 20004
800-327-0200 ▪ 202-628-9100
Web Site: www.interconti.com
E-mail: washington@interconti.com

Room Rates:	$350–$505. Senior citizen's discount.
Pet Charges or Deposits:	None.
Rated: 5 Paws 🐾🐾🐾🐾🐾	341 guest rooms and 37 suites. Fitness facility, restaurant and lounge, featuring national jazz musicians.

Meticulously restored to its 1904 grandeur, the Willard is a national landmark that has hosted presidents and others dignitaries. Guest accommodations reflect the charm of the past, while providing all the modern conveniences you expect today. Each lavishly appointed suite features a separate dining room, sitting area and kitchen.

Consistently rated one of the best restaurants in Washington, the elegant Willard Room offers fine contemporary French-American cuisine.

Located two blocks from the White House, the Willard is set amidst Washington's most fashionable shops, restaurants and museums.

Washington, D.C.

Please Note: *Pets must be on a leash at all times and may be restricted to certain areas. For directions, use fees, pet charges and general information, contact the numbers listed below.*

Parks General Information

National Park Service
Public Information Officer
U.S. Department of Interior
1100 Ohio Drive Southwest
Washington, D.C. 20242
202-619-7222

Anacostia Park encompasses 750 acres of parkland and offers visitors a bird sanctuary, tennis courts, basketball courts, soccer and baseball fields, a swimming pool, a skating rink and pavilions, fishing and biking.

Rock Creek Park, located in northwestern Washington, consists of 1,754 acres of parkland. Visitors to the park will enjoy bridle paths, a riding center, tennis courts, picnic areas, golfing, athletic fields and bicycle and jogging trails. For more information, call 202-282-1063.

Maryland (District of Columbia Vicinity)

Chesapeake and Ohio Canal National Historical Park follows the Maryland shore of the Potomac River from Georgetown in Washington, D.C., to Cumberland. For more information, please contact the Superintendent by writing to P.O. Box 4, Sharpsburg, MD 21782, or by phoning 301-739-4200.

Virginia (District of Columbia Vicinity)

GREAT FALLS

Great Falls Park encompasses 800 acres and is off Interstate 495. Take exit 13 at the end of Old Dominion Drive. Here you will find picnic areas and a visitors' center. For more information, call 703-285-2966.

Continued on next page

Veterinary Care in Washington, D.C.

Acacia Animal Clinic
3508 Connecticut Avenue Northwest
Washington, D.C. 20011
202-244-8595

Adams Morgan Animal Clinic
2112 18th Street Northwest
Washington, D.C. 20009
202-638-7470

Animal Clinic of Anacostia
2210 Martin Luther King, Jr. Avenue
Washington, D.C. 20020
202-889-8900

Animal Clinic of Brookland
3428 Ninth Street Northeast
Washington, D.C. 20017
202-269-4850

Animal Clinic of Capital Hill
1240 Pennsylvania Avenue Southeast
Washington, D.C. 20003
202-543-2288

Collins Hospital For Animals
1808 Wisconsin Avenue Northwest
Washington, D.C. 20007
202-659-8830

Dupont Veterinary Clinic
2022 P Street Northwest
Washington, D.C. 20036
202-466-2211

Friendship Hospital For Animals
4105 Brandywine Street Northwest
Washington, D.C. 20016
202-363-7300

Georgetown Veterinary Hospital
2916 M Street Northwest
Washington, D.C. 20007
202-333-2140

Jane's Veterinary Clinic
520 Eighth Street Southeast
Washington, D.C. 20003
202-543-6699

Kindcare Animal Hospital
3622 12th Street Northeast
Washington, D.C. 20017
202-635-3622

MacArthur Animal Hospital
4832 MacArthur Boulevard Northwest
Washington, D.C. 20007
202-337-0120

Petworth Animal Hospital
4012 Georgia Avenue Northwest
Washington, D.C. 20011
202-723-7142

Ross Veterinary Hospital
5138 MacArthur Boulevard Northwest
Washington, D.C. 20016
202-363-1316

Southeast Animal Hospital
2309 Pennsylvania Avenue Southeast
Washington, D.C. 20020
202-584-2125

Continued from previous page

ROCKVILLE

Rock Creek Regional Park is located 4 miles east of Rockville on State Route 28, then 2 miles north on Muncaster Mill Road to Avery Road. This 1,740-acre park offers a nature center, archery, golf, nature trails, picnic areas, hiking and bicycle trails, boating, boat rentals and fishing. For more information, call 301-948-5053 or 301-495-2525.

TRIANGLE

Prince William Forest Park consists of 18,571 acres along Quantico Creek. It is located off Interstate 95. Take exit 150, then go a quarter mile west on State Route 619. Here you will find camping, picnic areas, hiking and bicycle trails, fishing, winter sports and a visitors' center. For more information, call 703-221-7181.

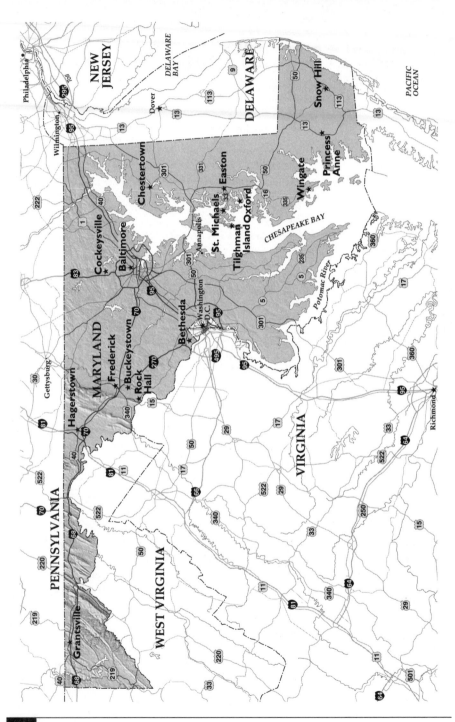

Admiral Fell Inn

Admiral Fell Inn
888 South Broadway
Baltimore, Maryland 21231
800-292-4667 ▪ 410-522-7377
Web Site: www.admiralfell.com
E-mail: pet@admiralfell.com

Room Rates:	$135–$195, including continental breakfast. AAA and AARP discounts.
Pet Charges or Deposits:	$75 per day. Sorry, no cats.
Rated: 3 Paws 🐾🐾🐾	75 guest rooms and 5 suites. Three restaurants.

T his historic urban inn is located downtown at water's edge in historic Fell's Point, Baltimore's original deep-water port. This lively and colorful community is renowned for its Belgian block streets and brick sidewalks, and its many antique shops, boutiques, art galleries, pubs and gourmet restaurants.

Comprised of eight adjoining buildings, some of which date back more than 200 years, the Admiral Fell Inn is just a water taxi ride away from Baltimore's acclaimed Inner Harbor attractions as well as Little Italy, Oriole Park at Camden Yards, museums, theaters and other cultural activities.

Guest rooms are custom-designed with Federal Period furnishings, each with a modern bathroom, color cable television and air conditioning. The two-story suites feature fireplaces and Jacuzzis.

Biltmore Suites Hotel

Biltmore Suites Hotel
205 West Madison Street
Baltimore, Maryland 21201
800-868-5064 ▪ 410-728-6550
Web Site: www.inn-guide.com/biltmoresuites

Room Rates:	$99–$139, including deluxe continental breakfast. Call for discounts.
Pet Charges or Deposits:	$20 per stay. Small pets only.
Rated: 3 Paws 🐾🐾🐾	26 guest rooms and 17 suites.

T he Biltmore Suites Hotel is a small luxury hotel providing guests with distinctive services and contemporary luxuries. Thoughtful details include mini-bars in every room or suite, the Wall Street Journal and USA Today, complimentary limousine and 24-hour concierge service, in a setting of elegance, with world-class accommodations. Your car is valet-parked, your bags are placed in your room, dinner reservations are made at the most popular restaurants and the staff is dedicated to your service.

A full European breakfast and an evening reception featuring an international wine tasting are compliments of the Biltmore. The hotel is located a few blocks from the central business district within the historic Mount Vernon area, adjacent to Antique Row and within walking distance of the Inner Harbor and Oriole Park at Camden Yards.

Residence Inn—Bethesda Downtown

Residence Inn—Bethesda Downtown
7335 Wisconsin Avenue
Bethesda, Maryland 20814
800-331-3131 ▪ 301-718-0200

Room Rates:	$159–$199, including continental breakfast and weekday social hour. AAA, AARP and Entertainment discounts.
Pet Charges or Deposits:	$5 per day. $100 non-refundable fee.
Rated: 3 Paws 😺😺😺	187 guest suites. Outdoor pool, exercise room, sauna. Full spa nearby.

These spacious suites provide all the comforts and conveniences you'll need, including fully equipped kitchen, large living room, fireplace, private entrance, efficient work space with computer hookup, multi-phone lines and laundry facilities.

Start your day off with a complimentary continental breakfast, then move on to the fitness facilities for a workout before heading off for business or a day of sightseeing.

Catoctin Inn and Conference Center

Catoctin Inn and Conference Center
3613 Buckeystown Pike
Box 243
Buckeystown, Maryland 21717
800-730-5550 ▪ 301-874-5555
Web Site: www.catoctininn.com
E-mail: catoctin@fred.net

Room Rates:	$85–$150, including full breakfast. AAA and AARP discounts.
Pet Charges or Deposits:	Manager's prior approval required.
Rated: 3 Paws ❀❀❀	19 guest rooms and 1 suite on 4 acres. Hot tub. Restaurant.

T he Catoctin Inn, circa 1780, offers a variety of distinctive cottages and guest rooms with special touches to make your stay cozy and comfortable. From antique elegance to local folk-art furnishings, each guest room is individually decorated and uniquely furnished. Amenities include handmade quilts, gas fireplaces, two-person whirlpool bathtubs, mini refrigerators and coffeemakers.

As a guest of the Inn you are invited to enjoy a full country breakfast each morning, served in the dining room or on the sun porch. The breakfast includes homemade granola, muffins and breads, as well as fresh fruit, juice, coffee and tea. Scrumptious French toast or fluffy pancakes with bacon or sausage round out the menu. Share afternoon tea in the parlor, furnished with family antiques, or lose yourself in the spacious library, graced with marble fireplaces and filled with books and magazines.

River Run at Rolph's Wharf

River Run at Rolph's Wharf
1008 Rolph's Wharf Road
Chestertown, Maryland 21620
800-894-6347 ▪ 410-778-6389
E-mail: rolphs@aol.com

Room Rates: $75–$115, including continental breakfast.
Pet Charges or Deposits: Manager's prior approval required. Credit card number for
                         deposit.
Rated: 3 Paws   6 guest rooms on 6 acres on the Chester River.

T his 1830s Victorian home, situated amid 6 acres on the scenic Chester River, is only three miles from historic Chestertown. You have your choice of six charming, air-conditioned guest rooms, all with private baths.

A continental breakfast is included, with home-baked breads, fresh-squeezed orange juice, cereal, hot coffee and tea.

Tidewater Inn and Conference Center

Tidewater Inn and Conference Center
101 East Dover Street
Easton, Maryland 21601
800-237-8775 ▪ 410-822-1300
Web Site: www.tidewaterinn.com
E-mail: info@tidewaterinn.com

Room Rates:	$95–$170. AAA and AARP discounts.
Pet Charges or Deposits:	Dogs are not allowed in guest rooms, but are kept in kennels on property. Sorry, no cats. Manager's prior approval required.
Rated: 3 Paws 🐾🐾🐾	114 guest rooms and 6 suites. Refrigerators, pool.

From the moment you enter the lobby of the Tidewater Inn, you feel like a guest in a fine home. Warm, rich mahogany doors, fine 18th-century reproduction furniture, the glow of brass lamps and crackling, open fireplaces invite you to relax and enjoy your visit.

Located in Easton, Maryland, where the tree-lined streets invite you to explore a patchwork of charming antique shops and boutiques. Guests can relax at the outdoor pool or take advantage of excellent nearby golfing, fishing and sailing.

Turning Point Inn

Turning Point Inn
3406 Urbana Pike
Frederick, Maryland 21701
301-831-8232

Room Rates:	$80–$150, including a hearty country breakfast.
Pet Charges or Deposits:	Manager's prior approval required.
Rated: 3 Paws 🐾🐾🐾	5 guest rooms and 2 cottages on 5 acres. Restaurant.

T he Turning Point Inn is a lovely Edwardian-era estate home with Georgian features. Built in 1910, and set back on five acres of tree-studded lawn, the home reflects the gracious elegance of a bygone era.

Accommodations feature beautifully appointed bedrooms "out of the pages of *House Beautiful*," as appreciative guests have written. Two guest cottages are located behind the Inn, offering a comfortable living room downstairs and a large bedroom with a king-sized bed and bath upstairs.

The Turning Point Restaurant specializes in contemporary cuisine that utilizes the essence of Mediterranean, Southern and Asian flavors. A nationally acclaimed wine list is offered to complement the menu.

Walnut Ridge Bed and Breakfast

Walnut Ridge Bed and Breakfast
92 Main
P.O. Box 368
Grantsville, Maryland 21536
888-419-2568 ▪ 301-895-4248
Web Site: www.walnutridge.net
E-mail: walnutridge@usa.net

Room Rates:	$75–$125, including full breakfast. AAA discount.
Pet Charges or Deposits:	$10 per day. Small pets only. Manager's prior approval required.
Rated: 3 Paws 🐾🐾🐾	2 guest rooms, 1 suite and 1 log cabin.

Walnut Ridge is a quaint, quiet, romantic getaway spot in historic Grantsville, in Garrett County, Maryland. The circa 1864 farmhouse is lovingly furnished with antiques, quilts, family heirlooms and country collectibles. Enjoy fireside chats, sing along with the antique player piano, stroll through the theme gardens, relax on the front porch swing, or enjoy hot tubbing under the stars within the garden gazebo.

Walnut Ridge Bed and Breakfast is a small inn offering two rooms, a country suite and even a log cabin. Each room offers a private bath, a cozy sitting area, and a desk or work area. Some rooms boast a fireplace or kitchen. In all, comfort abounds with feather-bed toppers, flannel sheets and handmade quilts.

Four Points Sheraton

Four Points Sheraton
1910 Dual Highway
Hagerstown, Maryland 21740
800-325-3535 ▪ 301-790-3010
Web Site: www.fourpoints.com
E-mail: fourpointshagerstown@erols.com

Room Rates:	$89–$149, including continental breakfast. AAA and AARP discounts.
Pet Charges or Deposits:	No pets over 100 lbs. $75 refundable deposit.
Rated: 3 Paws 🐾🐾🐾	104 guest rooms, 2 Jacuzzi suites. Disabled facilities available. Replays Sports Bar and restaurant, fully equipped fitness/exercise room with Jacuzzi and sauna.

Nicknamed "The Hub City" for its central location, near Harpers Ferry National Park, Gettysburg, the Eastern Panhandle of West Virginia and Central Pennsylvania, Hagerstown is only a short drive from Baltimore, Maryland, and Washington, D.C.

Comfortably spacious guest rooms feature remote-control TVs with complete cable package, telephones with built-in computer jacks and individually controlled in-room heat/air conditioning. All Executive Rooms are equipped with desks and plush sitting areas to make your stay more comfortable.

Residence Inn by Marriott

Residence Inn by Marriott
10710 Beaver Dam Road
Hunt Valley, Maryland 21030
410-584-7370

Room Rates:	$125–$159, including continental breakfast. AAA and AARP discounts.
Pet Charges or Deposits:	$5 per day. $100 refundable deposit.
Rated: 3 Paws 🐾🐾🐾	96 guest rooms and 96 guest suites. Outdoor pool, Jacuzzi, laundry valet.

I f you need accommodations for a short business trip or an extended family vacation, with plenty of space and the comforts of home, then this Residence Inn fits the bill. Here, your suite will be larger than the normal hotel room, with the convenience of a fully equipped kitchen and a private sleeping area.

Start your morning with a complimentary buffet breakfast. For aquatic relaxation, the pool or the Jacuzzi may call you. Golfing at Longview Golf Course Pine Ridge is nearby.

Combsberry

Combsberry
4837 Evergreen Road
Oxford, Maryland 21654
410-226-5253
Web Site: www.combsberry.com
E-mail: info@combsberry.com

Room Rates:	$250–$395, including full breakfast and cocktail/tea hour.
Pet Charges or Deposits:	$50 refundable deposit. Manager's prior approval required.
Rated: 4 Paws	5 guest rooms and 2 suites on 9 acres with formal gardens.

Set among mature magnolias and arching willows on the banks of Island Creek, Combsberry is one of Talbot County's premier historic homes, designed for unsurpassed comfort and privacy.

The unusual stair tower, hidden cellar and eight-arched fireplaces represent unique period design. All guest rooms provide splendid water views and are beautifully appointed with custom furnishings, fireplaces and large baths with Jacuzzis.

At Combsberry you will enjoy the kind of gracious hospitality and casual elegance for which the Eastern Shore of Maryland is well known. After a day of exploring the many sights in nearby Oxford, Easton and St. Michaels, returning home to Combsberry refreshes your spirit with the best of yesterday and today.

Waterloo Country Inn

Waterloo Country Inn
28822 Mount Vernon Road
Princess Anne, Maryland 21853
410-651-0883
Web Site: www.waterloocountryinn.com
E-mail: innkeeper@waterloocountryinn.com

Room Rates: $105–$225, including a full breakfast.
Pet Charges or Deposits: None. Manager's prior approval required.
Rated: 4 Paws 🐾🐾🐾🐾 3 guest rooms and 2 suites on 38 acres. Outdoor pool.

Step back in time and share the elegance and beauty of this fully restored, historic 1750s hidden jewel, which is listed on the National Register of Historic Places. The luxurious pre-Revolutionary waterfront estate is situated on a tidal pond, a habitat for wildlife and birds, with trails for walking. An outdoor pool, canoes and bicycles give you the opportunity to enjoy the serene, peaceful atmosphere.

Guest rooms feature antique furnishings with some Victorian reproductions. The Inn offers luxury suites with Jacuzzis and charming guest rooms, including handicapped-accessible accommodations. All rooms are comfortably appointed. Some have fireplaces and all offer private baths, TVs, telephones and air conditioners.

In the morning you will awake to a complimentary gourmet breakfast. An elegant lounge and dining room with fireplaces add to the comfort and charm of this Inn.

Huntingfield Manor Bed and Breakfast

Huntingfield Manor Bed and Breakfast
4928 Eastern Neck Road
Rock Hall, Maryland 21661
410-639-7779
Web Site: www.huntingfield.com
E-mail: manorlord@juno.com

Room Rates:	$85–$130, including continental breakfast. AAA discount.
Pet Charges or Deposits:	Manager's prior approval required.
Rated: 3 Paws 🐾🐾🐾	4 guest rooms, I suite and I cottage.

Huntingfield Manor provides comfortable lodging in a one-room wide, 136-foot long, telescope-type farmhouse. The Manor is a working farm dating back to the middle 1600s. Guest rooms are spacious, with private baths and king-sized beds. Huntingfield also provides a number of common rooms for guests to enjoy. A continental breakfast is served each morning on the 18-foot Amish-made cherry table.

The location of Huntingfield Manor allows you to explore the unspoiled shoreline of Chesapeake Bay, the Chester and Sassafras Rivers for fishing, crabbing, sailing, power boating and water sports. Enjoy the Eastern Neck Wildlife Refuge, which offers miles of trails for hiking and opportunities for birdwatching. The country roads are a delightful way to view old churches and historical points of interest from a bicycle.

River House Inn

River House Inn
201 East Market Street
Snow Hill, Maryland 21863
410-632-2722
Web Site: www.riverhouseinn.com
E-mail: innkeeper@riverhouseinn.com

Room Rates:	$100–$175, including full breakfast. AAA and AARP discounts.
Pet Charges or Deposits:	None
Rated: 3 Paws 😺😺😺	6 guest rooms, I suite and I cottage on two acres.

T reat yourself to a casual yet elegant getaway at the River House Inn, a spacious National Register Victorian home on the beautiful Pocomoke River. Located on Maryland's Eastern Shore in the village of Snow Hill, where you can be as active or relaxed as you choose, the possibilities are endless.

The River House Inn has three guest buildings in a lovely rambling setting on more than two acres of rolling lawn leading down to the river. It provides modern amenities along with all the charm of fireplaces in spacious rooms, plus plenty of porches to relax on.

All guest rooms have air conditioning, queen-sized beds and private baths. The 1890 Carriage Barn is now a deluxe private cottage with whirlpool tub, porch, microwave, mini-fridge, coffeemaker and television.

Inn at Perry Cabin

Inn at Perry Cabin
308 Watkins Lane
St. Michaels, Maryland 21663
800-722-2949 ▪ 410-745-2200
Web Site: www.perrycabin.com
E-mail: perrycbn@friend.ly.net

Room Rates:	$295–$895, including full breakfast and afternoon tea.
Pet Charges or Deposits:	$50 per day. Manager's prior approval required.
Rated: 5 Paws 🐾🐾🐾🐾🐾	35 guest rooms and 6 Master suites on 25 acres. Indoor pool and health facility. Restaurant.

Within easy reach of Washington, D.C., Baltimore and Philadelphia is St. Michaels, a small town that seems to live in a time warp. It slumbers on a beautiful cove off Chesapeake Bay. When you visit the Inn at Perry Cabin, built just after the War of 1812, you can easily imagine you've taken leave of the twentieth century.

It is easy to see why Sir Bernard Ashley, co-founder of Laura Ashley, chose this charming house and location for the first of his new Ashley Inns in America. Inside the Inn, all the principal rooms face the bay. English and American antiques are elegantly offset by understated, classic Laura Ashley fabrics and wallpapers.

Recent additions include an indoor pool and health facility with exercise room, sauna and steam room. The Inn's excellent food is based on the riches of the locality: fresh fish and produce and Chesapeake Bay specialties, mixed with fine international fare.

Tilghman Island Inn

Tilghman Island Inn
21384 Coopertown Road
Tilghman Island, Maryland 21671
800-866-2141 • 410-886-2141
Web Site: www.tilghmanisland.com/tii

Room Rates:	$95–$150.
Pet Charges or Deposits:	None.
Rated: 3 Paws 🐾🐾🐾	20 guest rooms and 2 suites on 5 acres. Private tennis court, swimming pool, docking facilities. Restaurant and lounge.

You will have magnificent views of Chesapeake Bay and waterfowl-filled marshes from this intimate waterfront resort, located in the heart of "waterman's country." Spacious guest rooms are individually decorated and all feature private baths.

The hallmark of the Tilghman Island Inn is the cuisine. Their intuitive style and spectacular presentations take local produce and Eastern Shore seafood to new heights. The carefully selected wine list has been designed to complement the menu, featuring quality and value wines from California, Europe, South America and Australian. Be sure to check out the winemakers' weekend schedule and cooking classes.

Wingate Manor Bed and Breakfast

Wingate Manor Bed and Breakfast
2335 Wingate-Bishop's Head Road
Wingate, Maryland 21675
888-397-8717 ▪ 410-397-8717
E-mail: wingatebb@aol.com

Room Rates: $65–$115, including full breakfast and use of bikes.
Pet Charges or Deposits: Limit two dogs. Sorry, no cats.
Rated: 3 Paws 🐾🐾🐾   6 guest cottages.

Among the rivers, pine forest, islands and wetlands of southern Dorchester County, Maryland, stands the historic Wingate family residence. This 1897 home is the subject of several books. Carefully restored, Wingate Manor is comfortably furnished in Victorian decor, offering a comfortable and relaxing atmosphere.

This unique bed and breakfast caters to bicyclists, birders, boaters and those interested in relaxing on Maryland's Eastern Shore. Bicycles are available at no charge. Enjoy kayaking or canoeing on our waters, or take the family on a fishing excursion into the Bay.

Furnished with period pieces and decorated to complement their location and views, guest rooms provide different and inviting settings. Settle into the living room to read, listen to music from the antique player piano or perhaps warm up by the wood stove with old and new friends.

Breakfast is a memorable experience.

Maryland

Please Note: *Pets must be on a leash at all times and may be restricted to certain areas. For directions, use fees, pet charges and general information, contact the numbers listed below.*

General Information

Maryland Office of Tourism Development
Redwood Tower, 9th Floor
217 East Redwood Street
Baltimore, Maryland 21202
800-394-5725

Maryland Department of Natural Resources
Fisheries Administration
580 Taylor Avenue
Annapolis, Maryland 21401
800-688-3467

National Seashore Areas

ASSATEAGUE ISLAND

Assateague Island National Seashore, located 6 miles south of Ocean City via State Route 611 on Assateague Island, consists of 39,500 acres of parkland and offers camping, picnic areas, hiking and bicycle trails, boating, fishing, swimming and a visitors' center.

State Parks General Information

Maryland Department of Natural Resources
State Forest and Parks Service
580 Taylor Avenue
Annapolis, Maryland 21401
410-260-8186

State Parks

CUMBERLAND

Green Ridge Forest State Park, 22 miles east of Cumberland off Interstate 68, Exit 64, occupies 38,811 acres of historic parkland. You will find camping, picnic areas, hiking and bicycle trails, boating, a boat ramp, fishing, winter sports and a visitors' center.

Rocky Gap State Park, located 6 miles east of Cumberland on Interstate 68, encompasses 113 acres of scenic parkland. You will find ice-skating, nature trails, camping, picnic areas, hiking and bicycle trails, boating, a boat ramp, boat rentals, fishing, swimming and a visitors' center.

ELLICOTT CITY

Patapsco State Park, west of Ellicott City along the Patapsco River from Baltimore to Liberty Dam on U.S. Highway 40, has 12,699 acres of parkland. It includes camping, picnic areas, hiking and bicycle trails, fishing and winter sports.

GRANTSVILLE

Savage River Forest State Park, located south of Interstate 68 and U.S. Highway 40 near Grantsville, encompasses 52,819 acres of parkland. It has camping, picnic areas, hiking and bicycle trails, boating, a boat ramp, fishing and winter sports.

HAVRE DE GRACE

Susquehanna State Park, 3 miles north of Havre de Grace on State Route 155, has 2,639 acres of historic and scenic parkland. It offers camping, picnic areas, hiking and bicycle trails, boating, a boat ramp, fishing and winter sports.

LUKE

Big Run State Park is located 11 miles northwest of Luke on Savage River Road. It has camping, picnic areas, hiking and bicycle trails, boating, a boat ramp and fishing.

NORTH EAST

Elk Neck State Park, 9 miles south of North East on State Route 272, consists of 2,188 scenic acres of parkland with bird watching, nature trails, camping, picnic areas, hiking and bicycle trails, boating, a boat ramp, boat rentals, fishing, swimming, winter sports and a visitors' center.

OAKLAND

Swallow Falls State Park, located 9 miles northwest of Oakland on Herrington Manor-Swallow Falls Road, encompasses 257 acres, including Maryland's highest waterfall. You will find cross-country skiing, nature trails, camping, picnic areas, hiking and bicycle trails, fishing and winter sports.

POINT LOOKOUT

Point Lookout State Park is on the southern tip of the western shore of Maryland, on State Route 5. This historic 528-acre park offers camping, picnic areas, hiking and bicycle trails, boating, a boat ramp, boat rentals, fishing, swimming and a visitors' center. For more information, call 301-872-5688.

SNOW HILL

Milburn Landing State Park, located 8 miles west of Snow Hill off State Route 12, encompasses 370 acres of parkland. The park has camping, picnic areas, hiking and bicycle trails, boating, a boat ramp and fishing.

THAYERVILLE

Deep Creek Lake State Park, 2 miles northeast of Thayerville, is Maryland's largest freshwater lake. It has 1,818 acres of parkland with cross-country skiing, nature and snowmobile trails, camping, picnic areas, hiking and bicycle trails, boating, a boat ramp, boat rentals, fishing, swimming, winter sports and a visitors' center.

Other Recreational Sites

BRUNSWICK

Brunswick Campsite is located on the C&O Canal towpath in Brunswick. This 24-acre park offers camping, picnic areas, hiking and bicycle trails, boating, a boat ramp and fishing.

CLINTON

Louise F. Cosca Park, on Thrift Road near Clinton, has 500 acres of parkland. It has camping, picnic areas, boat rentals, fishing, hiking trails and a visitors' center.

ROCKVILLE

Rock Creek Regional Park is located 4 miles east of Rockville on State Route 28, then 2 miles north on Muncaster Mill Road to Avery Road. This 1,740-acre park offers a nature center, archery, golf, nature trails, picnic areas, hiking and bicycle trails, boating, boat rentals and fishing. For more information, call 301-948-5053 or 301-495-2525.

Veterinary Care in Maryland

A

Aberdeen Vet Clinic
728 South Philadelphia
 Boulevard
Aberdeen, MD 21001
410-272-0655

**Anne Arundel
Veterinary Clinic**
2138 Generals Highway #B
Annapolis, MD 21401
410-224-0331

**Bay Ridge Animal
Hospital**
2246 Bay Ridge Avenue
Annapolis, MD 21403
410-268-6994

**Olde Towne Veterinary
Hospital**
1900 West Street
Annapolis, MD 21401
410-266-6880

**Bay Hills Animal
Hospital**
1292 Bay Dale Drive
Arnold, MD 21012
410-757-1169

**Arnold Veterinary
Hospital**
1414 Ritchie Highway
Arnold, MD 21012
410-757-7645

B

Abbey Animal Hospital
8858 Bel Air Road
Baltimore, MD 21236
410-256-0742

Animal Care Clinic
5009 Hartford Road
Baltimore, MD 21214
410-426-5300

**Animal Hospital of
Perry Hall**
9022 Bel Air Road #2
Baltimore, MD 21236
410-256-4888

**Animal Medical
Hospital**
7688 Bel Air Road
Baltimore, MD 21336
410-661-9200

**Anne Arundel
Veterinary Hospital**
4800 Ritchie Highway
Baltimore, MD 21225
410-789-0060

Ardmore Veterinarian
3130 Loch Raven Road
Baltimore, MD 21218
410-889-2230

**Baltimore Animal
Hospital**
5853 York Road
Baltimore, MD 21212
410-433-2540

**Bel Air Road Dog and
Cat Hospital**
6207 Bel Air Road
Baltimore, MD 21206
410-485-7373

**Beltway Animal
Hospital**
8702 Loch Raven Boulevard
Baltimore, MD 21286
410-825-5040

Catonsville Cat Clinic
823 Templecliff Road
Baltimore, MD 21208
410-602-1191

Liberty Animal Clinic
8130 Liberty Road
Baltimore, MD 21244
410-655-6500

**Metrocenter Animal
Clinic**
858 Park Avenue
Baltimore, MD 21201
410-962-1605

**Northwind Animal
Hospital**
10016 Harford Road
Baltimore, MD 21234
410-668-4806

**Parkville Animal
Hospital**
8600 Hartford Road #C
Baltimore, MD 21234
410-668-1040

**Patterson Park Dog
and Cat Hospital**
4128 South Robinson Street
Baltimore, MD 21224
410-276-3693

Pet Wellness Clinic
5004 Ritchie Highway
Baltimore, MD 21225
410-636-0044

**Pulaski Veterinary
Clinic**
9707 Pulaski Highway
Baltimore, MD 21220
410-686-6310

**Rosedale Animal
Hospital**
7611 Philadelphia Road
Baltimore, MD 21237
410-866-6100

**Schulmeyer Animal
Hospital**
4138 East Joppa Road #H
Baltimore, MD 21236
410-256-7297

**Towson Veterinary
Hospital**
716 York Road
Baltimore, MD 21204
410-825-8880

Vinson Animal Hospital
1030 York Road
Baltimore, MD 21204
410-828-7676

Vinson Animal Hospital
3015 Greenmount Avenue
Baltimore, MD 21218
410-235-5374

**West Baltimore Animal
Hospital**
3108 Frederick Avenue
Baltimore, MD 21229
410-233-7447

**Westview Animal
Hospital**
5800 Johnnycake Road
Baltimore, MD 21207
410-744-4800

**Whetstone Point
Veterinary**
827 East Fort Avenue
Baltimore, MD 21230
410-752-7122

**York Road Animal
Hospital**
4703 York Road
Baltimore, MD 21212
410-435-1120

**American Holistic
Veterinary**
2214 Old Emmorton Road
Bel Air, MD 21015
410-569-0795

**Animal Clinic of
Harford County**
2214 Old Emmorton Road
Bel Air, MD 21015
410-549-7777

**Bel Air Veterinary
Hospital**
1501 South Tollgate Road
Bel Air, MD 21015
410-838-4900

Benson Veterinary Hospital
1321 Bel Air Road
Bel Air, MD 21014
410-877-7666

Festival Veterinary Clinic
5 Bel Air South Parkway # N
Bel Air, MD 21015
410-569-7387

Vetsmart Pet Hospital & Health
602 Boulton Street
Bel Air, MD 21014
410-638-9832

Beltsville Veterinary Hospital
4246 Powder Mill Road
Beltsville, MD 20705
301-937-3020

Berlin Animal Hospital
10302 Old Ocean City
 Boulevard
Berlin, MD 21811
410-641-1841

Benson Animal Hospital
4981 Cordell Avenue
Bethesda, MD 20814
301-652-8818

Bradley Boulevard Veterinary Clinic
7210 Bradley Boulevard
Bethesda, MD 20817
301-365-5448

Currey Animal Clinic
5439 Butler Road
Bethesda, MD 20816
301-654-3000

Del Ray Animal Hospital
9301 Old Georgetown Road
Bethesda, MD 20814
301-564-1923

Hampden Lane Veterinary Office
4921 Hampden Lane
Bethesda, MD 20814
301-951-0300

Veterinary Holistic Care
4820 Moorland Lane
Bethesda, MD 20814
301-656-2882

Wisconsin Animal Clinic
9500 Wisconsin Avenue
Bethesda, MD 20814
301-493-4808

Bladensburg Animal Hospital
5634 Annapolis Road
Bladensburg, MD 20710
301-864-2640

Bel Air Veterinary Hospital
15511 Hall Road
Bowie, MD 20721
301-249-5200

Bowie Towne Veterinary Hospital
13801 Annapolis Road
Bowie, MD 20720
301-464-0402

VCA Bowie Animal Hospital
6804 Race Track Road
Bowie, MD 20715
301-262-8590

Brookeville Animal Hospital
22201 Georgia Avenue
Brookeville, MD 20833
301-774-9698

Buckeystown Veterinary Hospital
3820 Buckeystown Pike
Buckeystown, MD 21717
301-698-9930

Burtonsville Animal Hospital
15543 Old Columbia Pike
Burtonsville, MD 20866
301-421-9200

C

Alpine Animal Hospital
7732 Macarthur Boulevard
Cabin John, MD 20818
301-229-2400

Bayside Animal Hospital
2933 Ocean Gateway
Cambridge, MD 21613
410-228-1447

Paradise Animal Hospital
6433 Frederick Road
Catonsville, MD 21228
410-744-4224

Town and Country Animal Hospital
508 Railroad Avenue
Centreville, MD 21617
410-531-6500

Pet Vet Animal Hospital
12186 State Route 108
Clarksville, MD 21029
410-531-6500

Berwyn Animal Clinic
8904 Rhode Island Avenue
College Park, MD 20740
301-345-2010

Basin Run Animal Hospital
572 Firetower Road
Colora, MD 21917
410-658-5709

Cat and Dog Hospital of Columbia
7276 Cradlerock Way
Columbia, MD 21045
410-995-6880

VCA Lewis Animal Hospital
10665 State Route 108
Columbia, MD 21044
410-730-6660

Potomac Animal Hospital
13000 Winchester Road
 Southwest
Cumberland, MD 21502
301-777-3252

E

Animal Clinic of Talbot
417 Goldsborough Street
Easton, MD 21601
410-822-2922

Midshore Veterinary Service
602 Dutchmans Lane
Easton, MD 21601
410-820-9229

Reichardt Animal Hospital
125 Mayo Road
Edgewater, MD 21037
410-956-4500

South Arundel Veterinary Hospital
85 West Central Avenue
Edgewater, MD 21037
410-956-2932

Edgewood Veterinary Hospital
2007 Pulaski Highway
Edgewood, MD 21040
410-676-7800

North East Animal Hospital
1771 West Pulaski Highway
Elkton, MD 21921
410-398-8100

VCA Elkton Animal Hospital
400 West Pulaski Highway
Elkton, MD 21921
410-398-8777

Bethany Centennial Animal Hospital
10176 Baltimore National
 #111
Ellicott City, MD 21042
410-750-2322

F

Forest Hill Veterinary Clinic
6 West Jarrettsville Road
Forest Hill, MD 21050
410-838-6788

Hickory Veterinary Hospital
534 East Jarrettsville Road
Forest Hill, MD 21050
410-838-7797

Rock Spring Veterinary Clinic
1905 Rockspring Road
Forest Hill, MD 21050
410-838-6960

Forestville Animal Hospital
7307 Marlboro Pike
Forestville, MD 20747
301-736-5288

McClennan Veterinary Clinic
142 West Patrick Street #A
Frederick, MD 21701
301-663-6531

Opossom Pike Veterinary Clinic
1550 Opossomtown Pike
Frederick, MD 21702
301-662-2322

Yellow Springs Veterinary Clinic
8744 Yellow Springs Road
Frederick, MD 21702
301-663-8353

G

Airpark Animal Hospital
7600 Lindbergh Drive #H
Gaithersburg, MD 20879
301-990-8387

Montgomery Village Animal Hospital
19222 Montgomery Village Avenue
Gaithersburg, MD 20886
301-330-2200

Quince Orchard Veterinary Hospital
11910 Darnestown Road
Gaithersburg, MD 20878
301-258-0850

Walnut Hill Animal Hospital
615 South Frederick Avenue #D
Gaithersburg, MD 20877
301-977-8680

A Cat Clinic
13507 Clopper Road
Germantown, MD 20874
301-540-7770

Animal Clinic of Southgate
312 Hospital Drive #B
Glen Burnie, MD 21061
410-768-3396

Beltway Emergency Animal Hospital
11660 Annapolis Road
Glenn Dale, MD 20769
301-464-3737

Animal Medical Hospital
2465 Route 97
Glenwood, MD 21738
410-489-9677

H

Long Meadow Animal Hospital
19764 Longmeadow Road
Hagerstown, MD 21742
301-733-8400

Park Circle Animal Hospital
362 Virginia Avenue
Hagerstown, MD 21740
301-791-2180

Stoney Run Veterinary Hospital
1300 Hanover Road
Hanover, MD 21076
410-859-0085

Animal Hospital of Havre de Grace
2120 Pulaski Highway
Havre de Grace, MD 21078
410-272-8656

Three Notch Veterinary Hospital
55 Airport View Drive
Hollywood, MD 20636
301-373-8633

Padonia Veterinary Hospital
9827 York Road
Hunt Valley, MD 21030
410-666-7878

Prince Georges Animal Hospital
7440 Annapolis Road
Hyattsville, MD 20784
301-577-9400

K

Wheaton Animal Hospital
2929 University Boulevard West
Kensington, MD 20895
301-949-1520

Celebrie Veterinary Hospital
12301 Belair Road
Kingsville, MD 21087
410-592-2550

L

Animal Clinic of La Plata
6685 Glen Albin Road
La Plata, MD 20646
301-932-1881

Mid County Veterinary Clinic
6460 Crain Highway
La Plata, MD 20646
301-934-3220

New Carrollton Veterinary Hospital
7601 Good Luck Road
Lanham Seabrook, MD 20706
301-552-3800

Brenner Animal Hospital
10100 Washington Boulevard North
Laurel, MD 20723
301-725-5400

North Laurel Animal Hospital
9105 All Saints Road #P
Laurel, MD 20723
410-792-2692

Pautuxent Valley Animal Hospital
11200 Scaggsville Road
Laurel, MD 20723
301-490-1030

Rocky Gorge Animal Hospital
7515 Brooklyn Bridge Road
Laurel, MD 20707
301-776-7744

Breton Veterinary Hospital
22 Fenwick Street
Leonardtown, MD 20650
301-475-7808

Park Veterinary Clinic
1607 Great Mills Road
Lexington Park, MD 20653
301-863-9222

St. Marys Veterinary Hospital
22261 Three Notch Road
Lexington Park, MD 20653
301-862-2441

Lutherville Animal Hospital
506 West Seminary Avenue
Lutherville, MD 21093
410-296-7387

M

Middletown Veterinary Clinic
207 South Church Street #A
Middletown, MD 21769
301-371-6212

Benfield Animal Hospital
401 Headquarters Drive #107
Millersville, MD 21108
410-987-8300

Animal Health Center
806 Park Avenue
Mount Airy, MD 21771
410-795-9225

Country Veterinary Hospital
17591 Frederick Road
Mount Airy, MD 21771
301-829-0414

Taylorsville Veterinary Clinic
4339 Ridge Road # B
Mount Airy, MD 21771
410-875-5437

Palmer Animal Hospital
307 Main Street
Myersville, MD 21773
301-293-2121

N

Animal Care Clinic
11717 Old National Pike #12
New Market, MD 21774
301-865-0022

**New Market Animal
Hospital**
10609 Old National Pike
New Market, MD 21774
301-865-3232

O

**Pineview Veterinary
Hospital**
85 Pineview Drive
Oakland, MD 21550
301-334-8393

**Ocean City Animal
Hospital**
11843 Ocean Gateway
Ocean City, MD 21842
410-213-1170

Acacia Animal Clinic
17101 Quarter Horse Way
Olney, MD 20832
301-774-7361

**Town and Country
Animal Clinic**
2715 Olney Sandy Spring
 Road
Olney, MD 20832
301-774-7111

P

**Mt. Carmel Animal
Hospital**
17004 York Road
Parkton, MD 21120
410-343-0200

Carney Animal Hospital
9011 Hartford Road
Parkville, MD 21234
410-665-5255

**Animal Hospital of
Lake Shore**
4139 Mountain Road
Pasadena, MD 21122
410-435-7600

**Pasadena Animal
Hospital**
3007 Mountain Road
Pasadena, MD 21122
410-255-2300

**Post Road Veterinary
Clinics**
1098 Principio Furnace Road
Perryville, MD 21903
410-642-9255

**Pocomoke Animal
Hospital**
1139 Ocean Highway
Pocomoke City, MD 21851
410-957-0404

Worcester Animal Clinic
1402 Market Street
Pocomoke City, MD 21851
410-957-2413

Cecil Veterinary Clinic
43 Gutman Lane
Port Deposit, MD 21904
410-658-4356

**Falls Road Veterinary
Hospital**
10229 Falls Road
Potomac, MD 20854
301-983-8400

**Potomac Animal
Hospital**
10020 River Road
Potomac, MD 20854
301-299-4142

**Prince Frederick Animal
Hospital**
300 Solomons Island Road
 North
Prince Frederick, MD 20678
410-535-2590

**Somerset Animal
Hospital**
11279 Stewart Neck Road
Princess Anne, MD 21853
410-651-1044

Q

**Queenstown Veterinary
Hospital**
105 4H Park Road
Queenstown, MD 21658
410-827-6776

R

**Randallstown Animal
Hospital**
10022 Liberty Road
Randallstown, MD 21133
410-922-6043

**Main Street Veterinary
Hospital**
11617 Reisterstown Road
Reisterstown, MD 21136
410-526-7500

**Mountainside
Veterinary Hospital**
42 Westminster Road
Reisterstown, MD 21136
410-833-8085

**Reisterstown
Veterinary Center**
13030 Hanover Road
Reisterstown, MD 21136
410-833-0660

**TLC for Pets Veterinary
Hospital**
11809 Reisterstown Road
Reisterstown, MD 21136
410-833-1717

**All Creatures Veterinary
Service**
136 Sylmar Road
Rising Sun, MD 21911
410-658-9911

Lynn Animal Hospital
6215 Baltimore Avenue
Riverdale, MD 20737
301-779-1184

**Best Friends Veterinary
Hospital**
5100 Muncaster Mill Road
Rockville, MD 20855
301-977-1881

**Montgomery Animal
Hospital**
12200 Rockville Pike
Rockville, MD 20852
301-881-6447

S

**St. Michaels Veterinary
Clinic**
915 South Talbot Street
St. Michaels, MD 21663
410-745-5275

Animal Housecalls
3970 Doe Run Drive
Salisbury, MD 21804
410-543-1398

**McAllister Veterinary
Service**
235 Dykes Road
Salisbury, MD 21804
410-742-3935

**Salisbury Animal
Hospital**
925 Boundary Street
Salisbury, MD 21801
410-749-4393

**Wicomico Veterinary
Hospital**
1203 Mount Hermon Road
Salisbury, MD 21804
410-742-7543

**Severn Square
Veterinary Hospital**
2620 Annapolis Road #G
Severn, MD 21144
410-551-3702

**Telegraph Road Animal
Hospital**
7863 Telegraph Road
Severn, MD 21144
410-551-3100

**Severna Park
Veterinary Hospital**
542 Baltimore Annapolis
 Boulevard
Severna Park, MD 21146
410-647-8366

A Cat Practice
2816 Linden Lane
Silver Spring, MD 20910
301-587-0052

Ambassador Animal Hospital
7979 Georgia Avenue
Silver Spring, MD 20910
301-589-1344

Bonifant Animal Clinic
433 Bonifant Road
Silver Spring, MD 20905
301-236-0044

Briggs Chaney Animal Hospital
13850 Old Columbia Pike
Silver Spring, MD 20904
301-989-2226

Marymont Animal Hospital
24 Randolph Road
Silver Spring, MD 20904
301-384-1223

Norbeck Animal Clinic
2645 Norbeck Road
Silver Spring, MD 20906
301-949-6671

Silver Spring Animal Hospital
1915 Seminary Road
Silver Spring, MD 20910
301-587-6099

Solomons Veterinary Clinic
13872 South Solomons
  Island Road
Solomons, MD 20688
410-326-4300

Bay Area Veterinary Hospital
150 Kent Landing
Stevensville, MD 21666
410-643-7888

Deer Park Veterinary Hospital
3322 Ady Road
Street, MD 21154
410-452-8577

Banks Silver Hill Animal Hospital
3806 Old Silver Hill Road
Suitland, MD 20746
301-423-0550

Suitland Animal Clinic
4828 Silver Hill Road
Suitland, MD 20746
301-967-7222

Calvert Animal Hospital
1923 Skinners Turn Road
Sunderland, MD 20689
301-855-8525

South Carroll Veterinary Hospital
6220 Georgetown Boulevard
  #L
Sykesville, MD 21784
410-549-2345

T

Takoma Park Animal Clinic
7330 Carroll Avenue
Takoma Park, MD 20912
301-270-4401

Taneytown Veterinary Clinic
107 East Baltimore Street
Taneytown, MD 21787
410-756-2884

Thurmont Veterinary Clinic
224 N Church Street # J
Thurmont, MD 21788
301-271-3212

W

Charles County Veterinary Hospital
11759 Central Avenue
Waldorf, MD 20601
301-645-1120

Waldorf Animal Clinic
2242 Old Washington Road
Waldorf, MD 20602
301-645-2977

Animal Care Clinic
148 Walkers Village Way
Walkersville, MD 21793
301-898-7276

Poffenbarger Veterinary Clinic
10 Crum Road
Walkersville, MD 21793
301-898-5303

Walkersville Veterinary Clinic
10559 Glade Road
Walkersville, MD 21793
301-898-7676

Muddy Creek Animal Clinic
5518 Muddy Creek Road
West River, MD 20778
410-867-0770

Carroll County Veterinary Clinic
334 Gorsuch Road
Westminster, MD 21157
410-848-3100

Westminster Veterinary Hospital
269 West Main Street
Westminster, MD 21157
410-848-3363

Whaleyville Animal Hospital
8901 Whaleyville Road
Whaleyville, MD 21872
410-352-3311

Shawsville Veterinary Hospital
4534 Norrisville Road
White Hall, MD 21161
410-692-2800

Woodsboro Veterinary Clinic
9327 Gravel Hill Road #A
Woodsboro, MD 21798
301-898-7272

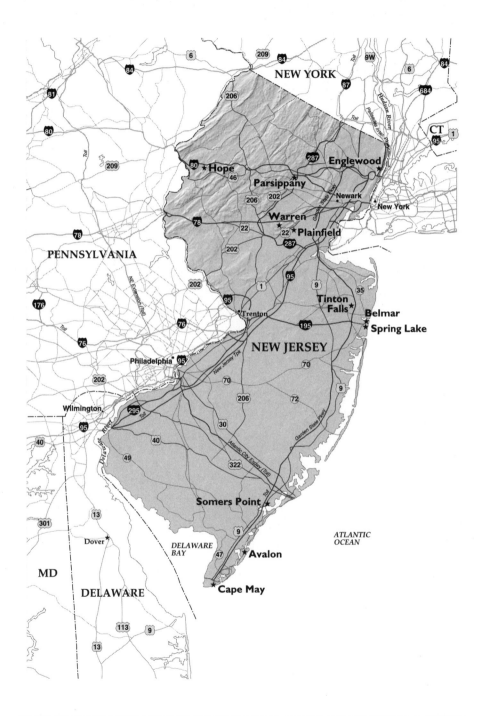

New Jersey

Sealark Bed and Breakfast

Sealark Bed and Breakfast
3018 First Avenue
Avalon, New Jersey 08202
609-967-5647
Web Site: www.sealark.com

Room Rates:	$60–$120, including full breakfast.
Pet Charges or Deposits:	Manager's prior approval required.
Rated: 3 Paws 🐾🐾🐾	6 guest rooms and 2 suites.

T he Sealark Bed and Breakfast is an attractively restored Victorian home that was built in the late 1800s by a wealthy Philadelphia widow. Guest rooms are light and airy with hardwood floors, oriental carpets and antiques. A common living room is shared by guests, in addition to a wrap-around porch furnished with rockers. Guests are encouraged to read, watch TV or enjoy a movie from the video collection.

Breakfast is a special treat in the morning, served either on the porch or by the fireplace in the parlor. The buffet begins with juices, fruits and cereals. Homemade cakes complement the main entrées such as eggs Florentine, crab-meat custard with tomato coulis, shrimp and cheese soufflé or stuffed baked French toast. The Sealark's meat dishes include a tasty apple sausage ring and corned beef hash.

Down the Shore Bed and Breakfast

Down the Shore Bed and Breakfast
201 Seventh Avenue
Belmar, New Jersey 07719
732-681-9023
Web Site: www.belmar.com/downtheshore

Room Rates:	$85, including full breakfast.
Pet Charges or Deposits:	Small pets only. Manager's prior approval required.
Rated: 3 Paws 🐾🐾🐾	3 guest rooms.

L ocated one block from the boardwalk and beach, Down the Shore Bed and Breakfast offers comfortable, air-conditioned, tastefully decorated guest rooms at reasonable rates. A parlor and a shaded porch are reserved for guests, where they can kick back with a good book, play games or watch TV. Each morning a full breakfast is served, included in your room rate.

The town of Belmar has much to offer—beaches, boat rentals, evening concerts and a variety of restaurant menus that feature everything from fresh seafood to home-style barbecue. Nearby, are thoroughbred racing at Monmouth Park, trotters at Freehold Raceway and world-class entertainment at the Garden States Arts Center.

Marquis de Lafayette Hotel

Marquis de Lafayette Hotel
501 Beach Drive
Cape May, New Jersey 08204
800-257-0432 • 609-884-3500

Room Rates:	$89–$329, including full breakfast. AAA and AARP discounts.
Pet Charges or Deposits:	$20 per day. $50 refundable deposit.
Rated: 3 Paws	30 guest rooms and 43 suites. Pool. Restaurant.

C ape May, the southernmost resort town on the New Jersey shore, sits at the end of the Garden State Parkway, 40 minutes south of Atlantic City. Its location at the tip of the peninsula that separates the Delaware Bay from the Atlantic Ocean makes for a remarkably moderate climate and enables visitors to watch the sun both rise and set over water.

Gracious hospitality, lovely decor, oceanfront rooms with spectacular views and the finest in dining and dancing. These are but a few of the reasons why you'll enjoy your stay here in the heart of Victorian Cape May's historic district.

Radisson Hotel Englewood

Radisson Hotel Englewood
401 South Van Brunt Street
Englewood, New Jersey 07631
201-871-2020
Web Site: www.radisson.com

Room Rates:	$99–$185. AAA discount.
Pet Charges or Deposits:	$100 refundable deposit. Manager's prior approval required.
Rated: 3 Paws 🐾🐾🐾	193 guest rooms and 1 suite. Indoor heated pool and exercise room. Restaurant and lounge.

S trategically situated on the Route 4 corridor, just four miles west of New York City, the comfortable Radisson Hotel is ideal for both the corporate and leisure traveler. You are less than 10 minutes from New York City, Yankee Stadium, the Meadowlands Sports Complex and Convention Center and some of the finest shopping, theaters and restaurants.

Guest rooms are spacious and well appointed with king-sized beds. Business Class rooms feature additional business amenities, including free full breakfast, in-room coffeemakers, pay-per-view movies, phone with computer data port and complimentary fax services.

Inn at Millrace Pond

Inn at Millrace Pond
313 Johnsonburg Road
P.O. Box 359
Hope, New Jersey 07844
908-459-4884

Room Rates:	$100–$160, including continental breakfast.
Pet Charges or Deposits:	Manager's prior approval required.
Rated: 3 Paws ❤❤❤	17 guest rooms on 23 acres. Tennis court, restaurant and Colonial tavern.

L ocated in the historic village of Hope, the Inn at Millrace Pond resides on 23 acres that date back to the 1770s. The main Inn building was a gristmill until the early 1950s.

Authentically decorated rooms, all with private baths, suggest the quiet elegance of Colonial America. Each guest room is tastefully decorated with Shaker-style furniture, complete with queen-sized beds.

Under the professional direction of Chef Troy Gullick, there are two dining rooms, which reflect exceptional gourmet continental cuisine. Upstairs is a more formal dining area, while the Colonial Tavern, with its bar and large stone fireplace, is located downstairs past the mill's old water wheel.

Hilton Parsippany

Hilton Parsippany
1 Hilton Court
Parsippany, New Jersey 07054
877-671-5744 ▪ 973-267-7373
Web Site: www.hilton.com

Room Rates:	$135–$675. AAA and AARP discounts.
Pet Charges or Deposits:	Manager's prior approval required. $50 refundable deposit.
Rated: 3 Paws ❀ ❀ ❀	504 guest rooms and 6 suites. Fitness center, jogging track, tennis courts, pools, basketball. Restaurant and lounge.

C onveniently located 25 minutes from Newark International Airport at the crossroads of Interstates 287 and 80, the Hilton Parsippany offers corporate and leisure travelers the best accommodations and most personalized service in the area. Downtown Morristown, New Jersey, is three miles away, while New York City is only 32 miles.

All guest rooms were recently renovated and a full-service Business Center was added to help meet the needs of corporate guests. The hotel's fitness center was upgraded as well, and is now open 24 hours.

Casual dining at The Harvest is available at the Hilton for breakfast, lunch and dinner. Full room service and special dietary and kosher meals are available upon request.

Pillars of Plainfield Bed and Breakfast

Pillars of Plainfield Bed and Breakfast
922 Central Avenue
Plainfield, New Jersey 07060
888 PILLARS ▪ 908-753-0922
E-mail: pillars2@juno.com

Room Rates:	$79–$99, including full breakfast, evening snacks and wine.
Pet Charges or Deposits:	$10 per day. Sorry, no cats. Manager's prior approval required.
Rated: 3 Paws 🐾🐾🐾	3 guest rooms and 1 suite. Refrigerators, microwaves, wood-burning fireplaces.

T he moment you drive through the wrought-iron gates, you'll know the Pillars is a special place. Surrounding the house are wildflowers, roses, dogwood, cherry trees and the rhododendrons and azaleas for which Plainfield is famous.

Once inside, in the grand foyer, you're greeted by a handsome circular staircase winding up three stories to a stained-glass skylight. Off the foyer you'll find the music room, with its nautical theme, wood-burning fireplace, organ, stereo and game table. You will enjoy a grand breakfast and your complimentary newspaper each morning in the dining room, with its oversized windows and colored glass.

This restored Victorian-Georgian mansion is nestled on a secluded acre of trees and wildflowers in the Van Wyck Brooks historic district. Golf, tennis and health clubs are nearby.

Residence Inn by Marriott

Residence Inn by Marriott
900 Hays Landing Road
Somers Point, New Jersey 08244
800-331-3131 ▪ 609-927-6400
Web Site: www.adnetint.com/residence
E-mail: resinnj@aol.com

Room Rates:	$79–$259, including continental breakfast buffet and an evening hospitality hour. AAA and AARP discounts.
Pet Charges or Deposits:	$50 per stay.
Rated: 3 Paws 😺😺😺	120 guest suites with fully equipped kitchens. Outdoor heated pool, sports court.

T he Residence Inn is aptly named, with its design resembling an upscale residential complex and its "home away from home" philosophy of customer service. With an inspired, home-like atmosphere, the low-rise buildings have private entrances on beautifully landscaped grounds, some with a view of the bay and protected wetlands. The accommodations are studio rooms and two-story penthouse suites, significantly larger than traditional hotel rooms and most with fireplaces.

Guests are treated to complimentary continental breakfast and an evening hospitality hour. For those who prefer home cooking, each guest room features a fully equipped kitchen, complete with appliances and utensils. Free grocery shopping service, as well as laundry and valet service, are arranged by the staff. In addition they offer free HBO and cable. VCR rentals and newly released movies are also available.

La Maison Bed and Breakfast and Gallery

La Maison Bed and Breakfast and Gallery
404 Jersey Avenue
Spring Lake, New Jersey 07762
732-449-0969
Web Site: www.bbianj.com/lamaison

Room Rates:	$115–$285, including full breakfast and happy hour.
Pet Charges or Deposits:	50% refundable deposit or $25 per day for dogs.
Rated: 5 Paws 🐾🐾🐾🐾🐾	5 guest rooms, 2 suites and 1 cottage; beach, pool, tennis, free access to fitness and spa facility.

T he reviews are in: "A top Northeast romantic escape…" states *USA Weekend.* "Even first-time guests feel as though they've returned to their favorite vacation home," says *Country Inns Magazine.* And one of 1998's Top 25 B&Bs in the nation, according to *America's Favorite Inns, B&Bs & Small Hotels.*

In the Victorian seaside village of Spring Lake, New Jersey, you will luxuriate in this quiet, French 1870s inn with an art gallery. Louis Philippe rooms with queen-sized sleigh beds and fluffy comforters combine with discreetly modernized private baths, air conditioning and cable TV. Awake each morning to a full breakfast of specialty omelets, Belgian waffles and French toast, accompanied by freshly squeezed orange juice, mimosas, cappuccino or espresso.

Residence Inn by Marriott

Residence Inn by Marriott
90 Park Road
Tinton Falls, New Jersey 07724
800-331-3131 ▪ 732-389-8100
Web Site: www.marriott.com

Room Rates:	$94–$175, including complimentary evening hospitality, grocery shopping service, daily newspapers and exercise facility.
Pet Charges or Deposits:	$10 per day. $175 per month for a studio suite. $275 per month for a penthouse suite.
Rated: 3 Paws 🐾🐾🐾	96 guest suites. Sports court, picnic and barbecue areas, same-day valet service, on-site laundry.

Located a few miles from the Jersey Shore beaches, the Residence Inn by Marriott offers handsomely furnished, comfortable and spacious guest suites. Each suite features separate sleeping and living areas, fully equipped kitchens, daily maid service, grocery shopping service, laundry facilities, work areas and meeting facilities, as well as the manager-hosted continental breakfast buffet and informal hospitality hour.

Upon check-in, pets receive complimentary pet dishes for their food and water, plus a special magnet for the room door to let housekeeping know you have a pet with you.

Somerset Hills Hotel

Somerset Hills Hotel
200 Liberty Corner Road
Warren, New Jersey 07059
800-688-0700 ▪ 908-647-6700
Web Site: www.shh.com
E-mail: shhotel@aol.com

Room Rates:	$115–$185. AAA and AARP discounts.
Pet Charges or Deposits:	$25 per day. Designated rooms only.
Rated: 3 Paws 🐾🐾🐾	108 guest rooms and 3 suites. Two restaurants and lounge.

Nestled in the Watchung Mountains, the Somerset Hills Hotel combines the warmth and attentive service of a fine country inn with the gracious dining, entertainment and accommodations you would expect of a grand urban hotel.

There is an abundance of activities and events to be enjoyed by all here. For two years running, World Class soccer has been a part of the Somerset Hills Hotel. The annual Far Hill Races every October are a must for horse lovers, and runners from all over the world come to compete in the Midland Run in nearby Far Hills every May.

Christine's Restaurant is inspired by the rich traditions and culinary creativity of Northern Italian cuisine. The Polo Lounge serves breakfast, lunch and dinner in a casual atmosphere.

New Jersey

Please Note: *Pets must be on a leash at all times and may be restricted to certain areas. For directions, use fees, pet charges and general information, contact the numbers listed below.*

National Recreation Area

Division of Parks and Forestry
State Park Service
501 East State Street, CN 404
Trenton, New Jersey 08625
800-843-6420 • 609-984-0370

Gateway National Recreation Area—Sandy Hook Unit is entered by the bridge from State Route 36 at Highlands. It encompasses 1,600 acres of parkland with picnic areas, hiking trails, fishing, swimming and a visitors' center.

State Parks

Division of Parks and Forestry
State Park Service
501 East State Street, CN 404
Trenton, New Jersey 08625
800-843-6420 • 609-984-0370

BELLEPLAIN

Belleplain Forest State Park, located on County Road 550 at Belleplain, is a 12,165-acre park offering camping, picnic areas, hiking trails, boating, a boat ramp, boat rentals, fishing and swimming.

BLAIRSTOWN

Worthington Forest State Park, 16 miles northeast of Blairstown on Millbrook Road, consists of 5,770 acres of parkland with cross-country skiing, snowmobiling, camping, picnic areas, hiking trails, boating, a boat ramp, fishing and winter sports.

BRANCHVILLE

Stokes Forest State Park, located 3 miles north of Branchville on U.S. Highway 206, encompasses 15,482 acres of parkland. Visitors to the park will enjoy cross-country skiing, ice-skating, snowmobiling, bridle and nature trails, camping, picnic areas, hiking trails, boating, fishing, swimming and winter sports.

CAPE MAY

Cape May Point State Park has 190 acres of historic parkland and is located 2 miles west of Cape May on County Road 606. Visitors to the park will enjoy picnic areas, hiking trails, fishing, nature trails and a visitors' center.

CHATSWORTH

Penn Forest State Park is a 3,366-acre park, 5 miles southeast of Chatsworth off County Road 563. It has picnic areas, hiking and bridle trails, boating, a boat ramp and fishing.

CHESTER

Hacklebarney State Park is an 892-acre park located 3 miles southwest of Chester via U.S. Highway 206. The park includes picnic areas, hiking trails, fishing and winter sports.

CLINTON

Spruce Run State Park, 3 miles north of Clinton on State Route 31, is a 1,961-acre park offering camping, picnic areas, hiking trails, boating, a boat ramp, fishing, swimming and winter sports.

FARMINGDALE

Allaire State Park, located 1.5 miles west of Garden State Parkway, Exit 98, is a 3,062-acre historic park with cross-country skiing, bridle and nature trails, camping, picnic areas, fishing, hiking trails, winter sports, a nature center and a visitors' center. For more information, call 732-938-2371.

FORT DIX

Lebanon Forest State Park is a 31,879-acre park south of Fort Dix, off State Routes 70 and 72. Visitors to the park will find camping, picnic areas, hiking trails, fishing and swimming.

HACKETTSTOWN

Allamuchy Mountain State Park, 2 miles north of Hackettstown on County Road 517, is a 7,276-acre park with camping, picnic areas, hiking trails, fishing and winter sports.

HIGH BRIDGE

Voorhees State Park is a 613-acre park located 2 miles north of High Bridge on County Road 513. It offers camping, picnic areas, hiking trails and winter sports.

HOPE

Jenny Jump Forest State Park encompasses 1,387 acres, 3 miles east of Hope on County Road 519. It offers camping, picnic areas, hiking trails and fishing.

JERSEY CITY

Liberty State Park, located off the New Jersey Turnpike, Exit 14B, is a 1,114-acre park with picnic areas, boating, a boat ramp, fishing, swimming and a visitors' center. For more information, call 201-915-3400 or 201-915-3401.

LANDING

Hopatcong State Park, 2 miles north of Landing off Interstate 80, encompasses 113 acres of parkland with ice-fishing, ice-skating, snowmobiling, picnic areas, boating, a boat ramp, fishing, swimming and winter sports.

LEBANON

Round Valley State Park, located 2 miles south of Lebanon off U.S. Highway 22, consists of 3,639 acres of parkland with cross-country skiing, ice-fishing, ice-skating, wilderness camping, picnic areas, hiking trails, boating, a boat ramp, fishing, swimming and winter sports.

MATAWAN

Cheesequake State Park is a 1,284-acre park located 3 miles west of Matawan on State Route 34. The park offers cross-country skiing, camping, picnic areas, hiking and nature trails, fishing, swimming and winter sports.

NEW BRUNSWICK

Delaware and Raritan Canal State Park, 7 miles west of New Brunswick on County Road 514, consists of 3,723 acres of parkland with picnic areas, hiking and bicycle trails, boating, a boat ramp, boat rentals, fishing and winter sports.

Bull's Island Section State Park, located 3 miles north of Stockton on State Route 29, is a 79-acre park offering camping, picnic areas, hiking trails, boating, a boat ramp and fishing.

NEWTON

Swartswood State Park, 5 miles west of Newton on County Roads 622 and 619, encompasses 1,718 acres of parkland with ice-fishing, ice-skating, snowmobiling, camping, picnic areas, hiking trails, boating, a boat ramp, boat rentals, fishing, swimming and winter sports.

RINGWOOD

Ringwood State Park, located 2.5 miles north of Ringwood via Skyland Drive, County Road 511 and Sloatsburg Road, is a 6,199-acre park offering picnic areas, hiking trails, fishing and winter sports. It consists of three separate areas: Ringwood Manor, Shephard Lake and Skyland Section. For more information, call 973-962-7031.

Ringwood Manor is an 895-acre historic park with picnic areas, hiking trails, fishing and winter sports.

Shephard Lake is a 1,220-acre park offering ice-fishing, ice-skating, picnic areas, hiking trails, boating, a boat ramp, boat rentals, fishing, swimming and winter sports.

Skyland Section is a 4,084-acre park that has snowmobiling, hiking trails and winter sports.

SEASIDE PARK

Island Beach State Park, 3 miles south of Seaside Park on State Route 35, has 3,002 acres of parkland with picnic areas, hiking and nature trails, fishing and swimming. This park is a 10-mile strip from Seaside Park to Barnegate Inlet.

STRATHMERE

Corson's Inlet State Park is a 341-acre park, located just north of Strathmere on Ocean Drive. Visitors to the park will find hiking trails, boating, a boat ramp and fishing.

SUSSEX

High Point State Park is a 14,193-acre park, 8 miles northwest of Sussex on State Route 23. The scenic park offers cross-country skiing, ice-fishing, snowmobiling, hiking and nature trails, camping, picnic areas, boating, a boat ramp, fishing, swimming, winter sports and a visitors' center.

TRENTON

Washington Crossing State Park is an 841-acre park located 8 miles northwest of Trenton on State Route 29, then northeast on County Road 546. Visitors to the historic park can enjoy nature programs, picnic areas, hiking trails, winter sports and a visitors' center. For more information, call 609-737-0623.

Wharton Forest State Park is a 108,328-acre park 35 miles south of Trenton off U.S. Highway 206. It offers canoeing, ice-fishing, ice-skating, nature programs, camping, picnic areas, hiking and bridle trails, boating, a boat ramp, boat rentals, fishing, swimming and a visitors' center.

TUCKERTON

Bass River Forest State Park, located 3 miles west of Tuckerton on County Road 592, consists of 23,585 acres of parkland with horse rentals, camping, picnic areas, hiking trails, boating, a boat ramp, boat rentals, fishing, swimming and nature programs.

VERNON

Wawayanda State Park is an 11,332-acre park located 3 miles east of Vernon on County Road 94. The park offers cross-country skiing, ice-fishing, ice-skating, snowmobiling, picnic areas, hiking trails, boating, a boat ramp, boat rentals, fishing, swimming and winter sports.

VINELAND

Parvin State Park, 6 miles west of Vineland on County Road 540, is a 1,125-acre park with camping, picnic areas, hiking and nature trails, boating, a boat ramp, boat rentals, fishing, swimming and a visitors' center.

Other State Recreation Areas

FREEHOLD

Turkey Swamp County Park, located 4.5 miles south of Freehold via U.S. Highway 9, County Road 524 and Georgia Road, consists of 498 acres of parkland with ice-skating, an archery range, camping, picnic areas, hiking and nature trails, boating, boat rentals, fishing and winter sports.

LAKEWOOD

Ocean County State Recreation Area is in Lakewood on State Route 88. This 325-acre park offers golf, tennis, picnic areas, hiking and bicycle trails, boat rentals fishing, swimming and nature trails.

MAYS LANDING

Estell Manor County Park is a 1,700-acre park located 3 miles south of Mays Landing on State Route 50. Visitors to the park can enjoy picnic areas, hiking and bicycle trails, fishing, winter sports and a visitors' center.

Lake Lenape Park, located on Old Harding Highway in Mays Landing, consists of 1,900 acres of parkland with camping, picnic areas, hiking trails, boating, a boat ramp and fishing.

WEST ORANGE

South Mountain Reservation is a 2,047-acre park off Interstate 280, Exit 7, then 2 miles south on Pleasant Valley Way in West Orange. Visitors to the park can enjoy indoor ice-skating, bridle trails, picnic areas, hiking trails, fishing and winter sports.

Veterinary Care in New Jersey

A

Absecon Veterinary Hospital
51 North Shore Road
Absecon, NJ 08201
609-646-7013

Shore Veterinarians-Smithville
45 South New York Road #103
Absecon, NJ 08201
609-748-1133

Allendale Animal Hospital
120 West Allendale Ave
Allendale, NJ 07401
201-327-1045

Allentown Animal Hospital
65 North Main Street
Allentown, NJ 08501
609-259-3500

Allenwood Veterinary Hospital
3002 Atlantic Avenue
Allenwood, NJ 08720
732-528-7444

Alpha Veterinary Care
334 Third Avenue
Alpha, NJ 08865
908-454-8384

Andover Animal Hospital
234 Andover Road
Andover, NJ 07821
973-729-9145

Tranquility Large Animal Vet
221 Johnsonburg Road
Andover, NJ 07821
908-852-1300

Asbury Park Animal Hospital
1707 Asbury Avenue
Asbury Park, NJ 07712
732-774-4475

Seashore Animal Hospital
1107 State Route 35
Asbury Park, NJ 07712
732-531-1171

Waterford Veterinary Associates
514 Fifth Street
Atco, NJ 08004
609-768-3731

Atlantic Highlands Animal Hospital
77 Memorial Pkwy Rear
Atlantic Highlands, NJ 07716
732-291-4400

Audubon Veterinary Associates
247 South White Horse Pike
Audubon, NJ 08106
609-547-7256

Animal Hospital of Sussex County
169 US Highway 206
Augusta, NJ 07822
973-579-1155

Augusta Veterinary Hospital
11 Plains Road
Augusta, NJ 07822
973-948-3211

St. Georges Veterinary Hospital
10 Remsen Avenue
Avenel, NJ 07001
732-634-5242

B

Barnegat Animal Clinic
530 N Main Street
Barnegat, NJ 08005
609-698-2141

Basking Ridge Animal Hospital
340 South Finley Avenue
Basking Ridge, NJ 07920
908-766-4211

Animal Clinic of Bayonne
926 Broadway
Bayonne, NJ 07002
201-437-6666

Bayonne Animal Hospital
1170 Kennedy Boulevard
Bayonne, NJ 07002
201-339-0121

Bayonne Veterinary Medical
256 Broadway
Bayonne, NJ 07002
201-437-0100

Bayville Veterinary Hospital
251 Route 9
Bayville, NJ 08721
732-269-0003

Belle Mead Animal Hospital
876 US Highway 206
Belle Mead, NJ 08502
908-874-4447

Harlingen Veterinary Clinic
2162 US Highway 206
Belle Mead, NJ 08502
908-359-2000

Amity Animal Clinic
211 Washington Avenue
Belleville, NJ 07109
973-759-4304

Belmar Wall Animal Hospital
2306 Belmar Boulevard
Belmar, NJ 07719
732-681-5040

Bergenfield Animal Clinic
88 N Washington Avenue
Bergenfield, NJ 07621
201-385-5776

New Bridge Veterinary Practice
452 New Bridge Road
Bergenfield, NJ 07621
201-384-4699

Berkeley Heights Animal Hospital
269 Springfield Avenue
Berkeley Heights, NJ 07922
908-464-0023

Bernardsville Animal Hospital
41 Morristown Road
Bernardsville, NJ 07924
908-766-0041

Johnson Veterinary Service
341 Mine Brook Road
Bernardsville, NJ 07924
908-766-7959

Blackwood Animal Hospital
503 South Black Horse Pike
Blackwood, NJ 08012
609-227-8503

Blairstown Animal Hospital
29 Cedar Lake Road
Blairstown, NJ 07825
908-362-6430

Bloomfield Animal Hospital
709 Bloomfield Avenue
Bloomfield, NJ 07003
973-748-8042

Brookside Veterinary Clinic
522 Broad Street
Bloomfield, NJ 07003
973-748-6897

Bloomingdale Animal Hospital
138 Glenwild Avenue
Bloomingdale, NJ 07403
973-838-4141

Morris Hills Veterinary Clinic
708 Parsippany Boulevard
Boonton, NJ 07005
973-334-2240

Advanced Care Small & Exotic
1991 US Highway 22
Bound Brook, NJ 08805
732-764-9595

Green Valley Veterinary Service
23 Phillips Road
Branchville, NJ 07826
973-948-3885

Adamston Veterinary Clinic
437 Adamston Road
Brick, NJ 08723
732-920-1617

Brick Town Veterinary Hospital
251 Chambersbridge Road
Brick, NJ 08723
732-477-9440

Hopewell Veterinary Clinic
540 Shiloh Pike
Bridgeton, NJ 08302
609-451-0840

Wilwynn Animal Hospital
496 Greenwich Road
Bridgeton, NJ 08302
609-451-0789

Somerset Veterinary Group
1074 US Highway 22
Bridgewater, NJ 08807
908-725-1800

Brielle Animal Clinic
505 Highway 71
Brielle, NJ 08730
732-528-7800

Brigantine Animal Hospital
3105 W Brigantine Avenue
Brigantine, NJ 08203
609-266-0700

Browns Mills Animal Clinic
14 Pemberton Browns Mill Road
Browns Mills, NJ 08015
609-893-4662

Budd Lake Animal Clinic
141 US Highway 46
Budd Lake, NJ 07828
973-691-9333

Florence Veterinary Clinic
2116 Route 130 North
Burlington, NJ 08016
609-499-2023

Burlington Animal Hospital
1031 Route 130 South
Burlington, NJ 08016
609-386-4422

Schoolhouse Animal Hospital
2701 Mount Holly Road
Burlington, NJ 08016
609-387-0302

Sova Animal Hospital
1546 State Rt 23
Butler, NJ 07405
973-838-5528

C

Califon Animal Clinic
421 County Road 513
Califon, NJ 07830
908-832-7523

Pennsauken Animal Hospital
6717 S Crescent Blvd
Camden, NJ 08105
609-662-4450

Sheehan Veterinary Center
1594 Collings Road
Camden, NJ 08104
609-962-8080

Cape Veterinary Clinic
694 Petticoat Creek Lane
Cape May, NJ 08204
609-884-1729

Abri Animal Hospital
38 S Route 47
Cape May Court House, NJ 08210
609-465-1368

Cape Veterinary Hospital
305 Goshen Swainton Road
Cape May Court House, NJ 08210
609-465-9326

Parkway Veterinary Hospital
1173 S Route 9
Cape May Court House, NJ 08210
609-465-5590

Carlstadt Animal Clinic
413 Hackensack Street
Carlstadt, NJ 07072
201-939-1332

Carteret Animal Clinic
6 Cooke Avenue
Carteret, NJ 07008
732-541-5551

Cedar Grove Animal Hospital
370 Pompton Ave
Cedar Grove, NJ 07009
973-239-3500

Chatham Animal Hospital
14 Watchung Ave
Chatham, NJ 07928
973-635-4994

Cherry Hill Animal Hospital
1425 Marlton Pike E
Cherry Hill, NJ 08034
609-429-4394

Lexington Animal Hospital
1091 Raritan Road
Clark, NJ 07066
732-381-3700

Millstone Animal Hospital
39 Carrs Tavern Road
Clarksburg, NJ 08510
609-259-1955

New Jersey Equine Clinic
279 Millstone Road
Clarksburg, NJ 08510
609-259-9149

Clayton Veterinary Assoc
714 N Delsea Dr
Clayton, NJ 08312
609-881-7470

Clementon Animal Hospital
210 White Horse Pike
Clementon, NJ 08021
609-784-2304

Cliffside Animal Hospital
401 Palisade Ave
Cliffside Park, NJ 07010
201-943-2400

Clifton Dog & Cat Hospital
1315 Main Ave
Clifton, NJ 07011
973-772-6686

Clifton Pet General
1071 Paulison Ave Fl 1
Clifton, NJ 07011
973-478-0097

Foster Animal Hospital
1347 Broad St
Clifton, NJ 07013
973-777-0064

Veterinary Health Care Ctr
753 Van Houten Ave
Clifton, NJ 07013
973-472-8883

Spruce Run Veterinary Hospital
1730 State Route 31
Clinton, NJ 08809
908-735-8411

Closter Animal Hospital
137 Piermont Road
Closter, NJ 07624
201-768-0880

Colonia Veterinary Clinic
490 Inman Ave
Colonia, NJ 07067
732-382-6290

Colts Neck Animal Clinic
85 State Route 34 S
Colts Neck, NJ 07722
732-780-4211

Columbus Central Veterinary
3075 Route 206
Columbus, NJ 08022
609-298-4600

Carnegie Cat Clinic
332 Princeton Hightstown Road
Cranbury, NJ 08512
609-951-0400

Prospect-Applegarth Animal Hospital
2670 Route 130
Cranbury, NJ 08512
609-655-5545

Cranford Veterinary Hospital
1 Springfield Ave
Cranford, NJ 07016
908-272-5000

Cream Ridge Animal Clinic
163 Burlington Path Road # A
Cream Ridge, NJ 08514
609-758-3030

Cresskill Animal Hospital
39 Spring St
Cresskill, NJ 07626
201-568-7700

D

Animal Clinic of Morris Plains
3009 State Route 10
Denville, NJ 07834
973-366-3223

Denville Animal Hospital
279 U.S. Highway 46
Denville, NJ 07834
973-625-5300

E

Cranbury Veterinary Hospital
465 Cranbury Road
East Brunswick, NJ 08816
732-257-7200

East Brunswick Animal Hospital
44 Arthur Street
East Brunswick, NJ 08816
732-254-1212

Edgebrook Veterinary Hospital
777 Helmetta Boulevard
East Brunswick, NJ 08816
732-257-8882

Village Veterinary Hospital
180 Main Street
East Brunswick, NJ 08816
732-390-7337

Hanover Veterinary Hospital
33 Eagle Rock Avenue
East Hanover, NJ 07936
973-887-0522

East Orange Animal Hospital
152 Central Avenue
East Orange, NJ 07017
973-676-7799

Modern Animal Hospital
33 North Park Street
East Orange, NJ 07017
973-675-6456

Shrewsbury Animal Center
1008 Shrewsbury Avenue
Eatontown, NJ 07724
732-542-0007

Animal General
725 River Road
Edgewater, NJ 07020
201-313-7000

Just Cats Veterinary Care
141 State Route 27
Edison, NJ 08817
732-632-8200

Oak Tree Animal Clinic
32122 Oak Tree Road
Edison, NJ 08817
732-548-4411

Raritan Hospital for Animals
1850 Lincoln Highway
Edison, NJ 08817
732-985-0278

Cologne Animal Hospital
727 White Horse Pike
Egg Harbor City, NJ 08215
609-965-6008

Egg Harbor City Dog and Cat Clinic
128 Hamburge Avenue
Egg Harbor City, NJ 08215
609-965-5555 08215

VIP Animal Hospital
444 North Broad Street
Elizabeth, NJ 07201
908-289-7387

Meisels' Animal Hospital
268 Broadway
Elmwood Park, NJ 07407
201-797-5300

Emerson Animal Hospital
371 Kinderkamack Road
Emerson, NJ 07630
201-262-2950

Englewood Animal Hospital
43 North Dean Street
Englewood, NJ 07631
201-568-1751

Englewood Cliffs Veterinary
34 Sylvan Avenue
Englewood Cliffs, NJ 07632
201-461-8651

Animal Health Care of Malboro
299 US Highway 9
Englishtown, NJ 07726
732-972-3201

Aspen Veterinary Clinic
298 Franklin Lane #G
Englishtown, NJ 07726
732-431-5454

Country Animal Clinic
22 Water Street
Englishtown, NJ 07726
732-446-5446

Manalapan Animal Clinic
690 Tennent Road
Englishtown, NJ 07726
732-536-1888

F

Fair Haven Animal Hospital
770 River Road
Fair Haven, NJ 07704
732-758-9797

Fair Lawn Animal Hospital
24 Maple Avenue
Fair Lawn, NJ 07410
973-796-2621

Lincoln Avenue Cat Hospital
133 Lincoln Avenue
Fair Lawn, NJ 07410
973-427-0990

Valley Brook Veterinary Hospital
3 Saddle River Road
Fair Lawn, NJ 07410
973-796-5833

Fanwood Animal Hospital
70 South Avenue
Fanwood, NJ 07430
908-322-7500

Bedminster Animal Hospital
330 US Highway 202
Far Hills, NJ 07931
908-234-0650

Cranberry Woods Equine Vet Service
229 Cranberry Road
Farmingdale, NJ 07727
732-938-4272

Farmingdale Veterinary Clinic
11 Walnut Street
Farmingdale, NJ 07727
732-938-4375

Flanders Veterinary Clinic
286 US Highway 206
Flanders, NJ 07836
973-927-4948

Mountain Lakes Vet Housecall
14 Theresa Drive
Flanders, NJ 07836
973-625-4100

Clover Hill Animal Hospital
257 US Highway 202
Flemington, NJ 08822
908-806-4525

Countryside Veterinary Hospital
1025 County Road 523
Flemington, NJ 08822
908-788-1800

Flemington Veterinary Hospital
332 US Highway 202
Flemington, NJ 08822
908-782-5731

Florham Park Animal Hospital
207 Ridgedale Avenue
Florham Park, NJ 07932
973-966-1998

Hopelawn Animal Clinic
297 New Brunswick Avenue
Ford, NJ 08863
732-738-1338

Crossroads Animal Hospital
458 West Street
Fort Lee, NJ 07024
201-944-3244

Fort Lee-Oradel Veterinary
1540 Lemoine Avenue
Fort Lee, NJ 07024
201-947-2442

Franklin Lakes Animal Hospital
754 Franklin Avenue
Franklin Lakes, NJ 07417
201-848-1991

Central Monmouth Animal Hospital
154 South Street
Freehold, NJ 07728
732-462-1876

Freehold Veterinary Hospital
3700 Route 9 South
Freehold, NJ 07728
732-462-0572

Frenchtown Veterinary Clinic
711 Harrison Street
Frenchtown, NJ 08825
908-996-3350

G

Glen Rock Veterinary Hospital
857 Street
Glen Rock, NJ 07452
201-444-0032

Green Brook Animal Hospital
915 North Washington Avenue
Green Brook, NJ 08812
732-968-3311

H

Hackensack Animal Hospital
50 Hackensack Avenue
Hackensack, NJ 07601
201-487-2727

East Plane Animal Hospital
112 East Plane Street
Hackettstown, NJ 07840
908-850-9494

Garden State Veterinary Hospital
94 US Highway 46
Hackettstown, NJ 07840
908-852-3515

Hackettstown Animal Hospital
14 US Highway 46
Hackettstown, NJ 07840
908-852-3166

Haddon Veterinarian Clinic
2 Second Avenue
Haddon Heights, NJ 08035
609-547-0731

Hamburg Veterinary Clinic
59 Vernon Avenue
Hamburg, NJ 07419
973-827-2777

Shore Veterinarians
357 South White Horse Pike
Hammonton, NJ 08037
609-561-2802

Hampton Animal Hospital
174 Main Street
Hampton, NJ 07860
908-537-4241

Hawthorne Animal Hospital
1125 Goffle Road
Hawthorne, NJ 07506
973-427-5554

Greenwood Lake Animal Hospital
1925 Union Valley Road
Hewitt, NJ 07421
973-728-2233

Highland Park Animal Clinic
31 South Second Avenue
Highland Park, NJ 08030
732-247-3737

Park Veterinary Clinic
1018 Raritan Avenue
Highland Park, NJ 08030
732-819-8299

Plainsboro West Windsor Vet
332 Princeton Hightstown Road
Hightstown, NJ 08520
609-799-3110

Twin Rivers Animal Hospital
244 Franklin Street
Hightstown, NJ 08520
609-426-9625

Hillsdale Animal Hospital
201 Broadway
Hillsdale, NJ 07642
201-358-6520

Hillside Animal Hospital
1148 Liberty Avenue
Hillside, NJ 07205
908-289-1414

Hohokus Brookside Avenue Service
205 Brookside Avenue
Ho Ho Kus, NJ 07423
201-652-3424

Hohokus Veterinary Hospital
22 Sycamore Avenue
Ho Ho Kus, NJ 07423
201-652-1258

Animal Infirmary of Hoboken
600 Adams Street
Hoboken, NJ 07030
201-216-5777

Hoboken Animal Clinic
640 Washington Street
Hoboken, NJ 07030
210-963-3604

Bayshore Veterinary Hospital
2094 State Route 35
Holmdel, NJ 07733
732-671-3110

Holmdel Veterinary Clinic
959 Holmdel Road
Holmdel, NJ 07733
732-946-7163

Briarwood Veterinary Clinic
1100 US Highway 9
Howell, NJ 07731
732-780-4499

Edgewood Veterinary Hospital
6461 US Highway 9
Howell, NJ 07731
732-363-8247

Howell Animal Hospital
238 Alexander Avenue
Howell, NJ 07731
732-364-6900

Howell Veterinary Clinic
641 Fort Plains Road
Howell, NJ 07731
732-364-3421

I

Chancellor Animal Hospital
595 Chancellor Avenue
Irvington, NJ 07111
973-375-6618

Iselin Veterinary Hospital
450 State Route 27
Iselin, NJ 08830
732-283-2110

J

Jackson Veterinary Clinic
33 South New Prospect Road
Jackson, NJ 07305
732-363-0809

Animal Clinic and Hospital
603 West Side Avenue
Jersey City, NJ 07301
201-435-6424

K

Arlington Dog and Cat Hospital
857 Passaic Avenue
Kearny, NJ 07032
201-991-3664

County Veterinary Hospital
3176 State Route 27
Kendall Park, NJ 08824
732-422-7500

Paulus Animal Hospital
7 Allston Road
Kendall Park, NJ 08824
732-297-1212

Boulevard Veterinary Clinic
429 Kenilworth Boulevard
Kenilworth, NJ 07033
908-276-1661

Kenilworth Animal Hospital
741 Boulevard
Kenilworth, NJ 07033
908-245-8776

Community Animal Hospital
707 Washington Avenue
Keyport, NJ 07735
732-739-2111

Kinnelon Veterinary Hospital
160 Kennelon Road
Kinnelon, NJ 07405
973-492-5413

Voorhees Veterinary Clinic
1138 White Horse Road
Kirkwood, NJ 08043
609-435-8090

L

Jersey Shore Veterinary
1000 Highway 70
Lakewood, NJ 08701
732-363-3200

Ocean County Veterinary Hospital
838 River Avenue
Lakewood, NJ 08701
732-363-7202

Amwell Animal Hospital
1410 Route 179
Lambertville, NJ 08530
609-397-0981

Lambertville Animal Clinic
66 York Street
Lambertville, NJ 08530
609-397-3657

Animal Clinic of Country Lakes
106 Landing Road
Landing, NJ 07850
973-398-2400

Veterinary Care Center
175 Lakeside Boulevard
Landing, NJ 07850
973-398-4111

Golub Anima Hospital
1901 US Highway 46
Ledgewood, NJ 07852
973-691-1771

Willowbrook Animal Clinic
7 Chapel Hill Road
Lincoln Park, NJ 07035
973-872-8920

Linden Animal Hospital
936 East Elizabeth Avenue
Linden, NJ 07036
908-486-3092

Animal Emergency Clinic
312 Berlin Road North
Lindenwold, NJ 08021
609-784-6514

Mountainview Animal Hospital
351 Blockwood Clementon Road
Lindenwold, NJ 08021
609-346-1212

Linwood Animal Hospital
535 Maple Avenue
Linwood, NJ 08221
609-927-7022

Little Falls Animal Hospital
333 Main Street
Little Falls, NJ 07424
973-785-8223

Little Silver Animal Hospital
675 Branch Avenue
Little Silver, NJ 07739
732-842-8266

Monmouth Animal Hospital
115 Oceanport Avenue
Little Silver, NJ 07739
732-747-4522

Livingston Animal Hospital
619 West Mount Pleasant Avenue
Livingston, NJ 07039
973-992-8888

Bergen Passaic Animal Hospital
541 Westminster Place
Lodi, NJ 07644
973-772-4930

Long Branch Animal Hospital
224 Second Avenue
Long Branch, NJ 07740
732-571-4100

Califon Animal Clinic
15 Naughtright Road
Long Valley, NJ 07853
908-876-4688

Long Valley Veterinary Clinic
59 East Mill Road
Long Valley, NJ 07853
908-876-5434

M

Madison Veterinary Hospital
262 Main Street
Madison, NJ 07940
973-377-1515

Fardale Veterinary Hospital
346 Forest Road
Mahwah, NJ 07430
210-891-7956

Manahawkin Veterinary Hospital
655 Route 72 West
Manahawkin, NJ 08050
609-597-0080

Stafford Veterinary Hospital
211 Route 9 North
Manahawkin, NJ 08050
609-597-7571

Squan Animal Hospital
1427 Lakewood Road
Manasquan, NJ 08736
732-528-9199

Maple Shade Animal Hospital
845 East Main Street
Maple Shade, NJ 08052
609-779-8818

Maplewood Animal Hospital
2006 Springfield Avenue
Maplewood, NJ 07040
973-762-5000

Valley Veterinary Hospital
2006 Millburn Avenue
Maplewood, NJ 07040
973-763-3445

Margate Animal Hospital
9200 Ventnor Avenue
Margate City, NJ 08402
609-823-3031

Brook Meadow Veterinary Hospital
480 County Road 520
Marlboro, NJ 08302
732-946-8339

Marlboro Village Vet Clinic
26 North Main Street
Marlboro, NJ 08302
732-431-0717

County Line Veterinary Hospital
989 Route 73 South
Marlton, NJ 08053
609-988-0022

Evesham Veterinary Clinic
800 Route 73 South
Marlton, NJ 08053
609-983-9440

Marlton Animal Hospital
9 West Main Street
Marlton, NJ 08053
609-983-5350

Medford Veterinary Clinic
951 Tuckerton Road
Marlton, NJ 08053
609-983-5757

Parwkway Veterinary Hospital
40 Roosevelt Boulevard
Marmora, NJ 08223
609-390-0701

Rubin Veterinary Hospital
222 South Shore Road
Marmora, NJ 08223
609-390-0199

Martinsville Animal Hospital
1983 Washington Valley Road
Martinsville, NJ 08836
732-469-6272

Berg Animal Hospital
3 State Route 34
Matawan, NJ 07747
732-566-65500

Matawan Animal Hospital
251 Highway 516 #C
Matawan, NJ 07747
732-566-6363

Mays Landing Dog and Cat Clinic
907 Route 50
Mays Landing, NJ 08330
609-625-0699

Maywood Veterinary Clinic
138 West Pleasant Avenue
Maywood, NJ 07607
201-368-0607

Countryside Animal Hospital
190 Route 70
Medford, NJ 08055
609-953-3502

Medford Animal Hospital
45 Jackson Road
Medford, NJ 08055
609-654-6855

South Jersey Animal Hospital
204 Route 541
Medford, NJ 08055
609-654-0300

Village Veterinary Hospital
177 Church Road
Medford, NJ 08055
609-953-8733

Howard Veterinary Service
1 Knollwood Trail East
Mendham, NJ 07945
973-543-6665

Mendham Animal Hospital
571 State Route 24
Mendham, NJ 07945
973-879-5800

Mercerville Animal Hospital
720 Edinburg Road
Mercerville, NJ 08619
609-587-5863

Veterinary Care Clinic
3100 Quackerbridge Road
Mercerville, NJ 08619
609-890-6266

Amboy Avenue Veterinary Hospital
159 Amboy Avenue
Metuchen, NJ 08840
732-548-1991

Bound Brook Veterinary Clinic
95 Union Avenue
Middlesex, NJ 08846
732-356-1573

Middletown Animal Hospital
1330 State Route 35
Middletown, NJ 07748
732-671-1503

Ticehurst Animal Hospital
537 State Highway 35
Middletown, NJ 07748
732-741-0621

Midland Park Veterinary Hospital
577 Godwin Avenue
Midland Park, NJ 07432
201-444-6848

Ridgewood Veterinary Hospital
70 Goffle Road
Midland Park, NJ 07432
201-445-0030

Springmills Veterinary Hospital
72 Spring Mills Road
Milford, NJ 08848
908-995-4959

Millburn Veterinary Hospital
147 Millburn Avenue
Millburn, NJ 07041
973-467-1700

Milltown Animal Clinic
111 South Main Street
Milltown, NJ 07930
973-467-1700

Animal Clinic of Millville
2425 West Main Street
Millville, NJ 07930
609-825-8935

Animal Hospital of Millville
2206 North Delsea Drive
Millville, NJ 08332
609-825-3434

South Brunswick Animal Hospital
879 Georges Road
Monmouth Junction, NJ 08853
732-821-0040

Montague Veterinary Hospital
325 Clove Road
Montague, NJ 07827
973-293-7132

Cameron Animal Hospital
417 Bloomfield Avenue
Montclair, NJ 07042
973-744-2052

Montclair Animal Hospital
124 Watchung Avenue
Montclair, NJ 07042
973-744-1942

Montvale Animal Hospital
115 Chestnut Ridge Road
Montvale, NJ 07645
201-391-4342

Burl Moor-Driben Animal Hospital
104 Kings Highway
Moorestown, NJ 08057
609-235-2534

Marlboro Animal Hospital
382 Highway 79
Morganville, NJ 07751
732-591-1900

Community Animal Hospital
921 State Route 53
Morris Plains, NJ 07950
973-267-4220

Werner Animal Hospital
659 State Route 53
Morris Plains, NJ 07950
973-540-1433

Feline Health Center
22 Elm Street
Morristown, NJ 07747
973-285-5151

Morristown Animal Hospital
400 Western Avenue
Morristown, NJ 07747
973-539-2808

South Street Veterinary Hospital
467 South Street
Morristown, NJ 07747
973-538-5414

Bryan Animal Hospital
102 Burrs Road
Mt. Holly, NJ 08060
609-267-0304

Marne Veterinary Clinic
2127 Marne Highway
Mt. Holly, NJ 08060
609-267-1609

Mount Laurel Animal Hospital
220 Moorestown Mt. Laurel Road
Mount Laurel, NJ 08054
609-234-7626

Racoon Valley Animal Hospital
301 Bridgeton Pike
Mullica Hill, NJ 08062
609-478-6500

N

Neptune Animal Hospital
317 State Route 35 North
Neptune, NJ 07753
732-775-5619

Shark River Veterinary Hospital
2260 State Route 33
Neptune, NJ 07753
732-775-2444

Amwell Bird Hospital
625 Amwell Road
Neshanic Station, NJ 08853
908-369-7373

Garden State Veterinary Hospital
41 Main Street
Netcong, NJ 07857
973-347-3611

Paulus Animal Hospital
141 How Lane
New Brunswick, NJ 08901
732-545-2900

American Dog and Cat Hospital
47 Elizabeth Avenue
Newark, NJ 07101
973-824-8347

Fredon Animal Clinic
391 State Route 94 South
Newton, NJ 07860
973-383-0811

Newton Veterinary Hospital
116 Hampton House Road
Newton, NJ 07860
973-383-4321

Bergenline Animal Hospital
7706 Bergenline Avenue
North Bergen, NJ 07047
201-854-7330

North Bergen Animal Hospital
9018 Kennedy Boulevard
North Bergen, NJ 07047
201-868-3753

Branchburg Animal Hospital
1167 State Highway 288
North Branch, NJ 08876
908-707-0045

North Brunswick Veterinary
832 Livingston Avenue
North Brunswick, NJ 08902
732-828-8175

North Haledon Veterinary Care
475 High Mountain Road
North Haledon, NJ 07508
973-423-5656

Dog, Cat and Bird Clinic
692 Passaic Avenue
Nutley, NJ 07110
973-661-0441

Nutley Animal Hospital
274 Wasington Avenue
Nutley, NJ 07110
973-667-7772

O

West Milford Animal Hospital
45 Oak Ridge Road
Oak Ridge, NJ 07438
973-697-8890

Oakhurst Veterinary Hospital
225 Monmouth Road
Oakhurst, NJ 07755
732-531-1212

Oakland Animal Hospital
86 Ramapo Valley Road
Oakland, NJ 07436
201-337-7090

Ramapo Valley Animal Hospital
12 Terhune street
Oakland, NJ 07436
201-337-4870

Collingswood Veterinary Hospital
40 White Horse Pike
Oaklyn, NJ 08107
609-858-0551

Rothman Animal Hospital
718 Dwight Avenue
Oaklyn, NJ 08107
609-854-7575

Ocean City Veterinary Office
712 West Avenue
Ocean City, NJ 08226
609-391-9536

Old Bridge Veterinary Clinic
2400 County Road 516
Old Bridge, NJ 08857
732-679-1850

Route 516 Animal Hospital
2515 County Road 516
Old Bridge, NJ 08857
732-679-1551

Oradell Animal Hospital
481 Kinderkamack Road
Oradell, NJ 07649
201-262-0010

P

Fort Lee Animal Hospital
534 Tenth Street
Palisades Park, NJ 07650
201-944-0140

Farview Animal Clinic
429 North Farview Avenue
Paramus, NJ 07652
201-967-1881

Paramus Animal Clinic
54 Linwood Avenue East
Paramus, NJ 07652
210-445-3350

Park Ridge Animal Hospital
40 Park Avenue
Park Ridge, NJ 07656
210-391-9494

Animal Clinic of Parsippany
189 Parsippany Road
Parsippany, NJ 07054
973-386-1711

Animal Clinic of Passaic
37 Grove Street
Passaic, NJ 07055
973-471-3598

Parkview Animal Hospital
48 Main Avenue
Passaic, NJ 07055
973-473-4993

Blue Cross Dog and Cat Hospital
470 McLean Boulevard
Paterson, NJ 07501
973-881-0430

Pennington Veterinary Hospital
186 Pennington Harbourton Road
Pennington, NJ 08534
609-737-0010

Stoney Brook Animal Hospital
116 Titus Mill Road
Pennington, NJ 08534
609-737-2187

Westfield Animal Hospital
6928 Westfield Avenue
Pennsauken, NJ 08110
609-665-1858

Pennsville Veterinary Clinic
187 Churchtown Road
Pennsville, NJ 08070
609-678-2070

Harmony Animal Hospital
2200 Belvidere Road
Phillipsburg, NJ 08865
908-678-2070

Phillipsburg Veterinary Clinic
581 Memorial Parkway
Phillipsburg, NJ 08865
908-859-2552

Warren Animal Hospital
793 Uniontown Road
Phillipsburg, NJ 08865
908-859-0702

Hadley Cat Clinic
1100 Shelton Road
Piscataway, NJ 08854
732-572-9550

Piscataway Animal Clinic
13 Shelton Road
Piscataway, NJ 08854
732-968-6888

Pitman Animal Hospital
654 Delsea Drive
Pitman, NJ 08071
609-582-7500

Equine Trauma Center
630 County Road 513
Pittstown, NJ 08867
908-735-6131

Animal Medical Group
947 Prospect Avenue
Plainfield, NJ 07060
908-756-1488

Bayview Animal Hospital
201 Venice Avenue
Pleasantville, NJ 08232
609-646-7195

Galloway Animal Hospital
10 White Horse Pike
Pomona, NJ 08240
609-965-4400

Pompton Lakes Animal Hospital
9 Cannonball Road
Pompton Lakes, NJ 07742
973-835-4774

Annimal Clinic of Pequannock
591 Newark Pompton Turnpike
Pompton Plains, NJ 07444
973-676-0400

Carnegie Cat Clinic
730 Alexander Road
Princeton, NJ 08540
609-951-0400

Lawrence Hospital for Animals
3975 Princeton Pike
Princeton, NJ 08540
609-924-2293

Princeton Animal Hospital
3440 US Highway 1
Princeton, NJ 08540
609-520-2000

Point Pleasant Vet Hospital
646 Ocean Road
Point Pleasant Beach, NJ 08742
732-892-4647

R

Clark Animal Hospital
1075 Westfield Avenue
Rahway, NJ 07065
732-388-3379

Rahway Animal Hospital
175 West Grand Avenue
Rahway, NJ 07065
732-381-2700

Kavanagh Animal Hospital
190 North Franklin Turnpike
Ramsey, NJ 07446
201-372-1877

Ramsey Veterinary Hospital
3 Meadowbrook Road
Ramsey, NJ 07446
201-825-4545

Alliance Emergency Veterinary
540 West State Highway 10
Randolph, NJ 07869
973-328-2844

American Animal Hospital
1202 Sussex Turnpike
Randolph, NJ 07869
973-895-4999

Readington Animal Hospital
96 Readington Road
Readington, NJ 08770
908-534-4058

Red Bank Veterinary Hospital
210 Newman Springs Road
Red Bank, NJ 08063
732-747-3636

A & R Veterinary Hospital
365 Broad Avenue
Ridgefield, NJ 07657
201-945-67700

Cats Exclusive Veterinary
742 Bergen Boulevard
Ridgefield, NJ 07657
201-943-8100

Ridgefield Park Animal Hospital
215 Main Street
Ridgefield Park, NJ 07660
201-814-0095

Ridgewood Veterinary Hospital
320 East Ridgewood Avenue
Ridgewood, NJ 07450
201-447-6000

Mid-Atlantic Equine Medical
40 Frontage Road
Ringoes, NJ 08551
609-397-0078

Animal Clinic of Ringwood
130 Skyline Drive
Ringwood, NJ 07456
973-962-0600

Animal Health Care Hospital
1131 Greenwood Lake Turnpike
Ringwood, NJ 07456
973-728-5148

Ringwood Animal Hospital
72 Greenwood Lake Turnpike
Ringwood, NJ 07456
973-835-1112

Baysea Veterinary Hospital
1127 Route 47 South
Rio Grande, NJ 08242
609-886-2292

River Edge Animal Hospital
311 Kinderkamack Road
River Edge, NJ 07661
201-487-0118

River Vale Animal Hospital
684 Westwood Avenue
River Vale, NJ 07675
201-666-6447

North Jersey Animal Hospital
62 Hamburg Turnpike
Riverdale, NJ 07457
973-835-3733

Robbinsville Veterinary Clinic
1116 US Highway 130
Robbinsville, NJ 08691
609-890-1177

Rockaway Animal Clinic
328 US Highway 46
Rockaway, NJ 07866
973-627-0789

Animal Care of Roseland
215 Eagle Rock Avenue
Roseland, NJ 07068
973-228-4444

Elizabeth Veterinary Clinic
151 East Second Avenue
Roselle, NJ 07203
908-245-7853

Roselle Park Animal Hospital
422 East Westfield Avenue
Roselle Park, NJ 07204
908-245-0233

Rutherford Animal Hospital
22 Glen Road
Rutherford, NJ 07070
201-933-4111

S

Saddle River Animal Hospital
171 East Saddle River Road
Saddle River, NJ 07458
201-818-9660

Salem Veterinary Hospital
659 Salem Quinton Road
Salem, NJ 08079
609-935-1390

Sayrebrook Veterinary Hospital
1400 Main Street
Sayreville, NJ 08872
732-727-1303

Scotch Plains Animal Hospital
1919 US Highway 22
Scotch Plains, NJ 07076
908-322-5515

Sea Girt Animal Hospital
2129 Highway 35
Sea Girt, NJ 08750
732-449-9224

Secaucus Animal Hospital
1250 Paterson Plank Road
Secaucus, NJ 07094
201-867-4795

All Creatures Veterinary Care
352 Greentree Road
Sewell, NJ 08080
609-256-8996

Gloucester County Animal Hospital
354 Egg Harbor Road
Sewell, NJ 08080
609-582-2127

Cedar Brook Animal Hospital
223 New Brooklyn Cedarbrook Road
Sickerville, NJ 08081
609-629-7177

Animal Hospital of Somerdale
408 North White Horse Pike
Somerdale, NJ 08083
609-346-4242

Somers Point Veterinary Clinic
1 Braddock Drive
Somers Point, NJ 08244
609-927-8077

Cedar Lane Animal Clinic
1760 Easton Avenue
Somerset, NJ 08628
732-469-5133

Hillsborough Veterinary Hospital
210 US Highway 206 South
Somerville, NJ 08876
908-359-3161

Animal Hospital of Sayreville
257 Oak Street
South Amboy, NJ 08879
732-727-7739

South Orange Animal Hospital
66 Valley Street
South Orange, NJ 07079
973-763-2600

Plainfield Animal Hospital
2201 Park Avenue
South Plainfield, NJ 07080
908-755-2428

South River Veterinary Clinic
74 Main Street
South River, NJ 08882
732-257-4747

Highlands Veterinary Hospital
49 Woodport Road 07871
Sparta, NJ
973-726-8080

Veterinary House Calls
33 Summit Trail
Sparta, NJ 07871
973-729-7121

Byram Animal Hospital
8 US Highway 206
Stanhope, NJ 07874
973-347-7500

Animal Health Center
2402 State Route 57
Stewartsville, NJ 08886
908-859-3045

Stirling Veterinary Hospital
1158 Valley Road
Stirling, NJ 07980
908-647-2686

Roxbury Animal Hospital
21 State Route 10 East
Succasunna, NJ 07876
973-584-5167

Summit Dog and Cat Hospital
16 Morris Turnpike
Summit, NJ 07901
908-273-2200

Island Veterinary Clinic
1111 Long Beach Boulevard
Surf City, NJ 08008
609-494-4111

Sussex Veterinary Hospital
225 County Road 565
Sussex, NJ 07461
973-875-5811

Delaware Valley Veterinary
903 Kings Highway
Swedesboro, NJ 08085
609-241-1100

Swedesboro Animal Hospital
284 Kings Highway
Swedesboro, NJ 08085
609-467-0004

T

Bergen Animal Hospital
1680 Teaneck Road
Teaneck, NJ 07666
201-837-3470

West Deptford Animal Hospital
195 Hudson Avenue
Thorofare, NJ 08086
609-845-3594

Bayview Veterinary Hospital
574 Fischer Boulevard
Toms River, NJ 08753
732-270-4700

Cat Care Clinic
1747 Hooper Avenue #10
Toms River, NJ 08753
732-255-2208

Dover Veterinary Hospital
877 Fischer Boulevard
Toms River, NJ 08753
732-929-9090

Pleasant Plains Vet Hospital
1842 Lakewood Road
Toms River, NJ 08753
732-240-4488

Toms River Veterinary Hospital
769 Route 37 West
Toms River, NJ 08753
732-349-4599

Totowa Animal Hospital
819 Riverview Drive
Totowa, NJ 07512
973-256-3303

Montville Animal Clinic
6 White Hall Road
Towaco, NJ 07082
973-335-8007

Tranquility Veterinary Clinic
70 Kennedy Road
Tranquility, NJ 07879
908-852-7800

Chesterfield Veterinary Clinic
8 Newbold Lane
Trenton, NJ
609-298-3888

Ewing Veterinary Hospital
38 Scotch Road
Trenton, NJ
609-882-8090

Family Pet Veterinary Clinic
1676 Old Trenton Road
Trenton, NJ
609-443-1212

Hamilton Veterinary Hospital
18 East Park Avenue
Trenton, NJ
609-888-3400

Nottingham Animal Hospital
395 Highway 33
Trenton, NJ
609-587-0222

Paws and Claws
238 Ashmore Avenue
Trenton, NJ
609-989-7575

Quaker Bridge Animal Hospital
3710 Quakerbridge Road
Trenton, NJ
609-586-7799

Solomon Veterinary Hospital
1709 Nottingham Way
Trenton, NJ
609-587-5553

Trenton Veterinary Hospital
695 Pennington Avenue
Trenton, NJ
609-394-8171

Southern Ocean Animal Hospital
319 East Main Street
Tuckerton, NJ 08087
609-296-3655

Tuckerton Veterinary Clinic
500 North Green Street
Tuckerton, NJ 08087
609-296-7571

Animal Hospital at Washington
450 Hurffville Cross Keys Road
Turnersville, NJ 08012
609-589-1155

Black Horse Pike Hospital
4250 Route 42
Turnersville, NJ 08012
609-728-1400

U

Central Animal Hospital
1067 Commerce Avenue
Union, NJ 08802
908-686-6873

TLC Pet Doctor
1345 Stuyvesant Avenue
Union, NJ 08802
908-686-7080

Ambassador Veterinary Hospital
3714 Kennedy Boulevard
Union City, NJ 07087
201-863-4072

Animal Clinic
600 Kennedy Boulevard
Union City, NJ 07087
201-865-5473

Summit Animal Clinic
3130 Summit Avenue
Union City, NJ 07087
201-348-8653

V

Vernon Veterinary Hospital
346 State Route 94
Vernon, NJ 07462
973-764-3630

Marsh Hospital for Animals
299 Bloomfield Avenue
Vernona, NJ 07044
973-239-0774

Verona Animal Hospital
17 Grove Avenue
Verona, NJ 07044
973-239-1881

Animal Clinic of Tabernacle
314 Medford Lakes Road
Vincentown, NJ 08088
609-268-9570

Pinelands Veterinary Clinic
1909 Route 38
Vincentown, NJ 08088
609-265-0100

Blue Cross Animal Hospital
1117 North Delsea Drive
Vineland, NJ 08360
609-696-3388

Cumberland Veterinary Hospital
1951 South Lincoln Avenue
Vineland, NJ 08360
609-691-3500

East Oak Veterinary Hospital
1673 East Oak Road
Vineland, NJ 08360
609-696-4440

Main Road Veterinary Clinic
847 South Main Road
Vineland, NJ 08360
609-696-0395

Pet Vet Animal Clinic
1921 West Landis Avenue
Vineland, NJ 08360
609-563-0410

W

Waldwick Animal Hospital
68 Franklin Turnpike
Waldwick, NJ 07463
201-652-3113

All Paws Veterinary Hospital
1732 Highway 71
Wall, NJ 07719
732-449-8585

Animal Clinic of Warren
53 Mountain Boulevard
Warren, NJ 07059
908-561-3083

Warren Animal Hospital
8 North Road
Warren, NJ 07059
732-868-1818

Brass Castle Animal Hospital
263 State Route 31 South
Washington, NJ 07675
908-689-3267

North Jersey Animal Hospital
197 Hamburg Turnpike
Wayne, NJ 07470
973-595-8600

Pompton Valley Animal Hospital
1955 State Highway 23 South
Wayne, NJ 07470
973-305-3652

Wayne Animal Hospital
2411 Hamburg Turnpike
Wayne, NJ 07470
973-839-3737

Wayne Hills Animal Hospital
61 Berdan Avenue #1A
Wayne, NJ 07470
973-633-7550

Berlin Township Animal Clinic
151 Walker Avenue
West Berlin, NJ 08091
609-753-1005

West Caldwell Animal Hospital
706 Bloomfield Avenue
West Caldwell, NJ
973-226-3727

Eagle Rock Pet Care
612 Eagle Rock Avenue
West Orange, NJ 07052
973-736-1555

Main Street Pet Pals
275 Main Street
West Orange, NJ 07052
973-325-8838

Prospect Ridge Veterinary
492 Prospect Avenue
West Orange, NJ 07052
973-736-7810

West Orange Animal Hospital
360 Northfield Avenue
West Orange, NJ 07052
973-731-1222

West Trenton Animal Hospital
568 Grand Avenue
West Trenton, NJ 07304
609-771-0995

Westfield Animal Hospital
357 South Avenue East
Westfield, NJ 07090
908-233-6030

Pascack Animal Clinic
515 Washington Avenue
Westwood, NJ 07675
201-664-8744

Washington Pond Veterinary
60 Pascack Road
Westwood, NJ 07675
201-666-3776

Whippany Veterinary Hospital
539 State Highway 10 East
Whippany, NJ 07981
973-386-1380

Whiting Veterinary Clinic
108 Lacey Road #26
Whiting, NJ 08759
732-849-0408

Berg Veterinary Hospital
1816 Glassboro Road
Williamstown, NJ 08094
609-881-2668

Companion Animal Hospital
2071 North Black Horse Pike
Williamstown, NJ 08094
609-629-6969

Shore Veterinarian West
1056 South Black House Pike
Williamstown, NJ 08094
609-728-6613

Country Club Plaza Veterinary
320 Beverly Rancocas Road
Willingboro, NJ 08046
609-871-2000

Willingboro Veterinary Clinic
10 Sidney Lane
Willingboro, NJ 08046
609-871-1600

Woodbridge Veterinary Group
165 Main Street
Woodbridge, NJ 07095
732-636-5520

Gray Fox Animal Hospital
440 Glassboro Road
Woodbury Heights, NJ 08097
609-848-7070

Decktor Veterinary Hospital
174 Pierson Road
Woodstown, NJ 08098
609-769-1142

Tri-County Veterinary Clinic
816 Route 45
Woodstown, NJ 08098
609-769-0165

Woodstown Veterinary Hospital
1250 Route 40
Woodstown, NJ 08098
609-769-2788

Wrightstown Veterinary Clinic
6 Cebulka Drive
Wrightstown, NJ 08077
609-723-2933

Cropper Veterinary Service
310 Newtown Road
Wyckoff, NJ 07481
201-444-6254

Wyckoff Animal Clinic
358 Clinton Avenue
Wyckoff, NJ 07481
201-891-2220

Y

Yardville Animal Hospital
401 Route 156
Yardville, NJ 08620
609-585-6599

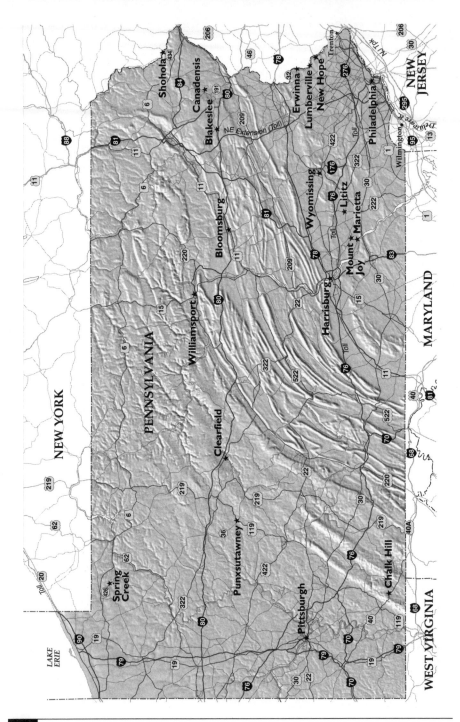

Pennsylvania

Blue Berry Mountain Inn

Blue Berry Mountain Inn
HC1, Box 1102
Thomas Road
Blakeslee, Pennsylvania 18610
717-646-7144
Web Site: www.blueberrymountaininn.com

Room Rates:	$90–$115, including full breakfast.
Pet Charges or Deposits:	$50 refundable deposit. Manager's prior approval required.
Rated: 3 Paws 🐾🐾🐾	6 guest rooms and 1 suite on 440 acres with lake. Indoor pool.

Nestled among mountains, streams, lakes and ponds on hundreds of acres of glacial wetlands is the Blue Berry Mountain Inn. Six modern, well-appointed guest rooms offer spectacular views of nature from each room.

A game room, a library, an indoor heated pool, an outside spa and an extraordinary Great Room that boasts a massive stone fireplace are available to guests. A full breakfast is served daily in the sun room, as well as tea and sweets in the afternoon. The Inn is friendly to the physically challenged.

Inn at Turkey Hill

Inn at Turkey Hill
991 Central Road
Bloomsburg, Pennsylvania 17815
717-387-1500
Web Site: www.enterpe.com/turkeyhill
E-mail: turkyinn@prolog.net (please, do not use E-mail for reservations)

Room Rates:	$95–$185, including continental breakfast.
Pet Charges or Deposits:	$15 per stay. Credit card refundable deposit. Treat bags provided for your pet.
Rated: 4 Paws 🐾🐾🐾🐾	16 guest rooms and 7 suites. Restaurant.

You would probably never suspect that a moment's drive from the Interstate would transport you into a world of peaceful strolls by a duck pond and personal wake-up calls.

This is an oasis along the highway, where continuous attention to detail is evident. It is apparent that the goal here is to make everyone feel pampered, whether you are eating a distinctive gourmet meal, or whether you are spending a night in one of the country cottages surrounding the informal courtyard or in the main house, an 1839 white brick farmhouse.

Fine dining at the Inn at Turkey Hill offers a creative, well-balanced menu in a relaxed, attractive setting.

Merry Inn

Merry Inn
Route 390
P.O. Box 757
Canadensis, Pennsylvania 18325
800-858-4182 ▪ 717-595-2011

Room Rates:	$90–$95, including full breakfast.
Pet Charges or Deposits:	$25 refundable deposit.
Rated: 3 Paws ❀❀❀	6 guest rooms. Outdoor hot tub.

Built Cape Cod-style in the 1940s as a boardinghouse, the Merry Inn was a private home for about twenty years, until 1994.

Owner-innkeepers Chris and Meredyth Huggard have decorated their Inn with comfortable, eclectic furnishings in a country and Victorian style. On the rear, second-level deck, "built over a piece of mountain," is a year-round hot tub that faces the woods. Awake each morning to Western or three-cheese omelets, stuffed French toast or apple or chocolate-chip pancakes served overlooking a brook.

You are within minutes of the Pocono Playhouse, Promised Land State Park, Alpine Mountain and Camelback ski areas. Area shopping, including candle factories and outlets, and white-water rafting, horseback riding and antiquing are nearby.

Pine Knob Inn

Pine Knob Inn
Route 447
Canadensis, Pennsylvania 18325
800-426-1460 ▪ 717-595-2532
Web Site: www.pineknobinn.com
E-mail: innkeepers@pineknobinn.com

Room Rates: $175–$225, including full breakfast and five-course, candlelit
                         dinner.
Pet Charges or Deposits: Manager's prior approval required.
Rated: 3 Paws 🐾🐾🐾   18 guest rooms. Outdoor pool and tennis court.

T his Civil War-period inn resides in the picturesque setting of the scenic Pocono Mountains. Nearby Promiseland State Park provides 8,000 acres of hiking trails, a lake and picnic areas. This location is a vacation land for sports enthusiasts and people seeking relaxation in a setting of tranquillity.

Lodge at Chalk Hill

Lodge at Chalk Hill
Route 40 East, Box 240
Chalk Hill, Pennsylvania 15421
800-833-4283 ▪ 724-438-8880
E-mail: thelodge@borg.pulsenet.com

Room Rates:	$73–$104, including continental breakfast. AAA and AARP discounts.
Pet Charges or Deposits:	$10 per day. Manager's prior approval required.
Rated: 3 Paws 🐾🐾🐾	61 guest rooms and 6 suites with kitchenettes.

he Lodge at Chalk Hill sits atop 37 lush acres in the heart of the scenic Laurel Highlands. Guest rooms and suites offer private decks, with views of the famous mountain foliage and scenic Lake Lenore.

Here you will enjoy whitewater rafting, premier bike trails, skiing and PGA golf. Shop a variety of unique galleries and boutiques or just relax and observe nature from your own private deck. Downhill and cross-country skiing and sleigh rides are within minutes of the Lodge.

Victorian Loft Bed and Breakfast and Cedarwood Lodge

Victorian Loft Bed and Breakfast and Cedarwood Lodge
216 South Front Street
Clearfield, Pennsylvania 16830
800-798-0456 ▪ 814-765-4805

Room Rates:	$95–$105, including full breakfast.
Pet Charges or Deposits:	$50 refundable deposit. Manager's prior approval required.
Rated: 4 Paws 🐾🐾🐾🐾	2 guest rooms, 1 suite, 1 mountain cabin. Kitchen, fireplaces, whirlpool.

T he Victorian Loft Bed and Breakfast is an elegant 1894 Victorian home, whose hosts offer warm hospitality and a friendly atmosphere. The house itself is located along the river in historic Clearfield, just minutes from the theater, restaurants and parks.

Featuring double-decker gingerbread porches, cherry and oak woodwork, stained glass and period furnishings, guest rooms are comfortable, air-conditioned and private. A memorable full breakfast is included with your night's stay and features homemade baked goods and freshly squeezed juice.

Cedarwood Lodge, for secluded privacy on 8 forested acres in the Moshannon State Forest, offers a charming post-and-beam, three-bedroom cabin, completely equipped with all the conveniences in a wilderness setting. There is a screened-in porch, deck, picnic table, gas grill and campfire, making this a wonderful base camp from which to explore the natural surroundings.

Golden Pheasant Inn

Golden Pheasant Inn
River Road, Route 32
Erwinna, Pennsylvania 18920
800-830-4GPI ▪ 610-294-9595
Web Site: www.goldenpheasant.com

Room Rates:	$75–$155, including continental breakfast.
Pet Charges or Deposits:	$10 per day. Manager's prior approval required.
Rated: 4 Paws 🐾🐾🐾🐾	6 guest rooms, 1 suite.

This magical country inn and restaurant is nestled between the Delaware River and the Pennsylvania Canal in Bucks County, Pennsylvania. Perfect for a weekend getaway or an exquisite country meal, the Golden Pheasant Inn is just over an hour from New York City or Philadelphia and only 20 minutes north of New Hope, Pennsylvania. Celebrating its tenth anniversary this year, this Inn remains a Bucks County gem.

Sleep soundly in one of the six romantic guest rooms or the cottage suite, featuring four-poster queen-sized canopy beds, private baths and a generous continental breakfast. All rooms have river and canal views and are furnished in French, English and American antiques. The cottage suite has a peaceful porch overlooking the Delaware Canal and comes equipped with a kitchenette and sitting room.

Sheraton Inn

Sheraton Inn
800 East Park Drive
Harrisburg, Pennsylvania 17111
800-644-3144 ▪ 717-561-2800

Room Rates:	$75–$135. AAA and AARP discounts.
Pet Charges or Deposits:	$10 per day. Manager's prior approval required.
Rated: 3 Paws 🐾🐾🐾	174 guest rooms and 11 suites. Pool, whirlpool, health club and sauna. Restaurant and lounge.

T he Sheraton Inn Harrisburg offers tastefully decorated rooms and suites. Each is complete with remote-control cable TV and direct dial phones with voice mail.

If winding down means working out, you'll enjoy the Sheraton Health Club, which includes a 13-station Nautilus System, workout machines, sauna and whirlpool.

Conveniently located near Pennsylvania government offices and Harrisburg's thriving business community, it is also close to some of the East's top vacation attractions, notably Hershey, Gettysburg and Lancaster County's Pennsylvania Dutch region.

General Sutter Inn

General Sutter Inn
14 East Main Street
Lititz, Pennsylvania 17543
717-626-2115

Room Rates:	$78–$108.
Pet Charges or Deposits:	One night's refundable deposit.
Rated: 3 Paws ❀❀❀	12 guest rooms and 4 suites, 2 restaurants, tavern, outdoor patio.

Founded in 1764 by the Moravian Church and known then as Zum Anker, or Sign of the Anchor, the Inn from its inception has been considered one of the finest in Pennsylvania. In 1803 and again in 1848 the Inn underwent significant structural changes, evolving into the handsome, three-story brick building of today.

The General Sutter Inn features 16 spacious rooms and suites decorated in antique country and Victorian style, two fine restaurants, a full-service tavern and a seasonal outdoor patio. Regional boutiques, interesting local crafts and a myriad of sights and pastimes are only steps from the front door.

Black Bass Hotel

Black Bass Hotel
3774 River Road
Lumberville, Pennsylvania 18933
215-297-5770
Web Site: www.blackbasshotel.com
E-mail: info@blackbasshotel.com

Room Rates:	$65–$175, including continental breakfast.
Pet Charges or Deposits:	Small dogs only.
Rated: 3 Paws ❀ ❀ ❀	7 guest rooms and 2 suites. Restaurants.

T he Black Bass Hotel was built as a fortified haven for river travelers in the turbulent days of the 1740s, when hostile Indian bands roamed the forests. It prospered as an inn for early traders and offered comfort to many travelers.

Though far more civilized today than when boatman and rafters called the inn home, there is the unmistakable sense of history here. Be it in the period-furnished guest rooms and suites, the fine dining rooms, the public room filled with 19th-century antiques and British royal memorabilia, or merely the facade or hallways of the building, there is a rekindling of Colonial spirit that is the very essence of the country inn.

As for provisions, the dining rooms of the Black Bass Hotel have earned a renowned reputation for their culinary reflections of European and American country traditions.

If you are one of those people who, when they imagine a country inn, conjure up the image of antique beds and good food, with a country store across the way, you will feel very much at home at the Black Bass Hotel.

B.F. Hiestand House

B.F. Hiestand House
722 East Market Street
Marietta, Pennsylvania 17547
717-426-1924
Web Site: www.authenticbandb.org

Room Rates:	$85–$105, including full breakfast and afternoon treats.
Pet Charges or Deposits:	$10 per day. Refundable deposit. Manager's prior approval required.
Rated: 4 Paws 🐾🐾🐾🐾	3 guest rooms and 1 suite.

Come experience the elegance of a bygone era in an 1887 High Queen Anne-style Victorian home while relaxing in the cozy, informal setting. This bed and breakfast offers first-class comfort and 19th-century charm, with twelve-foot ceilings and spacious bedrooms. Guest rooms feature stained glass windows, clawfoot bathtubs and handpainted tiles. Through the bedroom windows enjoy the views overlooking the vista of the York hills and river.

A full breakfast is served in the elegant mahogany dining room or on the enclosed sun porch. Welcome refreshments are served to you and your pet and beverages are available throughout the day.

Let your pet run in the enclosed back yard while you take in the tranquillity of the three parlors, verandah, enclosed sun porch and enclosed library porch. Take a ten-minute walk to the scenic Susquehanna River, where you can spend an afternoon fishing or hiking the trails.

Green Acres Farm Bed and Breakfast

Green Acres Farm Bed and Breakfast
1382 Pinkerton Road
Mount Joy, Pennsylvania 17552
717-653-4028
Web Site: www.castyournet.com/greenacres

Room Rates: $85, including full breakfast.
Pet Charges or Deposits: $5 per day. Sorry, no cats.
Rated: 3 Paws 🐾🐾🐾   7 guest rooms on 150-acre farm.

T his farm is truly family-friendly. From your arrival, your welcoming com-
mittee includes your hosts, along with a sociable group of kittens,
pygmy goats, sheep, peacocks, chickens and a pony. And the pigs won't
mind if you take a peek in the pens as well. Children will enjoy the trampo-
lines, volleyball and basketball courts, bicycles and a ride in the hay wagon.

The main farmhouse is furnished with antiques, offering comfortable air-
conditioned guest rooms with private baths. A large balcony and porch set the
relaxing tone, as you overlook the beautiful countryside.

Aaron Burr House

Aaron Burr House
80 West Bridge Street
New Hope, Pennsylvania 18938
215-862-2520

Room Rates:	$120–$220, including breakfast.
Pet Charges or Deposits:	$20 per day. Small dogs only. Sorry, no cats. Manager's prior approval required.
Rated: 4 Paws 🐾🐾🐾🐾	8 guest rooms and 2 suites with fireplaces. Pool and tennis club privileges.

T he Aaron Burr is an 1873 "Painted Lady"—a creamy yellow Bucks County Victorian, one block from the village center, that is on the National Register of Historic Places. A warm, friendly and hospitable inn, each one of its rooms and suites has a distinct personality.

Rooms are hand painted and stenciled by a New Hope artist. Guest rooms feature antiques, original art, scented English soaps, plush towels, extra pillows, plus handmade quilts and comforters. In addition, all have private baths and air conditioners. Most have brass ceiling fans, and some have fireplaces and four-poster canopy beds.

Days always begin with a generous homebaked breakfast and end with chocolates and a tot of Carl's secret-recipe almond liqueur.

Wedgwood Inn of New Hope

Wedgwood Inn of New Hope
III West Bridge Street
New Hope, Pennsylvania 18938
215-862-2570
Web Site: www.new-hope-inn.com
E-mail: stay@new-hope-inn.com

Room Rates:	$80–$225, including continental breakfast in bed and "Tea and Tidbits."
Pet Charges or Deposits:	$20 per day. Small dogs only. Manager's prior approval required. Sorry, no cats.
Rated: 3 Paws 🐾🐾🐾	10 guest rooms and 4 suites on two acres.

The Wedgwood Inn offers bed and breakfast lodgings year-round in a gracious 1870 Victorian as well as a historic Classic Revival stone manor house, circa 1833. Surrounded by two acres of beautifully manicured grounds, the Inn is only steps from the heart of New Hope's historic district.

The Victorian building features a large verandah, a porte-cochère and a gazebo. The Classic Revival plastered stone house boasts 26-inch stone walls, brick walkways through flowering gardens and a turn-of-the-century carriage house in the back yard.

Hardwood floors, lofty windows and antique furnishings recreate a warm, comfortable 19th century feeling among Wedgwood pottery, original art, handmade quilts and fresh flowers. Fresh fruit salad, hot croissants and homebaked goods are served each morning on the sunporch, in the gazebo or in your private bedroom.

Rittenhouse Hotel

Rittenhouse Hotel
210 West Rittenhouse Square
Philadelphia, Pennsylvania 19103
800-635-1042 ▪ 215-546-9000
Web Site: www.rittenhousehotel.com
E-mail: info@rittenhousehotel.com

Room Rates:	$190–$315.
Pet Charges or Deposits:	Call for refundable deposit.
Rated: 5 Paws ❀❀❀❀❀	87 guest rooms and 11 suites with kitchens. Health club and spa, 5 restaurants and lounge.

T he Rittenhouse Hotel has received the coveted AAA Five-Diamond Award every year since 1992. Located on the west side of Rittenhouse Square, this upscale residential area is within walking distance of luxurious shops, fine dining, museums and the business district.

Guest accommodations are oversized and exquisite, either overlooking the park or the cityscape to the west. Staterooms are decorated in country French themes, with Queen Anne chairs and writing desks, thick duvet-style bedspreads, beautiful marble baths and original artwork.

The Adolf Biecker Spa and Salon is Center City's premier health club and spa, with an indoor pool lit by an overhead skylight, extensive equipment, free weights and numerous aerobic machines. Take time to enjoy the sauna and steam room or indulge in the spa treatments of a facial, herbal and aromatherapy wraps, massage and manicure.

Warwick Hotel and Towers

Warwick Hotel and Towers
1701 Locust Street
Philadelphia, Pennsylvania 19103
800-523-4210 ▪ 215-735-6000
Web Site: www.warwickhotels.com
E-mail: phlwarwick@aol.com

Room Rates:	$199–$289. AAA, AARP and Entertainment Club discounts.
Pet Charges or Deposits:	$50 per stay.
Rated: 5 Paws 🐾🐾🐾🐾🐾	569 guest rooms and 49 suites.

This European boutique-style hotel is centrally located in the heart of Philadelphia's shopping and business district. Recently renovated from facade to furnishings, the Warwick now features such amenities as nightly turndown service with chocolates, and daily newspaper delivery.

All of the guest rooms are comfortable and nicely equipped to give a feeling of relaxed luxury. The hotel features a variety of facilities and services that are sure to meet the needs of both business and leisure travelers.

The Warwick is located near the Liberty Bell, Philadelphia Museum of Art and Philadelphia Zoo.

GreenTree Marriott

GreenTree Marriott
101 Marriott Drive
Pittsburgh, Pennsylvania 15205
800-525-5902 ▪ 412-922-8400
Web Site: www.marriott.com

Room Rates: $89–$119. AAA and AARP discounts.
Pet Charges or Discounts: None.
Rated: 3 Paws 🐾🐾🐾   463 guest rooms and 5 suites. Indoor and outdoor pools,
                          whirlpool, sauna and health club. Restaurant and lounge.

T he combination of a convenient location, along with comfortable guest rooms and amenities, make the Pittsburgh Marriott GreenTree a good lodging choice. The hotel is located just 3 miles from downtown and 14 miles from the greater Pittsburgh International Airport.

Guest rooms are commodious, with in-room movies, refrigerators and mini-bars, work desks, voice mail and data ports on the phones. Guest services include laundry valet, a full business center, concierge and room service.

The hotel offers both indoor and outdoor pools, with a whirlpool and sauna, a health club and access to golf at the Hickory Heights Golf Course.

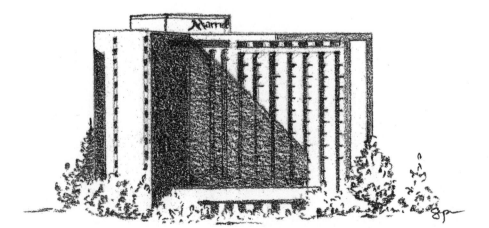

Hawthorn Suites Pittsburgh/Green Tree

Hawthorn Suites Pittsburgh/Green Tree
700 Mansfield Avenue
Pittsburgh, Pennsylvania 15205
800-527-1133 ▪ 412-279-6300
Web Site: www.hawthorn.com
E-mail: Pittsburghhs@cwixmail.com

Room Rates:	$79–$149, including continental breakfast and Manager's Reception. AAA and AARP discounts.
Pet Charges or Deposits:	$5 per day. $10–$50 nonrefundable deposit.
Rated: 3 Paws 🐾🐾🐾	151 guest suites. Outdoor pool and hot tub, sports court, barbecue grills, guest laundry.

E ach of the spacious suites features separate sleeping and living areas, many with fireplaces and full kitchens. In-suite conveniences include separate phone and modem lines, personal voice mail and oversized work areas. Nonsmoking and handicap-accessible suites are available on request.

A complimentary hot breakfast buffet is included daily in your room rate, as is the social hour Monday through Thursday, featuring hors d'oeuvres, beer, wine and soft drinks.

Guest laundry facilities with valet service are available, as is a grocery shopping service. The Hawthorn Suites offers airport shuttle service to Pittsburgh International Airport, which is about 14 miles away.

Pantall Hotel

Pantall Hotel
135 East Mahoning Street
Punxsutawney, Pennsylvania 15767
800-872-6825 ▪ 814-938-6600

Room Rates: $50–$85.
Pet Charges or Deposits: Manager's prior approval required.
Rated: 3 Paws ❀❀❀ 75 guest rooms and 2 suites.

From the first step inside the door, the historic Pantall Hotel welcomes you with its touches of small-town hospitality. All 75 guest rooms have modern conveniences such as cable television, air conditioning and newly renovated baths with showers.

The Coach Room of the Pantall Hotel serves fine food at breakfast, lunch and dinner, in a warm and comfortable setting. The room is filled with antiques, old and new framed prints, paintings and collector plates. An authentic Victorian Bar, made of curly maple-stained cherry with round, ornate columns and arches, has been recently restored here. If the bar could talk, it would fill volumes of history books. Hans Olson, a partner in the Olson & Fisher Drilling Company in the early 1900s, bought diamonds at the bar from dealers who would come from New York to meet him there.

Pegasus Bed and Breakfast

Pegasus Bed and Breakfast
Rural Route 2, Box 2066
Shohola, Pennsylvania 18458
717-296-4017

Room Rates:	$50–$100, including full breakfast.
Pet Charges or Deposits:	Manager's prior approval required.
Rated: 3 Paws 🐾🐾🐾	8 guest rooms and 2 suites with refrigerators and microwaves.

 Built as a country inn in 1910, Pegasus offers an ideal place for a relaxing getaway. Guests make themselves at home in the cozy living room, parlor game room, library or the big wraparound porch.

The Pegasus woodland is part of the tri-state forest and nature reserve surrounding Delaware River National Park, in the northeastern corner of the Pocono Mountains. The nearby Delaware River offers swimming and three-season floating in canoes, rafts, and kayaks—for beginners and whitewater experts. River, stream and lake fishing, golf, skiing and horseback riding are here to enjoy.

Spring Valley Bed and Breakfast and Horseback Riding

Spring Valley Bed and Breakfast and Horseback Riding
Rural Route I, Box 117
Spring Creek, Pennsylvania 16436
800-382-1324 ▪ 814-489-5415
Web Site: www.springvalleybandb.com
E-mail: kate@springvalleybandb.com

Room Rates:	$99–$159, including full breakfast, catered picnics and dinners.
Pet Charges or Deposits:	Call for refundable deposit. Horses welcome. Manager's prior approval required. Sorry, no cats.
Rated: 4 Paws 🐾🐾🐾🐾	4 guest suites on 175-acre farm.

T his unique bed and breakfast and horseback-riding facility is located in the foothills of the Allegheny National Forest in picturesque northwestern Pennsylvania. Each of the beautifully decorated, antique-filled suites, with private baths, private entrances and covered decks, affords sweeping views of hillsides, fields, pastures and hemlock forests. The adjoining stable provides the ambiance of grazing horses and trail riders on their way to explore the rolling woodlands beyond view.

In the morning, a gourmet breakfast is served in the dining room, with its cherry-board paneling and natural stone fireplaces. Evenings at this antique homesteaders' estate feature starry nights ands firelight.

Sheraton Inn Williamsport

Sheraton Inn Williamsport
100 Pine Street
Williamsport, Pennsylvania 17701
717-327-8231

Room Rates:	$70–$99. AAA, AARP and Quest discounts.
Pet Charges or Deposits:	None.
Rated: 3 Paws 🐾🐾🐾	146 guest rooms and 2 suites with whirlpool baths. Indoor swimming pool and courtyard, outdoor patio and volleyball court. Complimentary airport shuttle. Restaurant and lounge.

Conveniently located in downtown Williamsport, the hotel is just minutes from the Little League baseball museum and the World Series complex, golf courses, theater, stores, antique shops and the historic district. Spend a lazy afternoon cruising the Susquehanna on the Hiawatha Riverboat cruise or ride the trolley through "Millionaire's Row."

The Sheraton Inn features a delightful restaurant serving American-Continental cuisine, the hottest nightclub in town, an indoor heated swimming pool and an outdoor patio with volleyball court.

Sheraton Berkshire Hotel

Sheraton Berkshire Hotel
1741 Paper Mill Road
Wyomissing, Pennsylvania 19610
800-325-3535 ▪ 610-376-3811
Web Site: www.sheratonreadingpa.com

Room Rates:	$125–$197. AAA and AARP discounts.
Pet Charges or Deposits:	None.
Rated: 3 Paws 🐾🐾🐾	196 guest rooms and 59 suites. Indoor pool, saunas and whirlpool, putting green. Restaurant and lounge.

Sheraton guest rooms and suites are designed to appeal to the most discerning travelers. The tower guest rooms feature elegant furnishings, three phones, remote control color televisions, luxurious personal amenities and working desks with spacious conversation areas.

WHERE TO TAKE YOUR PET IN

Pennsylvania

Please Note: *Pets must be on a leash at all times and may be restricted to certain areas. For directions, use fees, pet charges and general information, contact the numbers listed below.*

National Parks General Information

Pennsylvania Fish and Boat Commission
P.O. Box 67000
Harrisburg, Pennsylvania 17106-7000
717-657-4518

Pennsylvania Game Commission
2001 Elmerton Avenue
Harrisburg, Pennsylvania 17110-9797
717-787-4250

National Recreation Areas

Delaware Water Gap National Recreation Area encompasses 70,000 acres and offers camping, picnic areas, boating, a boat ramp, fishing, swimming, hiking trails, winter sports and a visitors' center.

National Forest General Information

Forest Supervisor
Allegheny National Forest
P.O. Box 847
Warren, Pennsylvania 16365
800-280-2267—reservations
814-723-5150—information

National Forests

Allegheny National Forest consists of 516,000 acres in northwestern Pennsylvania and offers camping, picnic areas, boating, a boat ramp, boat rentals, fishing, swimming, hiking and bicycle trails, winter sports and a visitors' center. For more information, call 814-723-5150 or 800-280-2267.

Army Corps of Engineers

HUNTINGDON

Raystown Lake, located southwest of Huntingdon off State Route 26, occupies 29,300 acres of parkland with water-skiing, camping, picnic areas, hiking trails, boating, a boat ramp, boat rentals, fishing and swimming.

LAWRENCEVILLE

Cowanesque Lake, 3 miles west of Lawrenceville off State Route 15, encompasses 3,200 acres. You will find water-skiing, camping, picnic areas, boating, a boat ramp, fishing, swimming and winter sports.

MANSFIELD

Tioga-Hammond Lakes, located 12 miles north of Mansfield on U.S. Highway 15, consists of 6,700 acres. It has water-skiing, camping, picnic areas, hiking and bicycle trails, boating, a boat ramp, fishing, swimming and winter sports.

State Parks General Information

Pennsylvania Fish and Boat Commission
P.O. Box 67000
Harrisburg, Pennsylvania 17106-7000
717-657-4518

Pennsylvania Game Commission
2001 Elmerton Avenue
Harrisburg, Pennsylvania 17110-9797
717-787-4250

State Parks

ALTOONA

Prince Gallitzin State Park, 16 miles northwest of Altoona off State Route 53, consists of 6,249 acres of parkland with cross-country skiing, tobogganing, horse rentals, camping, picnic areas, boating, a boat ramp, boat rentals, fishing, swimming, hiking trails, winter sports and a visitors' center.

BEDFORD

Shawnee State Park, with 3,983 acres of parkland, is 9 miles west of Bedford, off U.S. Highway 30. Visitors to the park will enjoy cross-country skiing, snowmobiling, camping, picnic areas, hiking trails, boating, a boat ramp, boat rentals, fishing, swimming, winter sports and a visitors' center.

BELLEVILLE

Greenwood Furnace State Park is on 406 acres of parkland, located 5 miles northwest of Belleville, on State Route 305. You will enjoy snowmobiling, camping, picnic areas, hiking trails, fishing, swimming, winter sports and a visitors' center.

BUTLER

Moraine State Park is a 15,838-acre park 8 miles northwest of Butler off U.S. Highway 422. The park offers cross-country skiing, ice-boating, ice-fishing, snowmobiling, tobogganing, picnic areas, hiking and bicycle trails, boating, a boat ramp, boat rentals, fishing, swimming and winter sports.

CANADENSIS

Promised Land State Park, located 10 miles north of Canadensis on State Route 390, consists of 2,971 acres of parkland with cross-country skiing, snowmobiling, camping, picnic areas, boating, a boat ramp, boat rentals, fishing, swimming, hiking trails, winter sports and a visitors' center.

COLLEGEVILLE

Evansburg State Park, 2 miles east of Collegeville on U.S. Highway 422, has 3,349 acres of parkland with golfing, picnic areas, fishing, hiking trails and winter sports.

COOKSBURG

Cook Forest State Park is a 6,422-acre park located 1 mile north of Cooksburg off State Route 36, offering cross-country skiing, sledding, snowmobiling, horse rentals, camping, picnic areas, hiking trails, boating, a boat ramp, boat rentals, fishing, swimming, winter sports and a visitors' center.

CROYDON

Neshaminy State Park is a 330-acre park near Croydon, off State Route 132. Visitors to the park will find picnic areas, boating, a boat ramp, fishing and swimming.

DALLAS

Frances Slocum State Park encompasses 1,035 acres of parkland, located 4 miles east of Dallas off State Route 309. The park offers cross-country skiing, sledding, camping, picnic areas, hiking trails, boating, a boat ramp, boat rentals, fishing, swimming, winter sports and a visitors' center.

DOWNINGTOWN

Marsh Creek State Park is a 1,705-acre park 5 miles northwest of Downingtown off State Route 282. The park offers areas for ice-boating, ice-fishing, ice-skating, sledding, horse rentals, picnic areas, hiking trails, boating, a boat ramp, boat rentals, fishing, swimming and winter sports.

EBENSBURG

Yellow Creek State Park, located 18 miles northwest of Ebensburg on U.S. Highway 422, is a 2,891-acre park with cross-country skiing, sledding, snowmobiling, hiking trails, boating, a boat ramp, boat rentals, fishing, swimming, winter sports and a visitors' center.

ENTRIKEN

Trough Creek State Park is 3 miles north of Entriken off State Route 994. Visitors to the park will find snowmobiling, camping, picnic areas, hiking trails, fishing, winter sports and a visitors' center.

ERIE

Presque Isle State Park is a historic 3,200-acre park located 7 miles north of Interstate 90, exit 5 on Peninsula Drive. It has will find picnic areas, hiking and bicycle trails, boating, a boat ramp, boat rentals, fishing, swimming, winter sports and a visitors' center. For more information, call 814-833-7424.

FAYETTEVILLE

Caledonia State Park, 4 miles east of Fayetteville on U.S. Highway 30, is a historic 1,130-acre park offering cross-country skiing, camping, picnic areas, fishing, swimming, hiking and bicycle trails and winter sports. For more information, call 717-352-2164.

FORT LOUDON

Cowans Gap State Park is a 1,085-acre park north of Fort Loudon off State Route 75. Visitors to the park will find cross-country skiing, camping, picnic areas, hiking trails, boating, a boat ramp, boat rentals, fishing, swimming, winter sports and a visitors' center.

FORT WASHINGTON

Fort Washington State Park is a 493-acre park at 500 Bethlehem Pike in Fort Washington. The park offers cross-country skiing, sledding, picnic areas, hiking trails, fishing and a visitors' center.

FRANKFORT SPRINGS

Raccoon Creek State Park is a 7,323-acre park, 2 miles north of Frankfort Springs on State Route 18. It has cross-country skiing, camping, picnic areas, hiking trails, boating, a boat ramp, boat rentals, fishing, swimming, winter sports and a visitors' center.

FRANKLIN

Maurice K. Goddard State Park encompasses 1,075 acres of parkland, located 14 miles west of Franklin on U.S. Highway 62. The park offers picnic areas, hiking trails, boating, a boat ramp, boat rentals, fishing, winter sports and a visitors' center.

FRANKLIN FORKS

Salt Springs State Park is a 400-acre park 1 mile west of Franklin Forks off State Route 29. Visitors will find picnic areas, hiking and fishing.

GOULDSBORO

Gouldsboro State Park is a 3,050-acre park south of Gouldsboro. It offers picnic areas, hiking and bicycle trails, boating, a boat ramp, boat rentals, fishing, swimming and winter sports.

GRANTVILLE

Memorial Lake State Park, located 5 miles northeast of Grantville off U.S. Highway 22 and Interstate 81, is a 230-acre park with cross-country skiing, picnic areas, hiking trails, boating, a boat ramp, boat rentals, fishing and winter sports.

HANOVER

Codorus State Park encompasses 3,320 acres of parkland, 2 miles east of Hanover, off State Route 216. Visitors to the park will enjoy snowmobiling, tobogganing, camping, picnic areas, hiking trails, boating, a boat ramp, boat rentals, fishing, swimming and winter sports.

HOLLIDAYSBURG

Canoe Creek State Park is a 959-acre park, located 7 miles east of Hollidaysburg, off U.S. Highway 22. It has cross-country skiing, tobogganing, horse rentals, picnic areas, boating, a boat ramp, boat rentals, fishing, swimming, hiking trails, winter sports and a visitors' center.

JOHNSONBURG

Bendigo State Park, 3 miles northeast of Johnsonburg off U.S. Highway 219, is a 100-acre park offering tobogganing, picnic areas, fishing, swimming, and winter sports.

LAPORTE

Worlds End State Park encompasses 780 acres of parkland, located 7 miles northwest of Laporte on State Route 154. The park offers snowmobiling, camping, picnic areas, hiking trails, fishing, swimming, winter sports and a visitors' center.

LEHIGHTON

Beltzville State Park, 5 miles east of Lehighton off U.S. Highway 209, is a 2,972-acre park with cross-country skiing, tobogganing, picnic areas, hiking trails, boating, a boat ramp, boat rentals, fishing, swimming, winter sports and a visitors' center.

LEWISTOWN

Reeds Gap State Park, with 220 acres of parkland, is 13 miles northeast of Lewistown off U.S. Highway 322. The park offers tobogganing, camping, picnic areas, hiking trails, fishing, swimming and winter sports.

LIGONIER

Linn Run State Park, 10 miles southeast of Ligonier off State Route 34, consists of 565 acres of parkland with snowmobiling, picnic areas, fishing, hiking trails and winter sports.

MILROY

Penn Roosevelt State Park is a 41-acre park 10 miles west of Milroy off U.S. Highway and offers snowmobiling, camping, picnic areas, hiking trails, fishing and winter sports.

MILTON

Milton State Park, located on the island between Milton and West Milton, is a 77-acre park with picnic areas, hiking trails, boating, a boat ramp and fishing.

NEW ALEXANDRIA

Keystone State Park is a 1,190-acre park located 3 miles southeast of New Alexandria on State Route 981, offering snowmobiling, horse rentals, camping, picnic areas, hiking trails, boating, a boat ramp, boat rentals, fishing, swimming, winter sports and a visitors' center.

NEW CASTLE

McConnells Mill State Park, 8 miles southeast of New Castle off U.S. Highway 422, is a 2,534-acre park with picnic areas, hiking trails, fishing, winter sports and a visitors' center.

NEW GERMANTOWN

Fowlers Hollow State Park is a 104-acre park 4 miles south of New Germantown off State Route 274 on Upper Buck Ridge Road. The park offers areas for cross-country skiing, snowmobiling, camping, picnic areas, hiking trails, boat rentals, fishing and winter sports.

NEW HOPE

Ralph Stover State Park is a 45-acre park located 9 miles northwest of New Hope on State Route 32. It has areas for tobogganing, picnic areas, hiking trails, fishing and winter sports.

NEWPORT

Little Buffalo State Park is a 830-acre park, 4 miles southwest of Newport off State Route 34. Visitors will find cross-country skiing, tobogganing, picnic areas, hiking trails, boating, a boat ramp, boat rentals, fishing, swimming, winter sports and a visitors' center.

NEWTOWN

Tyler State Park, located 1.5 miles west of Newtown off State Route 413, consists of 1,711 acres of parkland with cross-country skiing, sledding, horse trails, picnic areas, boating, boat rentals, fishing, hiking and bicycle trails and winter sports.

NEWVILLE

Colonel Denning State Park, 9 miles north of Newville, off State Route 233, is a 273-acre park offering cross-country skiing, tobogganing, camping, picnic areas, hiking trails, fishing, swimming, winter sports and a visitors' center.

OIL CITY

Oil Creek State Park, located 4 miles north of Oil City, on State Route 8 via signs, is a 7,007-acre park with cross-country skiing, picnic areas, hiking and bicycle trails, fishing, winter sports and a visitors' center.

PAVIA

Blue Knob State Park is a 5,600-acre park 5 miles northwest of Pavia off State Route 869. The park has cross-country and downhill skiing, snowmobiling, camping, picnic areas, hiking trails, fishing, swimming and winter sports.

PENNSYLVANIA TURNPIKE

French Creek State Park, located 6 miles northeast of Pennsylvania Turnpike, exit 22 on State Route 345, is a 7,339-acre park with camping, picnic areas, hiking trails, boating, a boat ramp, boat rentals, fishing, swimming and winter sports.

PINE GROVE FURNACE

Pine Grove Furnace State Park is a 696-acre park at Pine Grove Furnace on State Route 233. Visitors to the park will find cross-country skiing, camping, picnic areas, hiking and bicycle trails, boating, a boat ramp, boat rentals, fishing, swimming, winter sports and a visitors' center.

QUAKERTOWN

Nockamixon State Park, located 5 miles east of Quakertown off County Roads 513 and 563, encompasses 5,283 acres of parkland with tobogganing, horse rentals, picnic areas, boating, a boat ramp, boat rentals, fishing, swimming, hiking and bicycle trails and winter sports.

ROSSVILLE

Gifford Pinchot State Park, 2 miles east of Rossville off State Route 74, is a 2,338-acre park offering cross-country skiing, camping, picnic areas, hiking trails, boating, a boat ramp, boat rentals, fishing, swimming, winter sports and a visitors' center.

SAXTON

Warriors Path State Park is a 334-acre park, located 1 mile south of Saxton on State Route 26. The park has picnic areas, hiking and bicycle trails, fishing and winter sports.

SHAMOKIN DAM

Shikellamy State Park, 1 mile north of Shamokin Dam, off State Route 11, is a 125-acre park with picnic areas, hiking and bicycle trails, boating, a boat ramp, boat rentals, fishing and winter sports.

SINNEMAHONING

Sinnemahoning State Park is a 1,910-acre park located 10 miles north of Sinnemahoning on State Route 872, offering snowmobiling, camping, picnic areas, hiking trails, boating, a boat ramp, boat rentals, fishing, swimming and winter sports.

SIGEL

Clear Creek State Park, 4 miles north of Sigel off State Route 949, encompasses 1,209 acres of parkland, with cross-country skiing, camping, picnic areas, a boat ramp, fishing, swimming, hiking trails, winter sports and a visitors' center.

SOMERSET

Kooser State Park is a 170-acre park located 10 miles west of Somerset on State Route 31. Visitors to the park will find cross-country skiing, camping, picnic areas, hiking trails, fishing, swimming and winter sports.

Laurel Hill State Park, 10 miles west of Somerset off State Route 31 near Trent, encompasses 3,935 acres of parkland with snowmobiling, camping, picnic areas, hiking trails, boating, a boat ramp, boat rentals, fishing, swimming, winter sports and a visitors' center.

STATE COLLEGE

Whipple Dam State Park is a 256-acre park located 12 miles south of State College, off State Route 26. The park offers areas for snowmobiling, picnic areas, hiking trails, boating, a boat ramp, fishing, swimming and winter sports.

TAMAQUA

Tuscarora State Park, 5 miles west of Tamaqua off State Route 309, encompasses 1,716 acres of parkland with tobogganing, picnic areas, boating, a boat ramp, boat rentals, fishing, swimming and winter sports.

TOBYHANNA

Tobyhanna State Park is a 5,440-acre park located 2 miles east of Tobyhanna on State Route 423. Visitors to the park will find snowmobiling, camping, picnic areas, hiking and bicycle trails, boating, a boat ramp, boat rentals, fishing, swimming and winter sports.

TROY

Mount Pisgah State Park, located 10 miles northwest of Troy off U.S. Highway 6, is a 1,302-acre park offering cross-country skiing, ice-fishing, ice-skating, sledding, snowmobiling, picnic areas, hiking trails, boating, a boat ramp, boat rentals, fishing, swimming, winter sports and a visitors' center.

UNIONTOWN

Ohlopyle State Park encompasses 18,719 acres of parkland, 14 miles east of Uniontown, on State Route 381. It offers snowmobiling, cross-country skiing, camping, picnic areas, hiking and bicycle trails, fishing, winter sports and a visitors' center.

UPPER BLACK EDDY

Delaware Canal State Park is located along a 60-mile stretch enar State Route 32 and its headquarters is in Upper Black Eddy. Visitors to the park will find cross-country skiing, sledding, picnic areas, hiking and bicycle trails, boat rentals, fishing and winter sports.

WAVERLY

Lackawanna State Park is 3 miles north of Waverly on State Route 407. It has tobogganing, camping, picnic areas, hiking trails, boating, a boat ramp, boat rentals, fishing, swimming and winter sports.

WEST CHESTER

Ridley Creek State Park, 7 miles east of West Chester via State Routes 3 or 352, is a 2,600-acre park with picnic areas, hiking and bicycle trails, fishing, winter sports and a visitors' center.

WEST MILTON

Milton State Park, located on the island between Milton and West Milton, is a 77-acre park offering picnic areas, hiking trails, boating, a boat ramp and fishing.

WHITE HAVEN

Hickory Run State Park, 5 miles southeast of White Haven on State Route 534, is a 15,500-acre park offering cross-country skiing, snowmobiling, camping, picnic areas, hiking trails, fishing, swimming, winter sports and a visitors' center.

WILCOX

Elk State Park, located 9 miles east of Wilcox, encompasses 3,192 acres of parkland with camping, picnic areas, boating, a boat ramp, fishing, hiking trails and winter sports.

WIND RIDGE

Ryerson Station State Park, 1 mile south of Wind Ridge off State Route 21, is a 1,164-acre park offering tobogganing, camping, picnic areas, hiking trails, boating, a boat ramp, boat rentals, fishing, swimming, winter sports and a visitors' center.

Other Recreation Areas

BUCK

Muddy Run is a 700-acre park located 4 miles north of Buck on State Route 372. The park offers camping, picnic areas, hiking and bicycle trails, boating, a boat ramp, boat rentals and fishing.

COATESVILLE

Hibernia Park consists of 800 acres, located 6 miles north of Coatesville on State Route 82, then west on Cedar Knoll Road. It offers camping, picnic areas, hiking and bicycle trails, fishing and a visitors' center.

CURWENSVILLE

Curwensville Lake is located 3 miles south of Curwensville on State Route 453. This 362-acre park offers cross-country skiing, camping, picnic areas, hiking trails, boating, a boat ramp, fishing, swimming, winter sports and a visitors' center.

EDINBORO

Edinboro Lake encompasses 240 acres of parkland on State Route 99 in Edinboro. It offers camping, picnic areas, bicycle trails, boating, a boat ramp, boat rentals, fishing, swimming and winter sports.

HAMLIN

Lake Wallenpaupack is a 5,700-acre park located 10 miles east of Hamlin off State Route 590. The park has horse rentals, camping, picnic areas, hiking trails, boating, a boat ramp, boat rentals, fishing, swimming, winter sports and a visitors' center.

HARVEYS LAKE

Harveys Lake is a 658-acre park and offers camping, picnic areas, boating, a boat ramp, boat rentals and fishing.

INDIANA

Blue Spruce Park, with 420 acres park, is 6 miles north of Indiana on State Route 110. The park offers picnic areas, hiking trails, boating, boat rentals, fishing, winter sports and a visitors' center.

LANDINGVILLE

Auburn Dam encompasses 187 acres of parkland, located 1 mile from Landingville. It has picnic areas, boating, a boat ramp and fishing.

MARTINS CREEK

Martins Creek consists of 225 acres, 3 miles north via State Route 611 North. It offers picnic areas, hiking trails, boating, a boat ramp and fishing.

MONTDALE

Chapman Lake, located near Montdale, has 98 acres of parkland with camping, picnic areas, boating, a boat ramp, fishing and swimming.

NEW ALEXANDRIA

Conemaugh River Lake is a 7,609-acre park located 8 miles north of New Alexandria, off State Route 981. The park offers picnic areas, hiking trails, boating, fishing and a visitors' center.

NOTTINGHAM

Nottingham is located a quarter of a mile south of Nottingham at 150 Park Road. Visitors will find 651 acres of parkland offering bird watching, cross-country skiing, camping, picnic areas, hiking trails, fishing, winter sports and a visitors' center.

READING

Felix Dam is a 3.5-mile area north of Reading at Tuckerton, via Tuckerton Road to Stoudts Ferry Bridge Road. Visitors to the park will find water-skiing, picnic areas, boating, a boat ramp and fishing.

SUNBURY

Lake Augusta is a 3,000-acre park near Sunbury. The park offers camping, picnic areas, boating, a boat ramp, boat rentals and fishing.

UNIONTOWN

Youghlogheny Reservoir is a 4,034-acre park located 20 miles southeast of Uniontown on U.S. Highway 40. The park offers camping, picnic areas, boating, a boat ramp, boat rentals, fishing, swimming and a visitors' center.

WARREN

Buckaloons Access Area is located 5 miles west of Warren at the junction of U.S. Highway 6 and 62. Visitors to the park will enjoy camping, picnic areas, hiking and bicycle trails, boating, a boat ramp, fishing, swimming and winter sports.

WATERFORD

Lake LeBoeuf consists of 70 acres 2 blocks south on Hazel Street in Waterford. It has camping, picnic areas, boating, a boat ramp, boat rentals, fishing and swimming.

WILLIAMSPORT

Susquehanna Park consists of 20 acres located on the Susquehanna River in Williamsport. Visitors will find picnic areas, boating, a boat ramp and fishing.

YORK

Lake Aldred, 25 miles southeast of York on State Route 425, is a 5,000-acre park offering camping, picnic areas, hiking trails, boating, a boat ramp, boat rentals, fishing and swimming.

Veterinary Care in Pennsylvania

A

Abingdon Animal Hospital
1626 Old York Road
Abingdon, PA 19001
215-659-0106

Albion Animal Center
11 Wells Avenue
Albion, PA 16401
814-756-4441

Alburtis Animal Hospital
122 Leady Aly
Alburtis, PA 18011
610-967-7387

Aliquippa Animal Hospital
924 Broadhead Road
Aliquippa, PA 15001
410-375-6658

Broadhead Veterinary Clinic
917 North Broadhead Road
Aliquippa, PA 15001
410-375-7753

Five Points Veterinary Clinic
4414 Broadhead Road
Aliquippa, PA 15001
410-375-7505

Abe Veterinary Hospital
2102 Walbert Avenue
Allentown, PA 18101
610-820-9224

Allentown Animal Clinic
2640 Walbert Avenue
Allentown, PA 18101
610-434-4470

Allentown Clinic for Cats
4090 West Tilghman Street
Allentown, PA 18101
610-398-3556

Lehigh Valley Animal Hospital
6350 Tilghman Street
Allentown, PA 18101
610-395-0328

Maple Hills Veterinary Hospital
862 Kressler Road
Allentown, PA 18101
610-395-3743

Maple Hills Veterinary Hospital
2025 Union Boulevard
Allentown, PA 18101
610-776-5050

Walbert's Animal Hospital
2061 Walbert Avenue
Allentown, PA 18101
610-434-7469

West Valley Animal Hospital
351 South Route 100
Allentown, PA 18101
610-530-0600

Duncan Manor Animal Hospital
1720 Ferguson Road
Allison Park, PA 15101
412-366-7374

North Hills Animal Hospital
3967 Route 8
Allison Park, PA 15101
412-486-1777

Lakemont Veterinary Clinic
1400 Circle Avenue
Altoona, PA 16601
814-946-4676

Pleasant Valley Animal Hospital
808 Pleasant Valley
  Boulevard
Altoona, PA 16601
814-946-0010

Veterinary Hospital of Altoona
232 Chestnut Avenue
Altoona, PA 16601
814-942-2182

Ambler Veterinary Clinic
419 North Spring Garden
  Street
Ambler, PA 19002
215-646-8095

Animal Clinic
308 Euclid Avenue
Ambler, PA 19002
215-641-1024

Mahoning Valley Animal Hospital
2967 Blakeslee Boulevard
  Drive West
Andreas, PA 18211
717-386-3088

Kiski Valley Animal Clinic
927 Old State Road
Apollo, PA 15613
412-478-4800

Ardmore Animal Hospital
24 East Athens Avenue
Ardmore, PA 19003
610-642-1160

Ivens Veterinary Hospital
60 Haverford Road
Ardmore, PA 19003
610-649-4242

Animal Emergency Hospital
4009 Market Street #E
Aston, PA 19014
610-494-6686

Avian and Exotic Animal Medical
4009 Market Street #E
Aston, PA 19014
610-494-2811

Pennell Veterinary Clinic
413 Marianville Road
Aston, PA 19014
610-497-4000

B

Bakerstown Animal Hospital
5814 Route 8
Bakerstown, PA 15007
412-443-8200

Avh Veterinary Group
1365 Ackermanville Road
Bangor, PA 18013
610-588-3121

St. Francis Veterinary Practice
2240 Community Drive
Bath, PA 18014
610-759-3883

Beaver Animal Clinic
357 State Street
Beaver, PA 16232
412-728-9020

Beaver Falls Animal Clinic
2702 Darlington Road
Beaver Falls, PA 15010
412-846-5505

College Hill Animal Clinic
3510 Fourth Avenue
Beaver Falls, PA 15010
412-847-7988

Kolbrooks Veterinary Clinic
1756 Nittany Valley Drive
Bellefonte, PA 16823
814-383-4415

Valley Veterinary Service
1132 Rostraver Road
Belle Vernon, PA 15012
412-929-5425

Bensalem Veterinary Hospital
3462 Bristol Pike
Bensalem, PA 19020
215-638-1595

Bridgewater Veterinary Hospital
1740 Byberry Road
Bensalem, PA 19020
215-638-9275

Croydon Animal Hospital
2014 State Road
Bensalem, PA 19020
215-788-6282

Bernville Veterinary Clinic
7135 Bernville Road
Bernville, PA 19506
610-488-0166

Blue Marsh Veterinary Clinic
56 Groff Road
Bernville, PA 19506
610-488-0559

Beach-Haven Veterinary Hospital
1998 Bowers Road #A
Berwick, PA 17316
717-759-1441

North Berwick Animal Hospital
735 West 17th Street
Berwick, PA 17316
717-759-0397

Berwyn Veterinary Center
1058 Lancaster Avenue
Berwyn, PA 19312
610-640-9188

Bethel Animal Clinic
8920 Lancaster Avenue
Bethel, PA 16226
717-933-4916

Bethel Park Cat Clinic
5861 Library Road
Bethel Park, PA 15102
412-835-8200

Lehigh Valley Animal Hospital
4505 Bath Pike
Bethlehem, PA 15757
610-865-9072

North Saucon Animal Hospital
3604 Route 378
Bethlehem, PA 15757
610-867-0800

Northside Animal Hospital
185 Mikron Road
Bethlehem, PA 15757
610-759-5922

Wright Veterinary Center
3247 Wimmer Road
Bethlehem, PA 15757
610-865-2611

Big Run Veterinary Service
319 East Main Street
Big Run, PA 15715
814-427-5004

Bloomsburg Veterinary Hospital
1924 Old Berwick Road
Bloomsburg, PA 17815
717-784-6440

Animal Hospital of Norristown
1660 Dekalb Pike
Blue Bell, PA 19422
610-272-6511

Cat Clinic and Feline Medical Center
1030 Dekalb Pike
Blue Bell, PA 19422
610-277-3672

Steinbach Veterinary Hospital
120 Skippack Pike
Blue Bell, PA 19422
215-646-0462

Conchester Animal Hospital
530 Conchester Road
Boothwyn, PA 19061
610-485-6007

Ironstone Veterinary Hospital
869 West Pine Ford Road
Boyertown, PA 19512
610-367-6446

Bradford Veterinary Clinic
829 West Washington Street
Bradford, PA 16881
814-362-2200

McKean County Animal Hospital
258 Seaward Avenue
Bradford, PA 16881
814-368-4711

Allegheny South Veterinary Service
444 Washington Avenue
Bridgeville, PA 15017
412-257-0909

Newport Animal Hospital
2416 Durham Road
Bristol, PA 19007
215-943-7175

Broadway Veterinary Hospital
912 Fifth Avenue
Brockway, PA 15824
814-265-1950

Broomall Animal Hospital
2518 West Chester Pike
Broomall, PA 19008
610-356-1758

Community Animal Hospital
2625 West Chester Pike
Broomall, PA 19008
610-353-6622

Bryn Mawr Veterinary Hospital
18 North Merion Avenue
Bryn Mawr, PA 15241
610-527-3484

Buckingham Animal Hospital
4871 York Road
Buckingham, PA 18912
215-794-8114

Valley Veterinary Clinic
2137 US Route 413
Buckingham, PA 18912
215-794-7598

Hilltop Animal Hospital
40 Steubenville Pike
Burgettstown, PA 15021
412-729-3460

Deer Creek Animal Hospital
388 Saxonburg Road
Butler, PA 16003
412-282-0006

Eastland Veterinary Hospital
127 Oneida Valley Road #100
Butler, PA 16003
412-293-2345

Suburban Animal Clinic
102 Thorncrest Drive
Butler, PA 16003
412-287-5289

C

Avian and Feline Hospital
3510 Trindle Road
Camp Hill, PA 17011
717-730-3755

Camp Hill Animal Hospital
3804 Market Street
Camp Hill, PA 17011
717-737-8669

Lower Allen Veterinary Clinic
943 Kranzel Drive
Camp Hill, PA 17011
717-975-9711

Canon Hill Veterinary Clinic
1953 Route 519 South
Canonsburg, PA 15317
412-746-4220

Carbondale Veterinary Hospital
198 Canaan Street
Carbondale, PA 18407
717-282-0744

Carlisle Large Animal Clinic
77 Shady Lane
Carlisle, PA 17013
717-249-7771

Carlisle Small Animal Clinic
25 Shady Lane
Carlisle, PA 17013
717-243-2717

Hillmount Animal Hospital
31 Westminster Drive
Carlisle, PA 17013
717-249-7272

Northside Veterinary Clinic
31 E Street
Carlisle, PA 17013
717-249-3313

Trindle Road Animal Hospital
1617 Trindle Road
Carlisle, PA 17013
717-243-8706

Chartiers Animal Hospital
1747 Railroad Street
Carnegie, PA 15106
412-279-7300

Maple Hills Veterinary
4951 Route 309
Center Valley, PA 18034
610-797-1300

Chadds Ford Animal Hospital
901 Baltimore Pike
Chadds Ford, PA 19317
6100-388-2141

Concord Pike Veterinary Hospital
12 Beaver Valley Road
Chadds Ford, PA 19317
610-459-4818

Ark Animal Hospital
1700 Horizon Drive
Chalfont, PA 18914
215-822-3636

Chalfont Animal Hospital
338 Park Avenue
Chalfont, PA 18914
215-822-2864

Best Friends Animal Hospital
1988 Lincoln Way West
Chambersburg, PA 17201
717-261-0520

Chambersburg Animal Hospital
1340 Lincoln Way East
Chambersburg, PA 17201
717-264-4712

Lincoln Way Animal Hospital
1986 Lincoln Way East
Chambersburg, PA 17201
717-264-2615

Tri-County Animal Medical Center
675 Mower Road
Chambersburg, PA 17201
717-267-2747

Providence Veterinary Hospital
2400 Providence Avenue
Chester, PA 19013
610-872-4000

Animal Health Clinic
211 Byers Road
Chester Springs, PA 19425
610-458-8789

Ludwigs Corner Veterinarian
298 Black Horse Road
Chesters Springs, PA 19425
610-458-8567

Atglen Veterinary Hospital
150 Pine Creek Drive
Christiana, PA 17509
610-593-6132

Baker Animal Hospital
3550 Valleyview Road
Clark, PA 16113
412-962-3557

Blue Cross Animal Hospital
1152 Lackawanna Trail
Clarks Summit, PA 18411
717-587-4025

Susquehanna Veterinary Clinic
217 West Pine Street
Clearfield, PA 16034
814-765-6541

Brandywine Valley Veterinary Hospital
2580 Strasburg Road
Coatesville, PA 19320
610-384-0731

Coatesville Veterinary Hospital
625 Blackhorse Hill Road
Coatesville, PA 19320
610-384-1681

Cochranton Veterinary Hospital
33124 US Highway 322
Cochranton, PA 16314
814-425-8311

Animal Medical Center
25 West Third Avenue
Collegeville, PA 19426
610-489-8982

Perkiomen Valley Veterinary Clinic
24 West Main Street
Collegeville, PA 19426
610-489-0220

Line Lexington Veterinary Hospital
1030 Bethlehem Pike
Colmar, PA 18915
215-822-8918

Columbia Animal Hospital
4081 Columbia Avenue
Columbia, PA 17512
717-684-2285

Donegal Animal Hospital
1493 Iron Bridge Road
Columbia, PA 17512
717-653-9396

St. Francis Animal Hospital
3935 Concordia Road
Columbia, PA 17512
717-684-3870

Moon Veterinary Hospital
991 Broadhead Road
Coraopolis, PA 15108
412-262-2100

Corry Veterinary Clinic
316 East Columbus Avenue
Corry, PA 16407
814-664-4046

Cranberry Veterinary Hospital
1 Odleview Road
Cranberry Township, PA 16046
412-776-2410

Gardens Plaza Veterinary Hospital
20325 Perry Highway #14
Cranberry Township, PA 16046
412-722-1870

Blue Cross Animal Hospital
115 Newportville Road
Croydon, PA 19021
215-788-9449

Ridley Veterinary Hospital
1408 Chester Pike
Crum Lynne, PA 19022
610-833-1252

D

Black Mountain Hospital
732 Center Hill Road
Dallas, PA 18612
717-675-3406

Dallas Veterinary Clinic
410 Machell Avenue
Dallas, PA 18612
717-675-0313

Ani-Care Animal Hospital
2740 South Queen Street
Dallastown, PA 17313
717-741-1320

Danboro Veterinary Clinic
4406 Point Pleasant Pike
Danboro, PA 18916
215-345-1120

Alpine Animal Clinic
321 Mill Street
Danville, PA 17821
717-271-1828

Animal Care Center
7 Enterprise Drive
Danville, PA 17821
717-275-6064

Leighow Veterinary Hospital
1221 Montour Boulevard
Danville, PA 17821
717-275-0202

Dauphin Animal Hospital
851 Peters Mountain Road
Dauphin, PA 17018
717-921-2100

Adamstown Veterinary Hospital
2481 North Reading Road
Denver, PA 17517
717-484-0440

Devon Veterinary Hospital
81 Lancaster Avenue
Devon, PA 19333
610-688-5224

Citywide Animal Clinic
315 Main Street
Dickson City, PA 18519
717-489-5208

Dillsburg Veterinary Center
305 North Baltimore #B
Dillsburg, PA 17019
717-432-7031

Timber View Veterinary Hospital
2054 Old York Road
Dillsburg, PA 17019
717-432-2513

Tri-County Animal Hospital
1512 Baltimore Road
Dillsburg, PA 17019
717-432-2453

Animal Clinic of Manchester
3760 Colonial Road
Dover, PA 17315
717-292-6444

Shiloh Veterinary Hospital
2401 Emigs Mil Road
Dover, PA 17315
717-764-1400

Animal Clinic at Thorndale
3915 East Lincoln Highway
Downingtown, PA 19335
610-873-4091

Downingtown Animal Hospital
5033 Horseshoe Pike
Downingtown, PA 19335
610-269-4209

Lionville Veterinary Clinic
389 West Uwchlan Avenue
Downingtown, PA 19335
610-269-0303

Animal Clinic
1960 South Easton Road
Doylestown, PA 18901
215-340-1838

Doylestown Animal Medical Clinic
800 North Easton Road
Doylestown, PA 18901
215-345-7782

Pheasant Run Animal Hospital
12 Peasant Road
Doylestown, PA 18901
215-348-9099

Dravosburg Veterinary Hospital
220 First Street
Dravosburg, PA 15034
412-466-4444

Clarks Ferry Veterinary Hospital
38 Benvenue Road
Duncannon, PA 17020
717-834-5534

Blair Animal Hospital
1308 Third Avenue
Duncansville, PA 16635
814-695-8478

Dunmore Dog and Cat Hospital
322 East Drinker Street
Dunmore, PA 18512
717-344-7651

E

East Stroudsburg Veterinary
353 Prospect Street
East Stroudsburg, PA 18301
717-421-0931

Easton Animal Hospital
2015 Sullivan Trail
Easton, PA 18040
610-252-8276

Thoreau Veterinary Hospital
929 Northampton Street
Easton, PA 18040
610-559-0728

William Penn Animal Hospital
3611 Nicholas Street
Easton, PA 18040
610-252-3222

William Penn Animal Hospital
2605 Nazareth Road
Easton, PA 18040
610-258-2618

Ebensburg Animal Hospital
815 Rowena Drive
Ebensburg, PA 15931
814-472-6263

Hilltop Animal Hospital
5377 Admiral Peary Highway
Ebensburg, PA 15931
814-472-8947

Edgemont Veterinary Clinic
5061 West Chester Pike
Edgemont, PA 17109
610-356-9334

Camboro Veterinary Hospital
13201 Cambridge Road
Edinboro, PA 16412
814-734-1628

Riverside Veterinary Hospital
520 South Second Avenue
Elizabeth, PA 17543
412-384-6884

Awad Animal Hospital
388 Hershey Road
Elizabethtown, PA 17022
717-367-0158

Elizabeth Area Animal Hospital
1096 West Bainbridge Street
Elizabethtown, PA 17022
717-367-7156

Elizabethville Veterinary Hospital
269 Camp Street
Elizabethville, PA 17023
717-362-3003

Community Animal Hospital
8023 Old York Road
Elkins Parks, PA 19027
215-635-2700

**Elkins Park
Veterinarian Hospital**
315 Township Line Road
Elkins Parks, PA 19027
215-379-2729

**Morgantown Veterinary
Clinic**
398 North Manor Road
Elverson, PA 19520
610-286-0009

**Ellwood Animal
Hospital**
728 Lawrence Avenue
Ellwood City, PA 16117
412-458-8882

**Emmaus Animal
Hospital**
1301 Chestnut Street
Emamaus, PA 18049
610-967-1512

Enola Animal Clinic
103 East Shady Lane
Enola, PA 17025
717-732-1121

**Conestoga Animal
Hospital**
113 Martindale Road
Ephrata, PA 17522
717-733-2155

**Ephrata Animal
Hospital**
776 East Main Street
Ephrata, PA 17522
717-733-1078

Aaa Animal Clinic
336 East 12th Street
Erie, PA 16503
814-452-2667

**Animal Ark Pet
Hospital**
3024 West 12th Street
Erie, PA 16505
814-838-7387

Animal Clinic
8465 Peach Street
Erie, PA 16509
814-868-5396

Erie Animal Hospital
3024 West 26th Street
Erie, PA 16506
814-838-7638

Glenwood Pet Hospital
3853 Peach Street
Erie, PA 16509
814-864-3019

**Twinbrook Veterinary
Hospital**
5065 Buffalo Road
Erie, PA 16510
814-899-6941

**Wintergreen Animal
Hospital**
8439 Wattsburg Road
Erie, PA 16509
814-825-6735

Valley Green Veterinary
1565 Potts Hill Road
Etters, PA 17319
717-938-8944

Animal Clinic
2 Marchwood Road #2
Exton, PA 19341
610-363-1595

**Colebrook Manor
Animal Hospital**
637 West Lincoln Highway
Exton, PA 19341
610-269-0255

Exton Pet Clinic
609 North Pottstown Pike
Exton, PA 19341
610-363-7479

F

**Delaware Valley Animal
Hospital**
266 Lincoln Highway
Fairless Hills, PA 19030
215-946-1111

**Muddy Veterinary
Service**
413 Ridge Road
Fawn Grove, PA 17321
717-862-1115

Dog and Cat Hospital
16 Heffner Road
Fleetwood, PA 19522
610-682-4774

**Oley Valley Animal
Clinic**
38 West Main Street
Fleetwood, PA 19522
610-944-6144

**Montgomery Animal
Hospital**
827 Bethlehem Pike
Flourtown, PA 19031
215-233-3958

**Thomas Animal
Hospital**
232 South Lehigh Avenue
Frackville, PA 17931
717-874-3312

Frazer Animal Hospital
530 Lancaster Avenue
Frazer, PA 15084
610-644-6996

**Main Line Veterinary
Clinic**
235 Lancaster Avenue
Frazer, PA 15084
610-695-0860

**Northeast Animal
Hospital**
513 Green Street
Freeland, PA 18224
717-636-1877

G

**Confederate Wood
Veterinary Hospital**
10 Confederate Drive
Gettysburg, PA 17325
717-334-1179

**Gettysburg Animal
Hospital**
996 Old Harrisburg Road
Gettysburg, PA 17325
717-334-2177

**Winter Spring Small
Animal**
910 Good Intent Road
Gettysburg, PA 17325
717-334-6840

**All Pets Animal
Hospital**
5007 Route 8
Gibsonia, PA 15044
412-444-600

Animal Hospital
1538 East Philadelphia
   Avenue
Gilbertsville, PA 19525
610-367-4744

**Patt Veterinary
Hospital**
1540 County Line Road
Gilbertsville, PA 19525
610-367-2572

**Gladwyne Veterinary
Hospital**
1014 Youngsford Road
Gladwyne, PA 19035
610-642-3102

**Old Trail Animal
Hospital**
84 Theatre Road
Glen Rock, PA 17327
717-235-7887

**Glenmoore Veterinary
Hospital**
3 Andover Road
Glenmoore, PA 19343
610-942-4404

**Chester Pike Animal
Hospital**
304 North Chester Pike
Glenolden, PA 19036
610-586-1344

**Glen Croft Veterinary
Hospital**
6 East Glenolden Avenue
Glenolden, PA 19036
610-583-2200

**Glenolden Animal
Hospital**
405 South Macdade
   Boulevard
Glenolden, PA 19036
610-237-6120

**Chestnut Hill
Veterinary Hospital**
903 Bethlehem Pike
Glenside, PA 19038
215-836-2950

Rau Animal Hospital
2135 Jenkintown Road
Glenside, PA 19038
215-884-0453

Greencastle Veterinary Hospital
862 Buchanan Trail East
Greencastle, PA 17225
717-597-3441

Green Lane Veterinary Hospital
3015 Main Street
Green Lane, PA 18054
215-234-0434

Family Pet Clinic
193 Haldey Road
Greenville, PA 15552
412-588-5290

Grove City Veterinary Clinic
218 Oak Street
Grove City, PA 16127
412-458-0750

H

Longmeadows Farm Clinic
94 Academy Road
Hamburg, PA 19526
610-562-3242

Clearview Animal Hospital
1035 High Street
Hanover, PA 17331
717-632-4757

Conewago Veterinary Clinic
3002 Hanover Pike
Hanover, PA 17331
717-632-4425

Countryside Veterinary Hospital
119 Impounding Dam Road
Hanover, PA 17331
717-637-6172

Hanover Veterinary Hospital
323 Broadway
Hanover, PA 17331
717-632-6711

Harleysville Veterinary Hospital
391 Main Street
Harleysville, PA 19938
215-256-4664

Hufnagel Veterinary Clinic
374 Perry Highway
Harmony, PA 16037
724-452-0910

Miller Animal Hospital
131 Old Little Creek Road
Harmony, PA 16037
724-452-7323

Animal Hospital
241 South Hershey Road
Harrisburg, PA 17112
717-652-1270

Capitol Area Animal Medical
6 North Progress Avenue
Harrisburg, PA 17109
717-652-0713

Colonial Park Animal Clinic
4905 Jonestown Road
Harrisburg, PA 17109
717-540-7140

Derry Animal Hospital
3761 Derry Street
Harrisburg, PA 17111
717-564-4470

Lockwillow Avenue Animal Clinic
27 North Lockwillow Avenue
Harrisburg, PA 17112
717-545-5803

Mountain View Animal Hospital
5821 Linglestown Road #A
Harrisburg, PA 17112
717-671-0797

Noah's Place Animal Hospital
6325 Chelton Avenue
Harrisburg, PA 17112
717-652-5923

County Line Veterinary Hospital
325 West County Line Road
Hatboro, PA 19040
215-675-0533

Hatboro Animal Hospital
242 south York Road
Hatbroro, PA 19040
215-443-7211

Gentle Cat Doctor of Haverford
644 Haverford Road
Haverford, PA 19083
610-649-2273

Haverford Animal Hospital
517 Lancaster Avenue
Haverford, PA 19083
610-525-1211

Delaware County Animal Medical Center
1200 West Chester Pike
Havertown, PA 19083
610-449-5100

Eagle Veterinary Clinic
212 North Eagle Road
Havertown, PA 19083
610-446-1404

Manoa Animal Hospital
1330 West Chester Pike
Havertown, PA 19083
610-853-4420

A & M Animal Clinic
137 North Wyoming Street
Hazleton, PA 18201
717-454-2466

Hazleton Veterinary Hospital
1092 North Church Street
Hazleton, PA 18201
717-454-7441

Saucon Valley Animal Hospital
1979 Leithsville Road
Helltertown, PA 18055
610-838-6644

Hermitage Veterinary Hospital
1500 North Hermitage Road
Hermitage, PA 16148
412-962-5725

Stefanick Veterinary Hospital
129 South Buhl Farm drive
Hermitage, PA 16148
412-347-5577

Young Veterinary Hospital
3816 East State Street
Hermitage, PA 16148
412-981-8770

Animal Health Care Center
948 East Chocolate Avenue
Hershey, PA 17033
717-533-6745

Hershey Veterinary Hospital
1016 Cocoa Avenue
Hershey, PA 17033
717-534-2244

Buck Road Animal Hospital
99 Buck Road
Holland, PA 18966
215-364-2997

Animal Clinic
801 Walnut Street
Hollidaysburg, PA 16648
814-695-1853

Mountain View Pet Hospital
103 Mountain Avenue
Hollidaysburg, PA 16648
814-941-2644

Kilwinning Veterinary Service
24 Buck Heights Road
Holtwood, PA 17532
717-284-2945

Honey Brook Anima Hospital
3784 Horseshoe Pike
Honey Brook, PA 19344
610-273-2055

Twin Valley Veterinary Clinic
7 Conestoga Avenue
Honey Brook, PA 19344
610-273-3230

Animal Medical Clinic
2544 US Route 30
Hookstown, PA 15050
412-573-1212

Horsham Veterinary Hospital
450 Central Avenue
Horsham, PA 19044
215-674-1738

CMI Veterinary Clinic
175 Veterinary Lane
Howard, PA 16841
814-625-2133

Hershire Animal Hospital
406 Middletown Road
Hummelstown, PA 17036
717-566-3703

Animal Clinic on Spruce Street
100 Spruce Street
Huntingdon, PA 16652
814-643-4403

Huntingdon Animal Hospital
601 Seventh Street
Huntingdon, PA 16652
814-643-2103

Bethayres Veterinary Hospital
2621 Philmont Avenue
Huntingdon Valley, PA 19006
215-947-5110

I

Imperial Animal Hospital
234 Main Street
Imperial, PA 15126
412-695-2475

Indian Springs Veterinary Clinic
1540 Indian Springs Road
Indiana, PA 15701
412-463-3549

J

Donaldson Animal Hospital
436 Lincoln Highway West
Jeannette, PA 15644
412-523-3302

Hopewell Veterinary Hospital
640 North Cedar Road
Jenkintown, PA 19046
215-379-2536

Rockledge Veterinary Clinic
2 South Sylvania Avenue
Jenkintown, PA 19046
215-379-1677

Penmar Veterinary Clinic
104 Donald Lane
Johnstown, PA 15904
814-269-3446

Richland Veterinary Hospital
1003 Eisenhower Boulevard
Johnstown, PA 15904
814-266-7912

K

Cat Veterinary of Kennett Square
550 School House Road
Kennett Square, PA 19348
610-444-2287

Kennett Square Veterinary Hospital
601 West State Street
Kennett Square, PA 19348
610-444-6141

Willowdale Veterinary Center
717 Unionville Road
Kennett Square, PA 19348
610-444-0352

Gulph Mils Veterinary Hospital
395 South Gulph Road
King of Prussia, PA 19406
610-265-6044

King of Prussia Veterinary
560 West Dekalb Pike
King of Prussia, PA 19406
610-265-4313

Suburban Veterinary Clinic
560 West Dekalb Pike
King of Prussia, PA 19406
610-265-5636

Kingston Veterinary Clinic
351 Wyoming Avenue
Kingston, PA 18704
717-288-3689

West Side Veterinary Hospital
576 Market Street
Kingston, PA 18704
717-288-8895

Northern Tier Veterinary Clinic
218 West Main Street
Knoxville, PA 16928
814-326-4145

Kutztown Animal Hospital
7 South Kemp Road
Kutztown, PA 19530
610-683-5353

L

Andorra Veterinary Clinic
638 Ridge Pike
Lafayette Hill, PA 19444
610-825-6622

Bridgeport Veterinary Clinic
1251 Ranck Mill Road
Lancaster, PA 17601
717-393-9074

Harrisburg Pike Animal Hospital
2449 Harrisburg Pike
Lancaster, PA 17601
717-892-7337

Leola Veterinary Clinic
2457 New Holland Pike
Lancaster, PA 17601
717-656-9754

Lincoln Highway Veterinary Clinic
1833 Lincoln Highway East
Lancaster, PA 17601
717-393-2444

Manheim Pike Veterinary Hospital
1669 Manheim Pike
Lancaster, PA 17601
717-569-6424

Manor Animal Hospital
2100 Stone Mill Road
Lancaster, PA 17601
717-393-5084

West Lancaster Animal Hospital
2110 Columbia Avenue
Lancaster, PA 17601
717-394-7713

Landenberg Veterinary Clinic
1611 New London Road
Landenberg, PA 19350
610-255-5372

Landisville Animal Hospital
3035 Harrisburg Pike
Landisville, PA 17538
717-898-1721

Animal Emergency and Critical
1900 Old Lincoln Highway
Langhorne, PA 19047
215-750-2774

Flowers Mill Veterinary Hospital
10 South Flowers Mill Road
Langhorne, PA 19047
215-752-1010

Veterinary Specialty and Emergency
1900 Old Lincoln Highway
Langhorne, PA 19047
215-750-7884

Gwynedd Veterinary Hospital
1615 West Point Pike
Lansdale, PA 19446
215-699-9294

Lansdale Animal Hospital
14 East Main Street
Lansdale, PA 19446
215-362-5150

North Penn Animal Hospital
1200 West Main Street
Lansdale, PA 19446
215-855-5853

Baltimore Pike Veterinary Hospital
708 East Baltimore Avenue
Landsdowne, PA 19050
610-623-8560

Emas Pet Hospital
107 East Baltimore Avenue
Landsdowne, PA 19050
610-626-3590

Jefferson Veterinary Hospital
446 Route 51
Large, PA 15025
412-384-7733

Lakeview Animal Hospital
809 Monastery Drive
Latrobe, PA 15650
412-537-5881

Latrobe Animal Clinic
1458 Clearview Drive
Latrobe, PA 15650
412-539-8531

Animal Clinic of Avon
1030 South Fifth Avenue
Lebanon, PA 18431
717-273-0171

East Lebanon Animal Clinic
429 East Cumberland Street
Lebanon, PA 18431
717-272-2453

Lebanon Valley Animal Hospital
2213 Cumberland Street
Lebanon, PA 18431
717-272-2515

Berks Animal Hospital
2648 Leisczs Bridge Road
Leesport, PA 19533
610-926-5363

Leesport Animal Hospital
216 Centre Avenue
Leesport, PA 19533
610-926-8866

Carbon County Animal Medical Center
43 Holiday Road
Lehighton, PA 18235
610-852-3660

Lehighton Animal Hospital
104 South Third Street
Lehighton, PA 18235
610-377-5574

Animal Hospital of Levittown
2230 Oxford Valley Road
Levittown, PA 19054
215-949-1010

Pets' Best Friend Veterinary Hospital
7029 Route 13
Levittown, PA 19054
215-547-5447

Animal Care Hospital
308 Hospital Drive
Lewisburg, PA 17837
717-524-7560

Lewisburg Veterinary Hospital
207 Fairground Road
Lewisburg, PA 17837
717-523-3640

Kish Veterinary Service
2098 US Highway 522 North
Lewistown, PA 17044
717-242-2415

Lewistown Veterinary Clinic
15 South Dorcas Street
Lewistown, PA 17044
717-242-2727

Pleasant View Veterinary Clinic
110 Electric Avenue
Lewistown, PA 17044
717-248-4703

Limerick Veterinary Hospital
345 West Ridge Pike
Limerick, PA 19468
610-489-2848

Linesville Veterinary Service
179 Airport Road
Linesville, PA 16424
814-683-5219

Lititz Veterinary Clinic
7 Toll Gate Road
Lititz, PA 17543
717-627-2750

Warwick Run Animal Clinic
788 Rothsville Road
Lititz, PA 17543
717-627-3411

Valley Veterinary Hospital
2847 Leechburg Road
Lower Burrell, PA 15068
412-339-1525

M

Mahanoy City Animal Clinic
539 East Centre Street
Mahanoy City, PA 15068
717-773-0922

Malvern Veterinary Hospital
545 South Warren Avenue
Malvern, PA 19355
610-647-2626

Spring Mill Veterinary
330 Conestoga Road
Malvern, PA 19355
610-644-6405

Sugartown Veterinary Hospital
605 Sugartown Road
Malvern, PA 19355
610-647-1266

Manheim Animal Hospital
30 South Main Street
Manheim, PA 17329
717-665-5465

White Oaks Veterinary Hospital
755 Lebanon Road
Manheim, PA 17329
717-665-2338

McDonald Animal Clinic
125 S McDonald Street
McDonald, PA 15057
412-926-4112

McKees Rocks Veterinary Clinic
908 Chartiers Avenue
McKees Rocks, PA 15136
412-771-8810

Brush Run Veterinary Clinic
450 Valleybrook Road
McMurray, PA 15317
412-941-4366

Hidden Valley Animal Clinic
100 Overlook Drive
McMurray, PA 15317
412-941-3900

Pleasant Valley Veterinary
211 East McMurray Road
McMurray, PA 15317
412-941-5484

Brooksvide Veterinary Clinic
448 North Street
Meadville, PA 16335
814-336-1352

Conneaut Lake Veterinary Clinic
14405 Conneaut Lake Road
Meadville, PA 16335
814-382-5446

Greener Pastures Veterinary
20594 Blooming Valley Road
Meadville, PA 16335
814-336-3161

Langdon's Town and Country Veterinary
18200 Conneaut Lake Road
Meadville, PA 16335
814-337-3271

Animal Emergency Medical Center
11 Willow Mill Park Road
Mechanicsburg, PA 17055
717-111-0001

Gettysburg Road Animal Hospital
1010 Wesley Drive #6
Mechanicsburg, PA 17055
717-697-7373

Good Hope Animal Clinic
6 Skyport Road #C
Mechanicsburg, PA 17055
717-766-5535

Lamb's Gap Animal Hospital
1806 Lambsgap Road
Mechanicsburg, PA 17055
717-732-9711

Mechanicsburg Veterinary Clinic
5244 East Trindle Road
Mechanicsburg, PA 17055
717-697-6856

Silver Springs Animal Clinic
5 Sample Bridge Road
Mechanicsburg, PA 17055
717-766-5980

Weber Veterinary Clinic
10 West Simpson Street
Mechanicsburg, PA 17055
717-766-5221

Willow Mill Veterinary Clinic
11 Willow Mill Park Road
Mechanicsburg, PA 17055
717-766-7981

Winding Hill Veterinary Clinic
1424 South Market Street
Mechanicsburg, PA 17055
717-697-4481

Aston Veterinary Hospital
3151 Pennell Road
Media, PA 19063
610-494-5800

Media Veterinary Hospital
695 South Baltimore Pike
Media, PA 19063
610-566-1936

Town and Country Veterinary Hospital
2800 Pennell Road #A
Media, PA 19063
610-459-2705

Crawford Veterinary Clinic
393 West Cornell Road
Mercer, PA 16038
412-662-5790

Burrows and Horst Veterinary Service
5643 Oakwood Drive
Mercersburg, PA 17236
717-328-5171

Middleburg Veterinary Service
37 US Highway 522 North
Middleburg, PA 16935
717-837-1212

Milford Veterinary
2170 Allentown Road
Milford Square, PA 18935
215-536-0141

Upper Dauphin Animal Hospital
132 Weaver Road
Millersburg, PA 17061
717-692-4791

Monogahela Animal Hospital
100 Van Voorhis Lane
Monongahela, PA 15338
412-258-8406

Monroeville Veterinary Hospital
232 Center Road
Monroeville, PA 15146
412-372-1100

Northern Pike Veterinary Hospital
4264 Northern Pike
Monroeville, PA 15146
412-373-8580

Montoursville Veterinary Hospital
416 Broad Street
Montoursville, PA 17754
717-368-5937

Morrisville Veterinary Hospital
822 West Trenton Avenue
Morrisville, PA 19067
215-295-5009

Stoney Creek Veterinary Hospital
701 Kedron Avenue
Morton, PA 19070
610-328-3600

Countryside Animal Hospital
430 North Main Street
Moscow, PA 18444
717-842-1414

Springbrook Pet Clinic
690 Swartz Valley Road
Moscow, PA 18444
717-842-4503

Munhall Veterinary Hospital
2110 West Street
Munhall, PA 15120
412-464-0893

Borderbrook Animal Hospital
3741 William Penn Highway
Murrysville, PA 15668
412-327-2200

East Suburban Animal Hospital
3895 William Penn Highway
Murrysville, PA 15668
412-325-3220

Myerstown Animal Hospital
410 South Broad Street
Myerstown, PA 17324
717-866-7515

N

Nanticoke Animal Hospital
226 South Market Street
Nanticoke, PA 18634
717-735-4744

Narberth Animal Hospital
815 Montgomery Avenue
Narberth, PA 19072
610-664-4114

Rainbow Pet Care Center
2201 Freeport Road
Natrona Heights, PA 15065
412-226-0333

Nazareth Veterinary Center
166 Bath Nazareth Pike
Nazareth, PA 18064
610-746-9080

William Penn Animal Hospital
678 Cherry Hill Road
Nazareth, PA 18064
610-759-8214

Kaufman's Veterinary Clinic
1718 Route 68
New Brighton, PA 15066
412-452-6151

New Britain Animal Clinic
341 West Butler Avenue
New Britain, PA 18901
215-340-0345

Apple Grove Veterinary Clinic
1725 Harlansburg Road
New Castle, PA 16101
412-656-1798

Castle Veterinary Clinic
2802 Ellwood Road
New Castle, PA 16101
412-652-1221

West Shore Veterinary Hospital
719 Limekiln Road
New Cumberland, PA 17070
717-774-0685

New Hope Veterinary Clinic
21 North Sugan Road
New Hope, PA 18938
215-862-2909

Crest View Animal Clinic
1928 New Ark Road
New London, PA 19360
610-255-5252

Country Doctor Veterinary Clinic
6418 Route 309
New Tripoli, PA 18066
610-298-2520

Dublin Veterinary Clinic
6 Spruce Court
Newtown, PA 18411
215-249-9800

Indian Walk Veterinary Center
1108 Wrightstown Road
Newtown, PA 18411
215-579-1779

Keystone Veterinary Hospital
428 Brownsburg Road
Newtown, PA 18411
215-598-3951

Newtown Veterinary Hospital
671 Newtown Yardley Road
Newtown, PA 18411
215-968-3895

Sycamore Veterinary Hospital
228 North Sycamore Street
Newtown, PA 18411
215-968-0509

Farrell Veterinary Clinic
108 Carlisle Road
Newville, PA 18914
717-776-6311

Cats Only Veterinary Hospital
1533 Dekalb Street
Norristown, PA 19401
610-279-2287

Garber Veterinary Hospital
2840 Swede Road
Norristown, PA 19401
610-272-1766

Metropolitan Veterinary Service
915 Trooper Road
Norristown, PA 19401
610-666-0995

Trooper Veterinary Hospital
7 North Park Avenue
Norristown, PA 19401
610-539-6820

North East Animal Hospital
9280 West Main Road
North East, PA 16428
814-725-8836

Countryside Veterinary Hospital
12249 Route 30
North Huntingdon, PA 15642
412-864-0939

Norwin Veterinary Hospital
12411 Route 30
North Huntingdon, PA 15642
412-864-6300

Shrader Veterinary Hospital
12720 Route 30
North Huntingdon, PA 15642
412-863-7501

East McKeesport Pet Hospital
1112 Lincoln Highway
North Versailles, PA 15137
412-824-1023

O

Old Forge Animal Hospital
904 South Main Street
Old Forge, PA 18158
717-457-1111

Oley Valley Animal Clinic
900 Blandon Road
Oley, PA 19547
610-987-6237

Hometown Animal Hospital
526 Burke Bypass
Olyphant, PA 18447
717-383-1950

Country Doctor Veterinary Clinic
6655 Farrier Road
Orefield, PA 18069
610-395-0650

Little Critters Veterinary
3746 Route 309
Orefield, PA 18069
610-481-9777

Meadowbrook Animal Hospital
4089 Durham Road
Ottsville, PA 18942
610-847-2776

Applebrook Veterinary Clinic
873 Market Street
Oxford, PA 17350
610-932-4430

Gum Tree Veterinary Clinic
402 Spruce Grove Road
Oxford, PA 17350
717-529-3070

Oxford Veterinary Hospital
2600 Baltimore Pike
Oxford, PA 17350
610-932-8757

P

Perkiomen Animal Hospital
919 Gravel Pike
Palm, PA 18070
215-679-7019

Little Gap Animal Hospital
2695 Little Gap Road
Palmerton, PA 18071
610-826-2793

Clark Veterinary Clinic
47 North Railroad Street
Palmyra, PA 18451
717-838-9563

Palmyra Animal Clinic
920 East Main Street
Palmyra, PA 18451
717-838-5451

Valley Animal Hospital
520 East Ridge Road
Palmyra, PA 18451
717-838-2643

Paoli Veterinary Care
1476 East Lancaster Avenue
Paoli, PA 19301
610-644-5360

Mid-Valley Veterinarian Hospital
10 Terrace Drive
Peckville, PA 18452
717-383-2566

Penn Hills Veterinary Hospital
12805 Frankstown Road
Penn Hills, PA 15235
412-795-1130

Runaway Farm Veterinary Hospital
10000 Tenth Street
Pennsburg, PA 18073
215-679-6219

Upper Bucks Animal Clinic
1815 Route 313
Perkasie, PA 18944
215-257-9995

Animal and Bird Clinic of Philadelphia
5542 Torresdale Avenue
Philadelphia, PA 19124
215-533-3726

Animal Medical Clinic
1401 South 13th Street
Philadelphia, PA 19147
215-463-1160

Animal and Bird Emergency Hospital
501 South Second Street
Philadelphia, PA 19147
215-627-8377

Bree's Animal Hospital
7436 Frankford Avenue
Philadelphia, PA 19136
215-338-3219

Broad Street Animal Hospital
5905 North Broad Street
Philadelphia, PA 19141
215-424-2470

Bustleton Avenue Animal Hospital
8120 Bustleton Avenue
Philadelphia, PA 19152
215-745-9000

Chelwayne Animal Hospital
5524 Wayne Avenue
Philadelphia, PA 19144
215-843-5952

Chestnut Hill Cat Clinic
8220 Germantown Avenue
Philadelphia, PA 19118
215-247-9560

Cottman Animal Hospital
1012 Cottman Avenue
Philadelphia, PA 19111
215-745-9030

Doctor Rude's Animal Hospital
3365 Frankford Avenue
Philadelphia, PA 19134
215-739-6401

Elmwood Animal Hospital
6206 Elmwood Avenue
Philadelphia, PA 19142
215-724-8808

Fairmount Animal Hospital
2315 Fairmount Avenue
Philadelphia, PA 19130
215-684-1439

Girard Veterinary Clinic
2806 West Girard Avenue
Philadelphia, PA 19130
215-232-0831

Knightswood Animal Hospital
12121 Knights Road
Philadelphia, PA 19154
215-632-2525

Mayfair Animal Clinic
2900 Hellerman Street
Philadelphia, PA 19149
215-332-9070

Mt. Airy Animal Clinic
114 East Mount Airy Avenue
Philadelphia, PA 19119
215-248-1886

Noah's Ark Animal Hospital
6801 Frankford Avenue
Philadelphia, PA 19136
215-624-7766

Northeast Animal Hospital
6503 Frankford Avenue
Philadelphia, PA 19135
215-624-8433

O'Neal Animal Hospital
4424 Market Street
Philadelphia, PA 19104
215-386-3293

Queen Village Animal Hospital
323 Bainbridge Street
Philadelphia, PA 19147
215-925-5753

Rhawnhurst Animal Hospital
7905 Bustleton Avenue
Philadelphia, PA 19152
215-333-8888

Roxborough Animal Hospital
6712 Ridge Avenue
Philadelphia, PA 19128
215-482-3037

Spruce Hill Veterinary Clinic
403 South 45th Street
Philadelphia, PA 19104
215-386-9100

Terry Animal Hospital
3606 Welsh Road
Philadelphia, PA 19136
215-624-6095

West Park Animal Medical Center
53000 Lancaster Avenue
Philadelphia, PA 19131
215-473-0210

Mt. Nittany Veterinary Clinic
500 South Centre Street
Philipsburg, PA 16866
814-342-1768

Allegheny North Veterinary
954 Perry Highway
Pittsburgh, PA 15237
412-364-5511

Castle Shannon Veterinary Hospital
3610 Library Road
Pittsburgh, PA 15234
412-885-2500

Fox Chapel Animal Hospital
1152 Freeport Road
Pittsburgh, PA 15238
412-781-6446

Greenfield Veterinary Hospital
611 Greenfield Avenue
Pittsburgh, PA 15207
412-422-7755

Greentree Animal Clinic
2080 Greentree Road
Pittsburgh, PA 15220
412-276-3311

Harts Run Animal Clinic
634 Dorseyville Road
Pittsburgh, PA 15238
412-963-8889

Kernick Animal Hospital
10753 Frankstown Road
Pittsburgh, PA 15235
412-242-2525

Lilac Veterinary Clinic
1039 Lilac Street
Pittsburgh, PA 15217
412-421-6700

North Boros Veterinary Hospital
2255 Babcock Boulevard
Pittsburgh, PA 15237
412-821-5600

Northview Animal Hospital
223 Siebert Road
Pittsburgh, PA 15237
412-364-5353

Penn Animal Hospital
2205 Penn Avenue
Pittsburgh, PA 15222
412-471-9855

Pittsburgh Animal Hospital
1117 Washington Boulevard
Pittsburgh, PA 15223
412-661-9817

Plum Animal Clinic
940 Unity Center Road
Pittsburgh, PA 15239
412-793-1118

Point Breeze Veterinary Clinic
6742 Reynolds Street
Pittsburgh, PA 15206
412-665-1810

Schenley Park Animal Hospital
3518 Boulevard of the Allies
Pittsburgh, PA 15213
412-683-3455

Shadyside Veterinary Clinic
235 Shady Avenue
Pittsburgh, PA 15206
412-661-5221

South Hills Animal Hospital
999 Killarney Drive
Pittsburgh, PA 15234
412-884-2434

South Sixty Animal Hospital
4167 Steubenville Pike
Pittsburgh, PA 15205
412-921-0600

Thornwood Veterinary Hospital
4211 Steubenville Pike
Pittsburgh, PA 15205
412-921-1474

Veterinary Emergency Clinic
882 Butler Street
Pittsburgh, PA 15223
412-492-9855

Pittston Animal Hospital
4 Oconnell Street
Pittston, PA 18640
717-655-2412

Pleasant Hills Pet Hospital
171 Green Drive
Pleasant Hills, PA 15236
412-655-8710

Allegheny Veterinary Emergency
1810 Route 286
Plum, PA 15239
412-325-1881

Golden Mile Animal Clinic
1835 Route 286
Plum, PA 15239
412-325-2661

Holiday Park Animal Hospital
1999 Route 286
Plum, PA 15236
412-327-7100

Plumsteadville Veterinary Clinic
6040 Easton Road
Plumsteadville, PA 18949
215-766-0388

Valley View Veterinary Clinic
2300 Mountain Road
Plymouth, PA 19401
717-287-9085

Hickory Veterinary Hospital
2303 Hickory Road
Plymouth Meeting, PA 19462
610-828-3054

Animal Hospital of Mount Pocono
1001 Route 940
Pocono Summit, PA 18346
717-839-8116

French Creek Veterinary Clinic
1424 Ridge Road
Pottstown, PA 19464
610-469-9700

Peterman Road Animal Hospital
1620 New Schuylkill Road
Pottstown, PA 19464
610-323-9454

Stowe Veterinary Clinic
571 West High Street
Pottstown, PA 19464
610-327-2617

Schuylkill Veterinary Hospital
1170 Route 61 Highway
South
Pottsville, PA 18837
717-622-1098

Prospect Park Veterinary Clinic
903 Lincoln Avenue
Prospect Park, PA 15834
610-461-7887

Q

Pleasant Valley Animal Hospital
1945 State Road
Quakertown, PA 18951
610-346-7854

Quakertown Veterinary Clinic
2250 Old Bethlehem Pike
Quakertown, PA 18951
215-536-6245

Tri-County Veterinary Emergency Service
2250 Old Bethlehem Pike
Quakertown, PA 18951
215-536-6245

Pennstar Veterinary Service
496 Solanco Road
Quarryville, PA 17566
717-786-1303

Solanco Veterinary Clinic
550 Solanco Road
Quarryville, PA 17566
717-786-5121

R

Animal Clinic of Reading
813 Elm Street
Reading, PA 17350
610-376-0065

Antietam Valley Animal Hospital
10 North Prospect Street
Reading, PA 17350
610-779-4796

Detwiler Animal Hospital
22 South Kenhorst Boulevard
Reading, PA 17350
610-777-6546

Exeter Veterinary Hospital
4955 Perkiomen Avenue
Reading, PA 17350
610-779-2300

Friends Veterinary Hospital
3208 Kutztown Road
Reading, PA 17350
610-939-9699

Springfield Veterinary Hospital
2 Princeton Avenue
Reading, PA 17350
610-777-7640

Big Valley Veterinary Clinic
101 Three Cent Lane
Reedsville, PA 17084
717-667-2000

Animal Clinic of Butler
827 Evans City Road
Renfrew, PA 16053
412-789-7000

Richboro Veterinary Hospital
700 Second Street Pike
Richboro, PA 18954
215-322-6776

Clover Farm Veterinary Hospital
3239 Route 40
Richeyville, PA 15358
412-632-3230

Ringtown Valley Veterinary
22 Apple Street
Ringtown, PA 17967
717-889-5023

Deer Lane Veterinary Clinic
620 Deer Lane
Rochester, PA 15074
412-728-6955

Hamilton Animal Hospital
1526 Easton Road
Rosyln, PA 16237
215-659-3611

S

Woodcock Dam Animal Clinic
21524 State Highway
Saegertown, PA 16433
814-763-66440

Sanatoga Animal Hospital
2814 East High Street
Sanatoga, PA 19464
610-326-6346

Saxony Animal Clinic
569 North Pike Road
Sarver, PA 16055
412-352-4250

Mountain Shadow Veterinary Service
64 Kiehner Road
Schuylkill Haven, PA 17972
717-739-4838

Keystone Mobile Veterinary Service
4150 Scotland Main Street
Scotland, PA 17254
717-261-9738

Aaa Animal Clinic
1107 South Washington
Avenue
Scranton, PA 18501
717-969-9778

Keyser Valley Animal Hospital
820 South Keyser Avenue
Scranton, PA 18501
717-961-5530

Scranton Animal Hospital
911 Providence Road
Scranton, PA 18501
717-347-0853

Veterinary Medical Center
3369 Birney Avenue
Scranton, PA 18501
717-344-1404

Alpha Veterinary Hospital
1430 Route 309
Sellersville, PA 18960
215-257-4717

Sewickley Veterinary Hospital
1104 Ohio River Boulevard
Sewickley, PA 15637
412-741-5550

Delco Veterinary Hospital
1301 Hook Road
Sharon Hill, PA 19079
610-586-1577

Trucksville Dog and Cat Hospital
215 South Memorial
  Highway
Shavertown, PA 19061
717-696-1146

Keystone Veterinary Service
110 Main Street
Shelocta, PA 15774
412-354-5200

Burnt Mill Veterinary Center
15154 Burnt Mill Road
Shippensburg, PA 17257
717-423-6536

Central Valley Veterinary Hospital
414 West King Street
Shippensburg, PA 17257
717-530-1060

Mt. Rock Animal Hospital
7473 Molly Pitcher Highway
Shippensburg, PA 17257
717-532-8599

Shippensburg Animal Hospital
93 Walnut Bottom Road
Shippensburg, PA 17257
717-532-5413

Berks Animal Hospital
10 Zions Church Road
Shoemakersville, PA 19555
610-562-2500

Shrewsbury Veterinary Clinic
85 East Forrest Avenue
Shrewsbury, PA 17758
717-428-3350

Hempfield Animal Hospital
3672 Marietta Pike
Silver Spring, PA 17575
717-285-7946

Sinking Spring Animal Hospital
21 Green Valley Road
Sinking Spring, PA 19608
610-670-5757

Skippack Animal Hospital
3865 Skippack Pike
Skippack, PA 19474
610-584-6300

Highland Animal Hospital
6415 Pennsylvania Route 873
Slatington, PA 18080
610-767-1100

Slippery Rock Veterinary Hospital
133 Branchton Road
Slippery Rock, PA 16101
412-794-8545

Smoketown Veterinary Hospital
2497 East Old Philadelphia
  Pike
Smoketown, PA 18951
717-394-5542

Sacksen Veterinary Service
274 Saddle Road
Somerset, PA 15330
814-352-7515

Somerset Veterinary Hospital
1322 Berlin Plank Road
Somerset, PA 15330
814-443-1323

Indian Valley Animal Hospital
28 Adams Avenue
Soudeton, PA 18964
215-723-3971

House Call Veterinarian
649 Ridge Road
Spring City, PA 19475
610-666-1686

Jasmine Veterinary Hospital
971 Pittsburgh Street
Springdale, PA 15144
412-274-0704

Animal Medical Hospital
1909 North Atherton Street
State College, PA 16801
814-234-0201

Centre Animal Hospital
1518 West Collage Avenue
State College, PA 16801
814-238-5100

JM Ritchie Veterinary Hospital
2790 West College Avenue
  #1000
State College, PA 16801
814-231-2666

Metzger Animal Hospital
1044 Benner Pike
State College, PA 16801
814-237-5333

Mt. Nittany Veterinary Hospital
200 Elmwood Street
State College, PA 16801
814-237-4272

State College Veterinary Hospital
1700 West College Avenue
State College, PA 16801
814-238-8181

University Drive Veterinary
1602 University Drive
State College, PA 16801
814-231-8387

Hopewell Veterinary Service
2 Trouts Lane
Stewartstown, PA 17363
717-993-2155

Mid Valley Mobile Veterinary
140 South Second Street
Sunbury, PA 17801
717-988-7811

Sunbury Animal Hospital
400 State Street
Sunbury, PA 17801
717-286-5131

T

Tamaqua Veterinary Hospital
131 West Broad Street
Tamaqua, PA 18252
717-668-6066

Berks County Mobile Veterinary
418 Crystal Rock Road
Temple, PA 19560
610-929-1035

VCA Muhlenberg Animal Clinic
4148 Kutztown Road
Temple, PA 19560
610-929-9896

Marley Veterinary Clinic
1120 Hydetown Road
Titusville, PA 16354
814-827-1778

Tunkhannock Veterinarian Clinic
125 East Tioga Street
Tunkhannock, PA 16351
717-836-5300

U

Natural Animal Veterinary
42 Waterford Street
Union City, PA 16438
814-438-3800

Bywood Animal Hospital
821 Garrett Road
Upper Darby, PA 19082
610-352-5470

Carlton Dog and Cat Hospital
137 South State Road
Upper Darby, PA 19082
610-352-2020

Delaware County Animal Hospital
301 South 69th Street
Upper Darby, PA 19082
610-352-6677

Market Upper Darby Animal Hospital
6421 Market Street
Upper Darby, PA 19082
610-352-9100

Township Line Animal Hospital
8510 Landsdowne Avenue
Upper Darby, PA 19082
610-789-2525

V

Twinbrook Animal Clinic
1120 Pittsburgh Road
Valencia, PA 16059
412-898-2300

Large Animal Veterinary Service
21409 Gospel Hill Road
Venango, PA 16049
814-398-8922

Verona Pet Hospital
1204 Milltown Road
Verona, PA 15147
412-793-2622

W

Blue Ridge Veterinary Clinic
1124 Myrtle Road
Walnutport, PA 18088
610-767-4896

Cherryville Animal Hospital
496 Willow Road
Walnutport, PA 18088
610-767-7505

Central Bucks Animal Hospital
491 West Bristol Road
Warminster, PA 18974
215-773-9494

Warminster Veterinary Hospital
405 York Road
Warminster, PA 18974
215-675-4319

Kinzua Veterinary Clinic
2029 Pennsylvania Avenue East
Warren, PA 18851
814-726-9720

Warren Veterinary Hospital
2848 Pennsylvania Avenue West
Warren, PA 18851
814-723-7123

Warrington Veterinary Clinic
1352 Easton Road
Warrington, PA 18976
215-343-4110

Chestnut Veterinary Clinic
850 West Chestnut Street
Washington, PA 15301
412-222-7040

East Maiden Animal Clinic
498 East Maiden Street
Washington, PA 15301
412-225-2312

Meadowlands Veterinary Hospital
1200 Washington Road
Washington, PA 15301
412-228-2040

Washington Animal Hospital
449 Washington Road
Washington, PA 15301
412-229-7100

Washington Crossing Hospital
1240 Route 532
Washington Crossing, PA 18977
215-493-5986

West Shore Animal Hospital
248 Belmont Street
Waymart, PA 18472
717-488-7488

Gateway Animal Hospital
103 East Swedesford Road
Wayne, PA 17748
610-687-9600

Radnor Veterinary Hospital
112 North Aberdeen Avenue
Wayne, PA 17748
610-687-1550

Waynesboro Veterinary Clinic
29 Philadelphia Avenue #A
Waynesboro, PA 17268
717-762-0221

Wellsboro Small Animal Hospital
23 Tioga Street
Wellsboro, PA 16901
717-724-1221

VCA Cacoosing Animal Hospital
5100 East Penn Avenue
Wernersville, PA 19565
610-678-2403

Hamilton Animal Care
6110 Hamilton Boulevard
Wescosville, PA 18106
610-395-0707

Animal Hospital
1353 Pottstown Pike
West Chester, PA 19380
610-692-7560

Chester County Cat Hospital
108 South High Street
West Chester, PA 19380
610-701-6369

East Goshen Veterinary Hospital
1506 Paoli Pike
West Chester, PA 19380
610-696-3303

Lenape Veterinary Clinic
1430 Lenape Road
West Chester, PA 19380
610-793-2589

Pet Clinic
1548 Wickerton Drive
West Chester, PA 19380
610-431-0345

Rocky Hill Veterinary Clinic
1601 Margo Lane
West Chester, PA 19380
610-431-1620

Sconnelltown Veterinary Clinic
415 South Birmingham Road
West Chester, PA 19380
610-696-7219

Targwood Animal Health Care
1819 West Strasburg Road
West Chester, PA 19380
610-486-6446

West Chester Animal Emergency
1141 West Chester Pike
West Chester, PA 19380
610-696-4110

West Chester Animal Hospital
1138 Pottstown Pike
West Chester, PA 19380
610-696-3476

West Chester Veterinary Medical
1141 West Chester Pike
West Chester, PA 19380
610-696-8712

Westtown Veterinary Clinic
1130 South Chester Road
West Chester, PA 19380
610-399-1012

Avalon Veterinary Hospital
310 East Baltimore Pike
West Grove, PA 19390
610-869-3766

Penn Animal Hospital
881 East Baltimore Pike
West Grove, PA 19390
610-869-3033

**West Hazelton
Veterinary Hospital**
45 East Monroe Avenue
West Hazelton, PA 18201
717-455-2580

**Animal Clinic of West
Lawn**
1917 Penn Avenue
West Lawn, PA 19609
610-678-7698

**West Middletown
Animal Hospital**
109 East Main Street
West Middletown, PA 15379
412-587-5667

**Animal Clinic of West
Mifflin**
4404 Kennywood Boulevard
West Mifflin, PA 15122
412-464-0385

Hope Veterinary Clinic
114 Mount Pleasant Road
West Newton, PA 15089
412-872-8644

**Bradford Hills
Veterinary Hospital**
13055 Perry Highway
Wexford, PA 15090
412-935-5827

**Tender Touch
Veterinary Hospital**
151 Wexford Bayne Road
Wexford, PA 15090
412-933-7387

**Wexford Veterinary
Hospital**
10309 Perry Highway
Wexford, PA 15090
412-935-5911

**Poco West Veterinary
Clinic**
332 Susquehanna Street
White Haven, PA 18661
717-443-9933

**White Haven Veterinary
Hospital**
400 Towanda Street
White Haven, PA 18661
717-443-0966

**White Oak Veterinary
Clinic**
3065 Jacks Run Road
White Oak, PA 15068
412-678-4042

Plains Animal Hospital
242 River Road
Wilkes Barre, PA 18702
717-829-4030

**Wyoming Valley
Veterinary Hospital**
770 Wilkes Barre Township
  Boulevard
Wilkes Barre, PA 18702
717-825-7617

**Animal and Avian
Hospital**
1828 East Third Street
Williamsport, PA 17701
717-323-9431

**Little's Veterinary
Hospital**
2075 Lycoming Creek Road
Williamsport, PA 17701
717-322-7811

**Loyalsock Animal
Hospital**
1900 Northway Road
Williamsport, PA 17701
717-326-1709

**Williamsport
Veterinary Service**
497 Northway Exit
Williamsport, PA 17701
717-326-1134

**Williamsport West
Veterinary Hospital**
3537 West Fourth Street
Williamsport, PA 17701
717-323-9588

**Willow Run Veterinary
Clinic**
320 Beaver Valley Pike
Willow Street, PA 17584
717-464-3424

**Willow Street Animal
Hospital**
2611 Willow Street Pike
Willow Street, PA 17584
717-464-4755

**Ackermanville
Veterinary Hospital**
205 North Broadway
Wind Gap, PA 18091
610-863-7111

**Conrad Weiser Animal
Hospital**
105 North Third Street
Womelsdorf, PA 19567
610-589-5019

Animal Care Center
2002 Wyoming Avenue
Wyoming, PA 18644
717-287-3329

**Forty Fort Animal
Hospital**
2002 Wyoming Avenue
Wyoming, PA 18644
717-287-5308

**Shoemaker Avenue
Animal Hospital**
692 Shoemaker Avenue
Wyoming, PA 18644
717-693-3196

**Wyomissing Animal
Hospital**
35 Commerce Drive
Wyomissing, PA 19610
610-372-2121

Y

Animal Healing Center
1724 Yardley Langhorne
  Road
Yardley, PA 19067
215-493-0621

**Flowers Mil Veterinary
Hospital**
1095 Reading Avenue
Yardley, PA 19067
215-493-3363

**Moontide Veterinary
Service**
955 Big Oak Road
Yardley, PA 19067
215-736-8885

**Animal Emergency
Clinic**
3256 North Susquehanna
  Trail
York, PA 17403
717-767-5355

**Animal Hospital of
West York**
3985 West Market Street
York, PA 17403
717-792-9278

**Community Animal
Hospital**
400 South Pine Street
York, PA 17403
717-845-5669

**Hill Street Veterinary
Hospital**
555 Hill Street
York, PA 17403
717-843-6060

**Leader Heights Animal
Hospital**
199 Leaders Heights Road
York, PA 17403
717-741-4618

**Market Street Animal
Hospital**
2200 West Market Street
York, PA 17403
717-792-2531

**Yorkshire Animal
Hospital**
3434 East Market Street
York, PA 17403
717-755-4935

Z

**Hidden Springs
Veterinary Hospital**
1335 North Gravel Pike
Zieglerville, PA 19492
610-287-5100

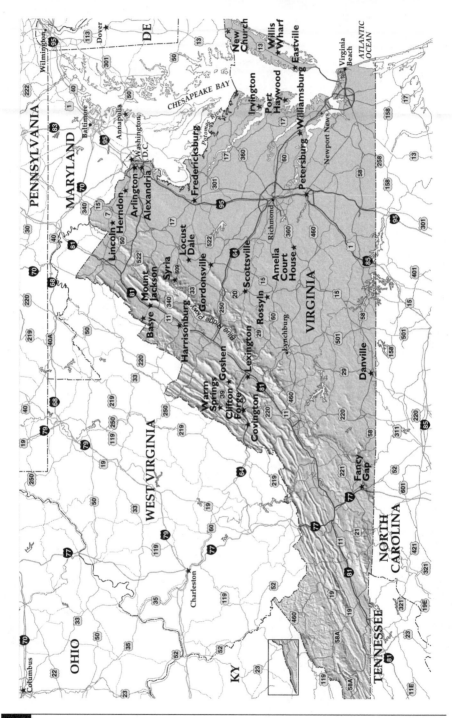

Virginia

Executive Club Suites

Executive Club Suites
610 Bashford Lane
Alexandria, Virginia 22314
800-535-CLUB ▪ 703-739-2582
Web Site: www.dcexeclub.com

Suite Rates:	$170–$190, including continental breakfast and evening reception. AAA discount.
Pet Charges or Deposits:	$25 per stay. $250 refundable deposit.
Rated: 3 Paws 🐾🐾🐾	78 guest suites. Health club and pool.

T he Executive Club accommodations and facilities are comparable to a luxury hotel, but at reasonable rates. Each suite is at least 650 square feet, with a floor plan that includes a living room, dining room, kitchen, bath and one or two bedrooms.

Queen Anne furnishings decorate this comfortable, apartment-size home throughout. Queen-sized beds, remote-controlled cable televisions and kitchens equipped with modern appliances, cookware and dinnerware are standard.

Continental breakfast and evening Club Room reception are complimentary, as are access to the Health Club, swimming pool and computer room.

Sheraton Suites—Alexandria

Sheraton Suites—Alexandria
801 North Asaph Street
Alexandria, Virginia 22314
800-325-3535 • 703-836-4700
Web Site: www.sheraton.com

Room Rates:	$99–$199. AAA and AARP discounts.
Pet Charges or Deposits:	$50 per stay. Pets must be 30 lbs. or less. Pet Policy must be signed.
Rated: 3 Paws 🐾🐾🐾	247 guest suites. Facilities for disabled. Indoor pool, hydrotherapy pool, exercise room. Restaurant and lounge. Complimentary airport transportation to and from National Airport.

Conveniently located for downtown Washington, D.C., and historic Old Town, the Sheraton Suites Alexandria offers comfortable, two-room suites with coffeemakers and mini-refrigerators.

Business travelers seek out Sheraton Hotels for the wide variety of services and amenities that help them stay productive while on the road. Guest rooms offer generous working desks, with Smart Rooms featuring ergonomically designed chairs, ample task lighting, extra electrical outlets, personalized voice mail and a combination printer/copier/fax machine. Other innovative services include the most flexible check-in and check-out program in the industry and "Body Clock Cuisine," to combat the effects of jet lag.

Benita's Bed and Breakfast

Benita's Bed and Breakfast
16620 Amelia Avenue
Amelia, Virginia 23002
804-561-6321
Web Site: www.bbonline.com/va/benita
E-mail: Davisr79@hotmail.com

Room Rates:	$50–$70, including full breakfast and evening dessert.
Pet Charges or Deposits:	Manager's prior approval required.
Rated: 3 Paws 🐾🐾🐾	4 guest rooms.

You'll find all the comforts of home at this bed and breakfast. Relax in a rocking chair on the front porch of this ante-bellum home or enjoy sitting by a warm fireplace in the winter. Snack on cookies and milk before you go to bed in one of the four guest rooms furnished with family antiques. In the morning feast on a hearty, Southern-style breakfast served in the dining room, or in bed if you like.

Area attractions include historic sites to explore, a treasure hunt for precious stones at the Morefield Mine, numerous antique stores to investigate and the Amelia wildlife area, which is great for fishing.

Executive Club Suites

Executive Club Suites
108 South Courthouse Road
Arlington, Virginia 22204
800-535-CLUB ▪ 703-522-2582
Web Site: www.dcexeclub.com

Suite Rates:	$170–$190, including continental breakfast and evening reception. AAA discount.
Pet Charges or Deposits:	$25 per stay. $250 refundable deposit.
Rated: 3 Paws 🐾🐾🐾	74 guest suites. Health club and pool.

Convenience and hospitality make the Executive Club Suites a good choice for the Washington, D.C., metropolitan area. Here you will find one-bedroom, one bedroom with den and two-bedroom suites—each with full kitchen and separate living areas and bedrooms.

Continental breakfast and evening Club Room receptions are complimentary. And access to the Health Club, swimming pool, computer room and meeting rooms are all part of the package.

Sky Chalet Mountain Lodge

Sky Chalet Mountain Lodge
Route 263
P.O. Box 300
280 Sky Chalet Lane
Basye, Virginia 22810
540-856-2147
Web Site: www.skychalet.com
E-mail: skychalet@skychalet.com

Room Rates:	$34–$79, including continental breakfast. AAA, AARP, AKC and ABA discounts.
Pet Charges or Deposits:	Manager's prior approval required.
Rated: 3 Paws 🐾🐾🐾	10 guest cabins and 2 suites, with fireplaces and spectacular views.

S ky Chalet is a warm, friendly place where travelers find good country food, refreshing spirits for the soul and a restful bed in a homey room. The proprietors are there to greet you as their guest, not as a stranger. Each morning a complimentary continental breakfast is delivered to your room.

Sky Chalet is a mountain lodge in its truest sense. First of all, it sits on the very top of a mountain, with views all around. It's rustic, it's old, and it does need work, but the rooms are clean and neat and very reasonably priced.

You are surrounded by hiking trails and woods, the George Washington National Forest and the Shenandoah National Park, in addition to antique and craft shops, skiing, golfing, horseback riding, tennis, swimming, canoeing and numerous lake activities.

Longdale Inn

Longdale Inn
6209 Longdale Furnace Road
Clifton Forge, Virginia 24422
800-862-0386 ▪ 540-862-0892
Web Site: www.symweb.com/longdale
E-mail:longdale@symweb.com

Room Rates:	$75 to $130, including full breakfast.
Pet Charges or Deposits:	Designated room only. Manager's prior approval required.
Rated: 3 Paws 🐾🐾🐾	8 guest rooms and 2 suites on 12 acres.

You enter through the stone gates, along the arched drive lined with flowering plum trees, to this dusty-rose Victorian mansion in the Allegheny Mountains. Here you will find twenty-three rooms, each superbly restored and uniquely decorated. On the first floor, laurel-leaf embellishments adorn the eleven-foot canvas ceilings, and guests can relax by the floor-to-ceiling windows. Snuggle in front of one of the inn's eight hand-painted marble fireplaces or read a favorite book beneath an original brass carbide chandelier. There are ten bedrooms and suites, furnished in Victorian, European or Southwestern decor.

Breakfast is offered in the dining room. Freshly brewed Allegheny Star coffee, fruit, juices and cereals, followed by the chef's entrée, are guaranteed to satisfy the heartiest appetite.

Twelve acres, rich with wildflowers and songbirds, surround Longdale Inn. One mile west of the Inn, Longdale National Recreation Area offers a variety of trails and a mountain lake for swimming. Nearby National Forest roads and trails are ideal for cross-country skiing and mountain biking.

Milton Hall Bed and Breakfast Inn

Milton Hall Bed and Breakfast Inn
207 Thorny Lane
Covington, Virginia 24426
540-965-0196

Room Rates:	$75–$140, including full breakfast. AARP discount.
Pet Charges or Deposits:	Manager's prior approval required.
Rated: 3 Paws 🐾🐾🐾	5 guest rooms and 1 suite on 17 acres.

Milton Hall, a unique English country manor, was built in 1874 in the Allegheny Mountains of western Virginia. The house presents an exotic contrast to its rustic surroundings, with its many gables, buttressed porch towers and Gothic trimmings. The house is spacious, but more of a large country home than a mansion.

Guest rooms are roomy with private baths, sitting areas and original fireplaces. Room rates include a full English breakfast, with menu highlights of fresh fruits in season, eggs prepared with herbs, Allegheny Mountain trout or local country-style sausage and red potatoes. Home-baked muffins are stuffed with fresh berries or apples in season.

Stratford Inn

Stratford Inn
2500 Riverside Drive
Danville, Virginia 24540
800-326-8455 ▪ 804-793-2500

Room Rates:	$50–$92, including full breakfast. AAA, AARP, AKC and ABA discounts.
Pet Charges or Deposits:	Small pets only.
Rated: 3 Paws ❤❤❤	151 guest rooms and 9 suites, with refrigerators, microwaves, pool, whirlpool and Jacuzzi. On-site fitness center. Restaurant.

T he rooms are spacious and comfortable and feature in-room coffee, free newspapers, hair dryers and other amenities, including room service. Suites are equipped with whirlpools, saunas, parlors and two baths.

The fitness facility features the treadmill, stepper and stationary bike. The heated pool, hot tub and sun deck are for guests to enjoy. Nearby is an indoor pool, steam room, Nautilus, racquetball and a fully equipped local health club. Just ask for a free pass at the front desk.

Windrush Farm Bed and Breakfast

Windrush Farm Bed and Breakfast
5350 Willow Oak Road
P.O. Box 1076
Eastville, Virginia 23347
757-678-7725

Room Rates:	$55–$65, including full breakfast.
Pet Charges or Deposits:	$10 per day. Horses welcome. Manager's prior approval required. Sorry, no cats.
Rated: 3 Paws 🐾🐾🐾	2 guest rooms on 3 acres. 5 Box-stall barn and horse pasture.

Here, you will enjoy the charm of an 1850s country house, the fragrance of a southern garden, and the pleasures of a working horse farm, in one of the oldest villages in Virginia. Stroll through two acres of lawns and gardens, graced by stately ash, maple and pecan trees.

Cozy guest rooms overlook the gardens and are comfortably furnished with American and English art and antiques. The upstairs sitting room features a fireplace, television and VCR. Breakfast is included and is served either on the screened porch or fireside, by the hearth.

Windrush Farm Bed and Breakfast offers easy access to a private beach on Chesapeake Bay and Kiptopeke State Park. Weekend trail rides with box lunches are available for guests who bring their own horses.

Doe Run Lodge Resort and Conference Center

Doe Run Lodge Resort and Conference Center
Milepost 189 Blue Ridge Parkway
P.O. Box 280
Fancy Gap, Virginia 24328
800-325-6189 ▪ 540-398-2212
Web Site: www.doerunlodge.com
E-mail: doerun@tcia.net

Room Rates:	$109–$254. AAA and AARP discounts.
Pet Charges or Deposits:	$45 refundable deposit.
Rated: 5 Paws 🐾🐾🐾🐾🐾	Cabins and chalets with refrigerators, microwaves, pool, Jacuzzi, hot tubs, tennis courts.

At Milepost 189, a spot between Roanoke and Fancy Gap, Virginia, at a place called Groundhog Mountain, you'll find an accommodating alpine lodge and resort where you can stop the world and imbibe the Appalachian experience. Doe Run Lodge offers an inviting retreat with comfortable accommodations nestled in a remote mountain setting along the Blue Ridge Parkway.

You'll find a pre-laid fire ready for your match when you arrive in any of the chalets or villas. The swimming pool and carpeted deck are comfortable throughout the season, and you can get even warmer in the adjacent saunas.

The rustically designed stone-and-timber lodge features top-rated dining, a fabulous wine cellar and a fully stocked bar. Floor-to-ceiling windows and a spacious granite patio add spectacular views at every meal.

Dunning Mills Inn

Dunning Mills Inn
2305-C Jefferson Davis Highway
Fredericksburg, Virginia 22401
540-373-1256

Room Rates:	$67–$90, including doughnuts and coffee. AAA discount.
Pet Charges or Deposits:	$2.50 per day per pet. $200 refundable deposit for stays of 30 days or longer.
Rated: 3 Paws 🐾🐾🐾	44 queen-sized suites. Refrigerators, microwaves, laundry facilities, pool.

T he Dunning Mills Inn features comfortable suites at reasonable rates. Each suite includes a fully equipped kitchen, dining area, living area and a spacious bedroom/bath. There are separate entrances to each suite, with convenient free parking.

While the Inn is centrally located on the Route 1 bypass in Fredericksburg, it is nestled near the woods, away from the noise and congestion of the highway. Most suites offer a wooded view and daily maid service.

Sheraton Inn Fredericksburg

Sheraton Inn Fredericksburg
2801 Plank Road
Fredericksburg, Virginia 22404
800-682-1049 ▪ 540-786-8321

Room Rates:	$79–$120. AAA and AARP discounts.
Pet Charges or Deposits:	$40 refundable deposit.
Rated: 3 Paws ❀❀❀	191 guest rooms and 9 suites. Olympic-sized outdoor pool, lighted tennis and basketball courts, fitness center. Restaurant and lounge.

T he land where the Sheraton Inn Fredericksburg Conference Center now stands was originally a dairy farm. The property was used to raise Aberdeen Angus cattle and the dairy barn accommodated 125 milk cows. It was this old barn that was renovated to form the main building of the Sheraton–Fredericksburg.

Great pains were taken to maintain the authenticity of the barn in spite of the extensive renovation necessary to prepare it for guests. This is the original barn. The exterior siding was replaced, but the metal roof is the original. On opening night it was found that the draft from air rising and falling in the tall cylinder silos literally fluttered the tablecloths of the guests seated below. Therefore, it was necessary to install false ceilings at a height of about 18 feet.

This unique hotel now features comfortable guest rooms, delicious food and recreational facilities.

Sleepy Hollow Farm Bed and Breakfast

Sleepy Hollow Farm Bed and Breakfast
16280 Blue Ridge Turnpike
Gordonsville, Virginia 22738
800-215-4804 ▪ 540-832-5555

Room Rates:	$65–$135, including full breakfast.
Pet Charges or Deposits:	$5–$10 per stay. Manager's prior approval required.
Rated: 4 Paws 🐾🐾🐾🐾	3 guest rooms and 3 suites. Refrigerator, microwave, whirlpool and Jacuzzi.

 njoy country life in a charming old farmhouse or in the chestnut cottage. The warmth and hospitality of Sleepy Hollow reflect Virginia's traditions.

Terraces, porches, a croquet lawn and rooms with views and fireplaces provide opportunities to relax in the family atmosphere. The main house with its antique furnishings and eclectic accessories offers a pleasing and comfortable place to relax.

Each morning a delicious country breakfast is served in the two dining rooms. Sleepy Hollow grows its own herbs, vegetables and flowers for cooking and for decorations.

Hummingbird Inn

Hummingbird Inn
30 Wood Lane
P.O. Box 147
Goshen, Virginia 24439
800-397-3214 ▪ 540-997-9065
Web Site: www.hummingbird.com
E-mail: hmgbird@hummingbird.com

Room Rates:	$105–$135, including full breakfast. AAA, AARP, AKC and ABA discounts.
Pet Charges or Deposits:	Sorry, no cats. Manager's prior approval required. $20 per stay. One night's refundable deposit.
Rated: 4 Paws 🐾🐾🐾🐾	5 guest rooms with whirlpools and fireplaces.

This unique Victorian villa, born in 1780 and completed in 1853, is just west of the scenic Goshen Pass on the western edge of the Shenandoah Valley. Here you will find country elegance amid perennial gardens and an old livery stable on the edge of a wide trout stream. The atmosphere is relaxed and informal.

Guest rooms are beautifully appointed with period antiques, natural linens, down comforters, ceiling fans, room air conditioners and thick, fluffy towels in modern bathrooms.

A typical gourmet breakfast features fresh fruit, entrées such as oven-baked French toast, cornmeal pancakes or Dutch babies, bacon, sausage or ham, potatoes or baked apples, coffee cake, muffins and scones. Guests have described the cuisine here as "five star" and "fabulous."

Village Inn

Village Inn
Route 1, Box 76
Harrisonburg, Virginia 22801
800-736-7355 ▪ 540-434-7355

Room Rates: $42–$58.
Pet Charges or Deposits: None.
Rated: 3 Paws 🐾🐾🐾   36 guest rooms and suites, many with decks and whirlpool
baths.

T he Village Inn of Harrisonburg is conveniently located on Highway 11, just off Interstate 81, in the picturesque Shenandoah Valley of Virginia. Opportunities for fun and recreation abound within easy reach of the Inn. Explore interesting underground caverns or experience the scenic beauty of famous Skyline Drive. The Valley's rich heritage is evident in the many historical monuments and markers along the roads and at the Civil War battlefield and museum in nearby New Market.

Guest rooms are spacious and comfortable, many with whirlpool baths and decks overlooking the scenic Virginia countryside. The Inn offers a pool and a playground as well as parking at your door for easy access.

Residence Inn by Marriott– Herndon/Reston

Residence Inn by Marriott—Herndon/Reston
315 Elden Street
Herndon, Virginia 20170
800-311-3131 ▪ 703-435-0044
Web Site: www.marriott.com

Room Rates:	$79–$189, including full breakfast. AAA and AARP discounts.
Pet Charges or Deposits:	$6 per day. $100 nonrefundable deposit.
Rated: 3 Paws 🐾🐾🐾	168 guest suites, some with fireplaces. Outdoor pool and whirlpool. Health club and full spa nearby.

Convenient to the Dulles International Airport, Residence Inn by Marriott dispels the myth that there's no place like home. When you have to be away from home on business or vacation, you will appreciate the inn's comforts and conveniences.

From the spacious accommodations (some with fireplaces), separate sleeping and living areas, fully equipped kitchens, laundry facilities, room service from local restaurants, work areas and meeting facilities, to the manager-hosted continental breakfast buffet and informal hospitality hour, you're bound to feel at home here.

For recreation, this retreat offers a heated outdoor pool and whirlpool. You are minutes from Great Falls Park and Tyson's Corner. Washington D.C. is twenty miles away.

The Tides Inn

The Tides Inn
480 King Carter Drive
Irvington, Virginia 22480
800-TIDES INN ▪ 804-438-5000
Web Site: www.tidesinn.com

Room Rates:	$130–$175.
Pet Charges or Deposits:	$10 per day.
Rated: 5 Paws 🐾🐾🐾🐾🐾	194 guest rooms and 10 suites, with a restaurant. 175-acre peninsula offering golf, tennis, yacht cruises and a pool.

The Tides Inn is a charming resort, tucked away from civilization and nestled on the Rappahannock River and Chesapeake Bay. Once a wonderful secret among friends, the Tides Inn has recently been recognized by *Condé Nast Traveler* readers as one of the premier resorts in the world.

Spoil yourself with a moonlight cruise aboard the exquisite private yacht, the *Miss Ann* or indulge in 45 holes of championship golf, including the Golden Eagle, rated one of the top ten golf courses in Virginia by *Golf Digest*. Delight in award-winning cuisine, a saltwater swimming pool, boating, bike-riding, tennis, dancing at the Chesapeake Club, luncheons and cocktails at poolside.

The area abounds in antique and craft shops, seafood markets and traditional boat-building. If nature is your interest, there are two excellent nature trails just minutes away that are a bird-watcher's paradise.

Applewood Inn

Applewood Inn
Buffalo Bend Road
P.O. Box 1348
Lexington, Virginia 24450
800-463-1902 ▪ 540-463-1962
Web Site: www.applewoodbb.com
E-mail: applewd@cfw.com

Room Rates:	$80–$130, including full breakfast, snacks and beverages.
Pet Charges or Deposits:	$20 per stay. Sorry, no cats.
Rated: 3 Paws 🐾🐾🐾	4 guest rooms on 35 acres. Llama trekking available.
	Refrigerators, microwaves, pool, whirlpool and hot tubs.

T his special home, perched high above scenic Buffalo Creek in Lexington, combines passive solar technology with historical and natural materials. In addition to four guest bedrooms, all with queen-sized beds and private baths, there is a hot tub with French doors opening out onto the hillside and an in-ground pool with views of the Blue Ridge Mountains. Porches span the entire front of the house on two levels, so that each bedroom opens onto a porch.

The property, consisting of 35 very private acres, has spectacular views of House Mountain and Short Hill, in addition to the Blue Ridge. It abuts more than 900 acres of the Rockbridge Hunt, for hiking and riding, and has access to Buffalo Creek for fishing and tubing. Birds and other wildlife are abundant.

Breakfast is heart-healthy, with whole-grain baked goods, such as hazelnut pancakes, wheat germ and cornmeal waffles, fresh fruit, herbal teas and coffee.

Creek Crossing Farm at Chappelle Hill

Creek Crossing Farm at Chappelle Hill
P.O. Box 18
Lincoln, Virginia 22078
540-338-7550
E-mail: creekcrossingfarm@erols.com

Room Rates:	$95–$115, including full breakfast.
Pet Charges or Deposits:	Credit card imprint. Horse boarding available.
Rated: 4 Paws 🐾🐾🐾🐾	2 guest rooms and 1 suite on 25-acre farm.

 ince 1773, Creek Crossing Farm at Chappelle Hill has been providing gracious hospitality to all who stay. The farm encompasses twenty-five acres, which are located in Virginia's Hunt Country, in a secluded valley just outside the present-day village of Lincoln. Walking trails wind around the creek and a cultivated blueberry field is part of the farm. Horses are boarded here.

Guests can choose from 3 exquisitely appointed rooms, each with a private bath, luxurious thick towels, a fluffy down comforter and all-natural cotton bedding.

Breakfast is served in the large, sunny, 40-foot kitchen or on the deck.

Inn at Meander Plantation

Inn at Meander Plantation
HCR 5, Box 460A
Locust Dale, Virginia 22948
800-385-4936 ▪ 540-672-4912
Web Site: www.meander.net

Room Rates: $95–$195, including full breakfast.
Pet Charges or Deposits: Horses welcome.
Rated: 5 Paws ❀❀❀❀❀ 3 guest rooms and 5 suites on 80 acres. Stables for horses.

Cradled in the heart of Jefferson's Virginia, the Inn at Meander Plantation offers a rare opportunity to experience the charm and elegance of Colonial living at its best. This historic country estate, which dates to 1766, allows guests to return to an earlier, more romantic time, when hospitality was a matter of pride and fine living was an art practiced in restful surroundings. Stroll through formal boxwood gardens or wander woods and fields where wildlife abounds. White rockers line both levels of the expansive back porches, providing peaceful respites for sipping afternoon tea, reading the latest novel or watching breathtaking mountain sunsets.

Guest rooms reflect the elegance and romance of a Virginia country estate, with four-poster queen-sized beds piled high with plump pillows and fluffy down comforters and beautifully appointed with period reproductions and antiques. Join your fellow guests in the formal dining room or under the arched breezeway on sun-warmed mornings for a full country gourmet breakfast.

Widow Kip's Country

Widow Kip's Country
355 Orchard Drive
Mount Jackson, Virginia 22842
800-478-8714 ▪ 540-477-2400

Room Rates:	$65–$85, including full breakfast. AAA, AARP, AKC and ABA discounts.
Pet Charges or Deposits:	None.
Rated: 4 Paws 🐾🐾🐾🐾	5 guest rooms and 2 cottages; fireplaces; pool, bicycles available.

T his lovingly restored 1830 gem rests on 7 rural acres in the Shenandoah Valley, with views of the Massanutten Mountains. The Widow Kip's is a serene and friendly home offering nostalgia and hospitality in five antique-filled bedrooms of the main house, all with original fireplaces and private baths. Locally crafted quilts grace the four-poster, sleigh and hand-carved Victorian beds. Children and pets are welcome in the two restored cottages that create a charming Williamsburg-style courtyard by the house.

Breakfast is a friendly family-style gathering in the dining room, and the common room welcomes you with backgammon or checkers and old movies on the VCR. A swimming pool is on the property and bikes are provided for rides through the apple orchards.

The Widow Kip's is a perfect jumping-off place for all that the Shenandoah has to offer: caverns, hiking, canoeing, antiquing, battlefields, golf, skiing, horseback riding and fishing on the property—as well as the fine restaurants in the area.

Garden and the Sea Inn

Garden and the Sea Inn
P.O. Box 275
New Church, Virginia 23415
800-842-0672 • 757-824-0672
Web Site: www.bbonline.com/va/gardensea

Room Rates:	$75–$165, including continental breakfast. AAA and AARP discounts.
Pet Charges or Deposits:	Manager's prior approval required.
Rated: 5 Paws 🐾🐾🐾🐾🐾	6 guest rooms with refrigerators, whirlpools, Jacuzzis. Fine dining.

T he romantic Garden and the Sea Inn, circa 1802, is located in New Church, Virginia, an area rich in history, architecture and natural beauty. The Inn offers the best of two worlds. Nestled in a quiet rural setting, it is just minutes from the barrier islands of Chincoteague and Assateague, home of the world-famous wild ponies and one of the most beautiful beaches on the East Coast.

Spacious guest rooms offer queen-sized beds with sitting areas, screened porches and double whirlpool baths. Fine dining at the Inn features a carefully selected menu, with entrées prepared with local produce and seafood from the farms and waters of the Eastern Shore. The menu changes frequently, with an extensive wine list to complement every dish.

Owl and the Pussycat

Owl and the Pussycat
405 High Street
Petersburg, Virginia 23803
888-733-0505 ▪ 804-733-0505
Web Site: www.ctg.net/owlcat
E-mail: owlcat@ctg.net

Room Rates:	$75–$105, including full breakfast.
Pet Charges or Deposits:	$10 per day. $20 refundable deposit.
Rated: 3 Paws 🐾🐾🐾	4 guest rooms and 2 guest suites.

This gracious Queen Anne-style mansion, with a two-story turret and balcony was built around 1895. The Owl and the Pussycat is graced with perennial flower beds and more than twenty herbs, tended to by the English innkeepers John and Juliette Swenson.

The Inn has many unique characteristics such as the original gas-light fixtures, eight fireplaces, all with different tiles and mantels, and polished "heart pine" floors with lovely rugs. Guest rooms are large and comfortable.

Many of Petersburg's attractions are just a brief stroll down High Street. Old Towne is close by, with shops, Civil War museums, antique emporiums and restaurants you can walk to in the evening.

Inn at Tabb's Creek Landing

Inn at Tabb's Creek Landing
Route 14
P.O. Box 219
Port Haywood, Virginia 23138
804-725-5136

Room Rates:	$95–$125, including full breakfast.
Pet Charges or Deposits:	$20 per day.
Rated: 4 Paws ❀❀❀❀	2 guest rooms and 2 suites. Outdoor pool. Restaurant.

Surrounded by water on three sides, the main house is an 1820s Colonial farmhouse on 38 acres, that has been renovated with the utmost care. The porches, where guests love to lounge, are flanked by ancient magnolias. Over 100 rose bushes perfume the cutting garden, which connects the guest cottage and swimming pool to the main house. The cottage contains two suites with private baths and water views.

Cabell and Catherine Venable are the innkeepers and have been involved in the hospitality business for twenty years. Previously they owned and operated a gourmet restaurant, wine shop, white-water rafting and dog sled companies in Jackson Hole, Wyoming. Catherine is a well-known producing artist and Cabell is a consultant and writer. They love children and pets, and allow both to visit with you at the Inn.

A new dimension in the Southern breakfast awaits you each morning, leaving no room for lunch.

Executive Club Suites

Executive Club Suites
1730 Arlington Boulevard
Rossyln, Virginia 22209
800-535-CLUB ▪ 703-525-2582
Web Site: www.dcexeclub.com

Suite Rates:	$150–$200, including continental breakfast and evening reception. AAA discount.
Pet Charges or Deposits:	$25 per stay. $250 refundable deposit.
Rated: 3 Paws ❀❀❀	55 guest suites. Health club and pool.

Whether traveling on business or pleasure, the Executive Club Suites is the next best thing to being home. These spacious guest suites provide you with all the comforts and conveniences you'll need, including fully equipped kitchens, large living rooms, private entrances and efficient work space with multi-line phones.

Start your day off with a complimentary continental breakfast, then move on to the fitness facilities for a workout before heading off for your day of sightseeing.

High Meadows Inn

High Meadows Inn
Route 4, Box 6
Scottsville, Virginia 24590
800-232-1832 ▪ 804-286-2218
Web Site: www.highmeadows.com

Room Rates:	$99–$185, including full breakfast. Call for discounts.
Pet Charges or Deposits:	$20 per stay. Manager's prior approval required.
Rated: 5 Paws 🐾🐾🐾🐾🐾	7 guest rooms and 7 suites. Refrigerators, microwaves, whirlpool, Jacuzzi and hot tub.

P art of what makes the High Meadows Inn unique is its duality as both a country inn and a vineyard. As Virginia's only Inn that combines its place on the National Register of Historic Homes with a renaissance farm vineyard (it's a leading producer of Pinot Noir grapes), High Meadows offers the discriminating guest a rare opportunity to look at 170 years of architectural history and twelve new, exciting years of viticultural happening.

High Meadows is a grand house, where guests are welcomed with champagne, and stay in individually appointed rooms, furnished with period antiques and art, each with a private bath. The rooms are romantic, each with a story—a fantasy place. The fifty surrounding acres of gardens, footpaths, forests and ponds guarantee privacy and quiet.

There are picnic baskets full of delightful tastes, good wine and poetry books, multicourse dinners and country breakfasts.

Graves' Mountain Lodge

Graves' Mountain Lodge
Route 670
Syria, Virginia 22743
540-923-4231

Room Rates:	$55–$110, including 3 meals per day.
Pet Charges or Deposits:	None.
Rated: 3 Paws 🐾🐾🐾	38 guest rooms, kitchens, Olympic-sized outdoor pool.

Graves' Mountain Lodge is nestled deep in the foothills of the Blue Ridge Mountains, near the end of the road in Syria, Virginia. Here you're invited to assume a leisurely pace as you enjoy some of life's simpler pleasures, such as hiking, fishing, tennis, swimming and some good, old-fashioned "porch-sitting." Take a stroll down the lane to observe the activities of the fruit orchard and cattle farm.

Guest accommodations range from the old farmhouse, where you can enjoy comfortable accommodations in an authentically rustic atmosphere, to guest cottages overlooking the river with beautiful mountain views and two or three bedrooms.

In the Lodge itself, you'll find the dining rooms, the gift shop and recreation lounges. At Graves' Mountain, nobody leaves the table hungry. You will enjoy tasty, down-home specialties prepared with foods fresh from the garden.

Anderson Cottage Bed and Breakfast

Anderson Cottage Bed and Breakfast
Old Germantown Road
Warm Springs, Virginia 24484
540-839-2974

Room Rates:	$60–$125, including full breakfast.
Pet Charges or Deposits:	Manager's prior approval required. Pets are allowed in the separate cottage. Sorry, no cats.
Rated: 3 Paws 🐾🐾🐾	2 guest rooms and 3 suites.

One of Bath County's oldest buildings, Anderson Cottage has been in the present owner's family since the 1870s. A rambling house, it is actually two buildings, log and clapboard. The original four rooms house an 18th century tavern. It has also been a girls' school and a summer inn. The 1820 brick kitchen is now a separate guest cottage.

Located in a quiet mountain village, long famous for its warm mineral springs, the emphasis here is on privacy and quiet relaxation. The rocking chairs on the porch and the hammock by the creek typify this place. Breakfast is served in the large dining room, with an open fire on chilly days, or in the comfortable country kitchen.

Three Hills Inn

Three Hills Inn
Route 220
P.O. Box 9
Warm Springs, Virginia 24484
888-234-4557 ▪ 540-838-5381
Web Site: www.3hills.com
E-mail: inn@3hills.com

Room Rates:	$69–$189, including full breakfast.
Pet Charges or Deposits:	$5 per pet. Manager's prior approval required.
Rated: 4 Paws 🐾🐾🐾🐾	3 guest rooms, 7 suites and 2 cabins on 42 acres.

Three Hills Inn, perched on 38 acres on Warm Springs Mountain, offers panoramic views of Warm Springs Gap and the Alleghenies beyond. The estate features a boxwood garden, extensive grounds and acres of woods and walking trails. A stuccoed portico graced with Ionic columns welcomes you to Three Hills Inn. The building retains many exquisite original details, including German crystal chandeliers, pocket doors and wainscot paneling, leaded glass bookcases and a grand staircase.

Guest accommodations range from hotel rooms and suites to cottages. Special surprises might include decks, stained glass windows, fireplaces and clawfoot tubs. All rooms include color TV and private baths. The manor house is decorated with antiques and period furnishings. Two charming dining rooms, with fireplaces and magnificent mountain views, afford a delightful setting for a relaxed dining experience.

This Inn provides a retreat for body, mind and spirit.

Heritage Inn

Heritage Inn
1324 Richmond Road
Williamsburg, Virginia 23185
800-782-3800 ▪ 757-229-6220
Web Site: www.heritageinnwmsb.com
E-mail: heritage@travelbase.com

Room Rates:	$40–$74, including continental breakfast from April to December. AAA and AARP discounts.
Pet Charges or Deposits:	Designated rooms only.
Rated: 3 Paws 🐾🐾🐾	54 guest rooms. Pool.

Heritage Inn, known for its warmth and charm, welcomes you to the colonial capital. Conveniently located on Richmond Road, Heritage Inn is close to the restored district, a short walk to the Bush Garden and major shopping and retail outlet centers.

Aesthetically appointed in a traditional style, most rooms feature two double beds or a king-sized bed with sleep sofa, soft lighting, writing desk and an armoire that conceals the television. All rooms offer a view of the pool and terrace.

Inn at 802

Inn at 802
802 Jamestown Road
Williamsburg, Virginia 23185
800-672-4086 ▪ 757-564-0845

Room Rates:	$115–$145, including full breakfast. AAA and AARP discounts.
Pet Charges or Deposits:	Manager's prior approval required. Call for refundable deposit.
Rated: 3 Paws 🐾🐾🐾	4 guest rooms.

T his new bed and breakfast, decorated in Colonial style, offers four bedrooms, each with its own private bath. Guest rooms are spacious, private, quiet and inviting, with reading chairs and period-style antiques and reproductions.

The common areas of the house include an extensive library with wood-burning fireplace, a large living room, a dining room and a delightful sun room that overlooks the garden and patio area.

A candlelight breakfast is served on fine china with crystal and silver. Menu highlights include sumptuous homemade pastries, sizzling hickory-smoked Virginia bacon, ham or sausage and variable mouth-watering entrées.

Ballard House Bed and Breakfast

Ballard House Bed and Breakfast
12527 Ballard Drive
Willis Wharf, Virginia 23486
757-442-2206
E-mail: ballardhouse@esua.com

Room Rates:	$60–$70, including full breakfast.
Pet Charges or Deposits:	$5 per day. Manager's prior approval required.
Rated: 3 Paws 🐾🐾🐾	4 guest rooms and 1 suite. Refrigerators, hot tub.

T his turn-of-the-century home is located in the peaceful fishing village of Willis Wharf on the Eastern Shore of Virginia. Owners Jo and Kim Penland encourage families to come have fun, relax and unwind. Sip a refreshing glass of mint tea while you swing on the front porch. Take a serene walk along the nature path in neighboring meadows. Relax with a leisurely soak in the hot tub. Ride around the wharf on a bicycle built-for-two. Make reservations for a boating excursion on Chesapeake Bay or to the Barrier Islands.

Awake each morning to a heart-healthy, low sodium and low cholesterol menu or a full-blown, hearty Southern breakfast. The E.L. Willis Country Store, a ten-minute walk away, serves delicious lunches offering local seafood specialties and dinner on Friday and Saturday nights. Several seafood restaurants are located within a short drive. Midnight raids on the icebox are encouraged here.

Virginia

Please Note: *Pets must be on a leash at all times and may be restricted to certain areas. For directions, use fees, pet charges and general information, contact the numbers listed below.*

National Parks General Information

National Park Service/Mid-Atlantic Region
143 South Third Street
Philadelphia, Pennsylvania 19106
215-597-3679

National Parks

Shenandoah National Park, located in western Virginia, encompasses 196,466 acres and offers horse rentals, camping, picnic areas, fishing, hiking trails, winter sports and a visitors' center.

National Forest General Information

Southern Region Information Office
1720 Peachtree Road Northwest
Atlanta, Georgia 30367-9102
800-280-2267—reservations
404-347-2384—information

National Forests

George Washington and Jefferson National Forests covers a total of 1,800,000 acres in western Virginia and the eastern edge of West Virginia. Together they offer camping, picnic areas, boating, a boat ramp, boat rentals, fishing, swimming, hiking and bicycle trails, winter sports and a visitors' center. For more information, write to the Forest Supervisor, 5162 Valleypoint Parkway, Roanoke, Virginia 24019, or phone 540-265-5100.

National Recreation Area General Information

National Park Service/Mid-Atlantic Region
143 South Third Street
Philadelphia, Pennsylvania 19106
215-597-3679

National Recreation Area

Mount Rogers National Recreation Area is located in southwestern Virginia. It encompasses 200,000 acres of parkland with camping, picnic areas, hiking and bicycle trails, fishing, swimming and a visitors' center.

State Parks General Information

Virginia State Parks
Department of Conservation and Recreation
203 Governor Street, Suite 302
Richmond, Virginia 23219
800-933-7275 • 804-225-3867

State Parks

APPOMATTOX

Holliday Lake State Park, located 6 miles east of Appomattox on State Route 24, then 4 miles east via State Route 626/629, is a 250-acre park with camping, a picnic area, hiking trails, boating, a boat ramp, boat rentals, fishing, swimming and a visitors' center.

BASSETT

Fairy Stone State Park is a 4,750-acre park located 8 miles west of Bassett on State Route 57, offering camping, picnic areas, hiking and bicycle trails, boating, a boat ramp, boat rentals, fishing, swimming, winter sports and a visitors' center.

BEDFORD

Smith Mountain Lake State Park encompasses 1,506 acres of parkland, located 26 miles south of Bedford, off State Route 43. Visitors to the park will enjoy camping, picnic areas, hiking trails, boating, a boat ramp, fishing, swimming, winter sports and a visitors' center.

BLUE RIDGE PARKWAY

Otter Creek State Park covers 552 acres, located at Mile 61. The park offers camping, picnic areas, hiking trails and fishing.

Peaks of Otter State Park encompasses 4,150 acres of parkland, located at Mile 66. The park has camping, picnic areas, hiking trails, fishing and a visitors' center.

Roanoke Mountain State Park has 65 acres of parkland, located at Mile 121. The park offers camping, picnic areas and hiking trails.

Rocky Knob State Park encompasses 4,200 acres of parkland, located at Mile 167. The park offers camping, picnic areas, hiking trails, fishing and a visitors' center.

BREAKS

Breaks Interstate State Park covers 4,200 acres of parkland, located 7 miles east of Breaks, on State Route 80. Visitors to the scenic park will enjoy camping, picnic areas, hiking trails, boating, fishing, swimming and a visitors' center. For more information, call 540-865-4413.

BURKEVILLE

Twin Lakes State Park, located 3 miles southwest of Burkeville off U.S. Highway 360 to State Route 612, is a 270-acre park offering camping, picnic areas, hiking trails, boating, a boat ramp, boat rentals, fishing and swimming.

CAPE HENRY

First Landing/Seashore State Park and Natural Area encompasses 2,770 acres of parkland, located at Cape Henry on U.S. Highway 60. The park has camping, picnic areas, hiking and bicycle trails, boating, a boat ramp, fishing, winter sports and a visitors' center.

CHESTERFIELD

Pocahontas State Park is a 7,604-acre park located 4 miles southwest of Chesterfield off State Route 655. The park offers camping, picnic areas, hiking and bicycle trails, boating, a boat ramp, boat rentals, fishing, swimming, winter sports and a visitors' center.

CLARKSVILLE

Occoneeche State Park encompasses 2,690 acres of parkland, 1.5 miles east of Clarksville on U.S. Highway 58. The park has camping, picnic areas, hiking trails, boating, a boat ramp and fishing.

CLIFTON FORGE

Douthat State Park, located 6 miles north of Clifton Forge on State Route 629, consists of 4,493 acres of parkland with camping, picnic areas, boating, a boat ramp, boat rentals, fishing, swimming, hiking trails, winter sports and a visitors' center.

CROAKER

York River State Park, 1 mile north of Croaker via State Route 607, then 2 miles east on State Route 606, is a 2,505-acre park with picnic areas, hiking and bicycle trails, boating, a boat ramp, fishing, winter sports and a visitors' center. For more information, call 757-566-3036.

CUMBERLAND

Bear Creek Lake State Park, located 5 miles west of Cumberland off U.S. Highway 60, encompasses 150 acres of parkland with camping, picnic areas, boating, a boat ramp, boat rentals, fishing, swimming and hiking trails.

DUFFIELD

Natural Tunnel State Park is a 649-acre park, 3 miles south on U.S. Highway 23, then east on County Road 871. The park offers camping, picnic areas, hiking trails, fishing, swimming, winter sports and a visitors' center. For more information, call 540-940-2674.

FREDERICKSBURG

Lake Anna State Park, located 25 miles southwest of Fredericksburg off State Route 208, is a 2,058-acre park with picnic areas, hiking trails, boating, a boat ramp, fishing, swimming, winter sports and a visitors' center.

MARION

Hungry Mother State Park is 3 miles northeast of Marion on State Route 16. Visitors to the park will find horse rentals, camping, picnic areas, hiking trails, boating, a boat ramp, boat rentals, fishing, swimming, winter sports and a visitors' center.

MONTROSS

Westmoreland State Park encompasses 1,295 acres of parkland, located 5 miles northwest of Montross on State Route 3. The park offers camping, picnic areas, hiking and bicycle trails, boating, a boat ramp, boat rentals, fishing, swimming, a swimming pool, winter sports and a visitors' center.

OWENS

Caledon Natural Area State Park has 2,600 acres, located on State Route 218, west of Owens. Visitors to the park will enjoy picnic areas, hiking trails, and a visitors' center.

PARIS

Sky Meadows State Park, located 1 mile south off State Route 17, is a scenic 1,618-acre park with primitive camping, picnic areas, hiking trails, winter sports and a visitors' center. For more information, call 540-592-3556.

RADFORD

Claytor Lake State Park, 4 miles south of Radford via Interstate 8, then 2 miles south on State Route 660, consists of 472 acres of parkland with horse rentals, camping, picnic areas, boating, a boat ramp, boat rentals, fishing, swimming, hiking trails, winter sports and a visitors' center.

SANDBRIDGE

False Cape State Park is a 4,750-acre park, southeast of Sandbridge via signs to Little Island Recreation Area. The park is accessible only by foot, bicycle or boat. Visitors to the park will find camping, hiking and bicycle trails, boating and fishing.

SCOTTSBURG

Staunton River State Park is a 1,277-acre park, located 9 miles southeast of Scottsburg, on State Route 344. Visitors to the park will find camping, picnic areas, boating, a boat ramp, boat rentals, fishing, swimming, hiking trails, winter sports and a visitors' center.

SURRY

Chippokes Plantation State Park is on the James River, 1.5 miles east via State Route 10, then 3 miles north on County Road 634. The historic park offers camping, picnic areas, hiking and bicycle trails, swimming and a visitors' center. For more information, call 757-294-3625.

VIRGINIA BEACH

Kiptopeke State Park is a 375-acre park that is 3 miles north of the Chesapeake Bay Bridge Tunnel from Virginia Beach on U.S. Highway 13, then west on State Route 704. Visitors to the park will find camping, picnic areas, hiking and bicycle trails, boating, a boat ramp, fishing, swimming and a visitors' center.

VOLNEY

Grayson Highlands State Park has 4,754 acres, west of Volney on U.S. Highway 58. The park offers camping, picnic areas, hiking trails, fishing, winter sports and a visitors' center.

WOODBRIDGE

Leesylvania State Park is a 508-acre park east of Woodbridge, off Interstate 95, at exit 156. Visitors to the park will find picnic areas, hiking trails, boating, a boat ramp, boat rentals and fishing.

Mason Neck State Park is a 1,804-acre park, located 1 mile north of Woodbridge on U.S. Highway 1, then 2.5 miles east on State Route 242. The park offers picnic areas, hiking trails, fishing, winter sports and a visitors' center.

WYTHEVILLE

Shot Tower/New River Trail State Park is off Interstate 77, exit 24, then 1.5 miles north on U.S. Highway 52. The historic park offers picnic areas, hiking and bicycle trails, fishing, swimming and a visitors' center. For more information, call 540-699-6778.

Other Recreation Areas

CENTREVILLE

Bull Run Regional Park is located 3 miles from Interstate 66, Centreville exit, off U.S. Highway 29. It offers miniature golf, a playground, camping, picnic areas, hiking trails, swimming and a visitors' center.

CHESAPEAKE

Northwest River Park is a 763-acre park that is 15 miles south on State Route 168, then 3.5 miles east on Indian Creek Road. The park offers a fragrance garden for the blind, horseback riding, canoeing, miniature golf, a playground, camping, picnic areas, hiking trails, boating, boat rentals, fishing and winter sports.

HAMPTON

Sandy Bottom Nature Park encompasses 456 acres of parkland, located off Interstate 64 at 1255 Big Bethel Road in Hampton. The park offers a nature center, a playground, camping, picnic areas, hiking and bicycle trails, boating, fishing and a visitors' center.

LEESBURG

Algonkian Regional Park is a 500-acre park that 11 miles east of Leesburg and 3 miles north of State Route 7. The park offers golf, miniature golf, a playground, picnic areas, hiking trails, boating, a boat ramp, fishing and swimming.

LORTON

Pohlck Bay Regional Park is located via Interstate 95 south to Lorton exit, south on U.S. Highway 1 to Gunston Road, then 3 miles east. It has golf, miniature golf, camping, picnic areas, hiking trails, boating, a boat ramp, boat rentals, fishing, swimming and a visitors' center.

MOUNT SOLON

Natural Chimneys Regional Park, is half a mile northwest of Mount Solon on State Route 731 and has comprises seven natural limestone towers. This 150-acre park offers nature trails, a swimming pool, jousting tournaments, camping, picnic areas, hiking and bicycle trails, swimming and a visitors' center. For more information, call 540-350-2510.

NEWPORT NEWS

Newport News City Park encompasses 8,330 acres of parkland located on State Route 143, half a mile west of the junction with State Route 105. It offers golf, jogging, an archery range, nature trails, paddleboating, camping, picnic areas, hiking and bicycle trails, boating, a boat ramp, boat rentals, fishing, winter sports and a visitors' center. For more information, call 757-596-8175.

RURAL RETREAT

Rural Retreat Lake is a 350-acre park located 4 miles southwest of Rural Retreat off Interstate 81. Take exit 60, go 4 miles east on Country Road 749, then 1 mile south on County Road 677. The park offers camping, picnic areas, hiking trails, boating, a boat ramp, boat rentals, fishing and swimming.

TRIANGLE

Prince William Forest Park consists of 18,571 acres along Quantico Creek, located off Interstate 95. Take exit 150, then a quarter mile west on State Route 619. Here you will find camping, picnic areas, hiking and bicycle trails, fishing, winter sports and a visitors' center. For more information, call 703-221-7181.

Veterinary Care in Virginia

A

Abingdon Animal Medical Center
19586 Dennison Drive
Abingdon, VA 24211
540-628-9655

Washington County Veterinary
17455 Sky King Drive
Abingdon, VA 24210
540-628-6861

Beacon Hill Cat Hospital
6610 Richmond Highway
Alexandria, VA 22306
703-765-6369

Sacramento Veterinary Hospital
8794 Sacramento Drive #D
Alexandria, VA 22309
703-780-2808

VCA Old Town Animal Hospital
425 North Henry Street
Alexandria, VA 22314
703-549-3647

Virginia-Maryland Veterinary
2660 Duke Street
Alexandria, VA 22314
703-823-3601

Village Veterinary Service
16419 Court Street
Amelia Court House, VA 23002
804-561-2244

Annandale Animal Hospital
7405 Little River Turnpike
Annandale, VA 22003
703-941-3100

Austin Veterinary Clinic
7323 Little River Turnpike
Annandale, VA 22003
703-941-5300

Arlington Animal Hospital
2624 Columbia Pike
Arlington, VA 22204
703-920-5300

Ballston Animal Hospital
5232 Wilson Boulevard
Arlington, VA 22205
703-528-2776

Suburban Animal Hospital
6879 Lee Highway
Arlington, VA 22213
703-532-4043

Ashburn Veterinary Hospital
20893 Stubble Road
Ashburn, VA 22011
703-729-9200

Ashcake Animal Clinic
9552 Kings Charter Drive
Ashland, VA 23005
804-550-2458

Oak Lawn Veterinary Clinic
11194 Oak Lawn Lane
Ashland, VA 23005
804-798-3944

B

Riggs Animal Hospital
626 Wood Avenue West
Big Stone Gap, VA 24219
540-523-0813

Blacksburg Animal Clinic
3960 South Main Street
Blacksburg, VA 22060
540-552-3911

North Main Small Animal Clinic
1407 North Main Street
Blacksburg, VA 24060
540-951-1002

Roseville Veterinary Clinic
26 Greenway Avenue South
Boyce, VA 22620
540-837-1334

Bristol Animal Clinic
930 Commonwealth Avenue
Bristol, VA 24201
540-466-4113

Burke Animal Clinic
6307 Lee Chapel Road
Burke, VA 22015
703-569-9600

Parkway Veterinary Clinic
5749 Burke Centre Parkway
Burke, VA 22015
703-323-9020

Village Veterinary Clinic
9544 Burke Road
Burke, VA 22015
703-978-8655

C

Caring Hands Animal Hospital
5659 Stone Road
Centreville, VA 22020
703-830-5700

Centreville Square Animal Hospital
14215 Centreville Square #L
Centreville, VA 22020
703-222-9682

Westfields Animal Hospital
5095 Westfields Boulevard
Centreville, VA 22020
703-378-3028

Animal Hospital of Ivy Square
2125 Ivy Road #2
Charlottesville, VA 22903
804-295-8387

Old Dominion Animal Clinic
811 Preston Avenue
Charlottesville, VA 22903
804-971-3500

Animal Medical Clinic
1020 Battlefield Boulevard North
Chesapeake, VA 23320
757-548-2000

Brentwood Veterinary Clinic
1236 George Washington Highway North
Chesapeake, VA 23323
757-487-2531

Centreville Animal Hospital
417 Centreville Turnpike South
Chesapeake, VA 23322
757-482-9410

Midway Veterinary Hospital
1646 South Military Highway
Chesapeake, VA 23320
757-543-3273

Veterinary Clinic of Chesapeake
837 Battlefield Boulevard South
Chesapeake, VA 23322
757-482-2181

Bermuda Hundred Animal Hospital
302 East Hundred Road
Chester, VA 23831
804-530-1513

Centralia Crossing Animal Hospital
9819 Chester Road
Chester, VA 23831
804-768-4212

Old Dominion Animal Clinic
4312 West Hundred Road
Chester, VA 23831
804-796-3647

Town and Country Veterinary Clinic
7416 Woodpecker Road
Chesterfield, VA 23838
804-590-1794

Town and Country Veterinary Clinic
1605 North Franklin Street
Christiansburg, VA 24073
540-382-5042

Riner Veterinary Service
3513 Riner Road
Christiansburg, VA 24073
540-382-2351

Amelia Bovine Clinic
2900 Esnora Lane
Church Road, VA 23833
904-265-5958

Academy Veterinary Clinic
17023 Jefferson Davis Highway
Colonial Heights, VA 23834
804-526-6567

Amberwood Veterinary Hospital
121 Sycamore Street
Culpeper, VA 22701
540-825-5303

Blue Ridge Animal Hospital
11298 James Monroe Highway
Culpeper, VA 22701
540-825-8353

D

Pet Health Clinic
430 Roanoke Road
Daleville, VA 24083
540-992-4550

Roanoke Valley Equine Clinic
1501 Greenfield Road
Daleville, VA 24083
540-992-3507

Animal Medical Center
2815 Riverside Drive
Danville, VA 24540
804-793-6477

Brosville Animal Clinic
10480 Martinsville Highway
Danville, VA 24541
804-685-2011

Mount Hermon Animal Clinic
3620 Franklin Turnpike
Danville, VA 24540
804-836-2499

Town and Country Veterinary Clinic
209 Washburn Drive
Danville, VA 24541
804-822-0020

Westover Animal Hospital
2918 Westover Drive
Danville, VA 24541
804-822-2235

Montclair Animal Hospital
4385 Kevin Walker Drive
Dumfries, VA 22026
703-878-3442

E

Animal Hospital of Emporia
715 North Main Street
Emporia, VA 23847
804-634-3936

F

Blue Cross Animal Hospital
8429 Lee Highway
Fairfax, VA 22031
703-560-1881

Pender Veterinary Clinic
4001 Legato Road
Fairfax, VA 22033
703-591-3304

Town and Country Animal Hospital
9780 Lee Highway
Fairfax, VA 22031
703-273-2110

Seven Corners Animal Hospital
6300 Arlington Boulevard
Falls Church, VA 22044
703-534-1156

Ridge Animal Hospital
1913 East Third Street
Farmville, VA 23901
804-392-8222

Botetourt Veterinary Hospital
2460 Roanoke Road
Fincastle, VA 24090
540-992-2711

White Oak Veterinary Service
9 Rickets Lane
Flint Hill, VA 22627
540-675-1138

Animal Care Clinic of Floyd
209 West Main Street
Floyd, VA 24091
540-745-2004

South Hampton Veterinary Clinic
26292 Delaware Road
Franklin, VA 23851
757-562-3606

Animal Emergency Clinic
1210 Snowden Street
Fredericksburg, VA 22401
540-371-0554

Chancellor Animal Clinic
5316 Plank Road
Fredericksburg, VA 22407
540-786-2282

Princess Anne Animal Hospital
2105 Princess Anne Street
Fredericksburg, VA 22401
540-373-8181

White Oak Animal Hospital
316 White Oak Road
Fredericksburg, VA 22405
540-374-0462

G

Scott Animal Clinic
425 East Jackson Street
Gate City, VA 24251
540-386-7280

Seneca Hill Veterinary Hospital
11415 Georgetown Pike
Great Falls, VA 22066
703-450-6760

Southside Large Animal Clinic
617 Andrew Road
Gretna, VA 24557
804-656-8232

H

Armistead Avenue Veterinary
531 North Armistead Avenue
Hampton, VA 23669
757-723-8571

Mercury Animal Hospital
2500 West Mercury Boulevard
Hampton, VA 23666
757-826-4951

Pembroke Animal Clinic
1316 East Pembroke Avenue
Hampton, VA 23669
757-722-2883

Todds Lane Veterinary Hospital
1309 Todds Lane
Hampton, VA 23666
757-826-7602

Veterinary Hospital
1619 West Pembroke Avenue
Hampton, VA 23661
757-723-9323

Spangler Veterinary Clinic
979 South High Street
Harrisonburg, VA 22801
540-434-3903

Valley Veterinary Hospital
498 University Boulevard #A
Harrisonburg, VA 22801
540-433-8387

Bull Run Veterinary Hospital
14840 Washington Street
Haymarket, VA 22069
703-754-4146

Tri City Animal Hospital
3412 Oaklawn Boulevard
Hopewell, VA 23860
804-541-7387

K

Potomac Ridge Animal Hospital
13413 Ridge Road
King George, VA 22485
540-775-3777

Veterinary Home Care
15437 Delaware Drive
King George, VA 22485
540-663-2681

L

All Creatures Animal Clinic
14700 Pocahontas Trail
Lanexa, VA 23089
804-966-2767

Catoctin Veterinary Clinic
108 Dry Mill Road Southwest
Leesburg, VA 22075
703-777-8447

Market Street Animal Clinic
210 East Market Street
Leesburg, VA 22075
703-777-6661

Rokus Veterinary Hospital
19275 James Monroe Highway
Leesburg, VA 22075
703-777-3758

Towne Animal Clinic
338 East Market Street
Leesburg, VA 22075
703-777-6350

Locust Grove Veterinary Clinic
4092 Germanna Highway
Locust Grove, VA 22508
540-972-3869

Central Virginia Veterinary Clinic
21084 Louisa Road
Louisa, VA 23093
540-967-1404

Lovingston Veterinary Hospital
8151 Thomas Nelson Highway
Lovingston, VA 22949
804-263-4881

Blue Mountain Animal Clinic
18 Luray Shopping Center
Luray, VA 22835
540-743-7387

Luray Clinic of Veterinary Medicine
1208 East Main Street
Luray, VA 22835
540-743-7298

Addison Animal Hospital
1818 Memorial Avenue
Lynchburg, VA 24501
804-846-2563

Animal Emergency Clinic
1000 Miller Park Square
Lynchburg, VA 24501
804-846-1504

Animal Hospital
1705 Memorial Avenue
Lynchburg, VA 24501
804-845-7021

Boonsboro Animal Hospital
6097 Boonsboro Road
Lynchburg, VA 24503
804-384-7799

Cat Clinic of Central Virginia
3709 Old Forest Road
Lynchburg, VA 24501
804-385-6324

Peakland Veterinary Hospital
5006 Boonsboro Road #1
Lynchburg, VA 24503
804-384-1009

Timberlake Animal Hospital
7819 Timberlake Road
Lynchburg, VA 24502
804-239-4475

Wildwood Animal Hospital
11400 Timberlake Road
Lynchburg, VA 24502
804-525-1044

M

Monelison Animal Clinic
115 Highview Drive
Madison Heights, VA 24572
804-929-1322

Manakin-Sabot Veterinary Clinic
15 Plaza Drive
Manakin Sabot, VA 23103
804-784-0040

Battlefield Animal Clinic
8138 Sudley Road
Manassas, VA 20109
703-361-0271

Prince William Animal Hospital
10227 Nokesville Road
Manassas, VA 20110
703-361-5223

Morganna Animal Clinic
9050 Liberia Avenue
Manassas, VA 20110
703-361-4196

Southside Animal Hospital
10464 Dumfries Road
Manassas, VA 20110
703-368-8284

Pet Centre Animal Hospital
8307 Yorkshire Lane
Manassas, VA 20110
703-368-9241

Marshall Veterinary Clinic
4216 Frost Street
Marshall, VA 22115
540-364-1409

Rectortown Equine Center
8446 Maidstone Road
Marshall, VA 22115
540-364-2632

McLean Animal Hospital
1330 Old Chain Bridge Road
McLean, VA 22101
703-356-5000

Old Dominion Animal Hospital
6719 Lowell Avenue
McLean, VA 22101
703-356-5582

Mayo and Rofe Equine Clinic
35355 Training Center Lane
Middleburg, VA 22117
540-687-6844

Middleburg Equine Clinic
35355 Millville Road
Middleburg, VA 22117
540-687-5249

Cedar Creek Animal Hospital
7714 Main Street
Middletown, VA 23228
540-869-7280

Midlothian Animal Clinic
14411 Sommerville Court
Midlothian, VA 23113
804-794-2099

Swift Creek Animal Hospital
2806 Fox Chase Lane
Midlothian, VA 23112
804-744-7222

Sycamore Veterinary Hospital
13137 Midlothian Turnpike
Midlothian, VA 23113
804-794-3778

Caroline Animal Hospital
17435 Richmond Turnpike
Milford, VA 22514
804-633-5958

Virginia Equine Service
100 Cloudcroft Drive
Monroe, VA 24574
804-384-0046

Baldwin Creek Animal Hospital
16500 Hull Street Road
Moseley, VA 23120
804-739-2933

Shen-Val Veterinary Service
2598 Cave Ridge Road
Mount Jackson, VA 22842
540-477-9333

N

New Market Veterinary Clinic
3673 Old Valley Pike
New Market, VA 22844
540-740-3500

Boulevard Veterinary Hospital
12620 Nettles Drive
Newport News, VA 23606
757-874-3200

Woodland Veterinary Hospital
13148 Jefferson Avenue
Newport News, VA 23608
757-877-2232

Nokesville Veterinary Clinic
12831 Fitzwater Drive
Nokesville, VA 22123
703-594-3216

Animal Care Center
1228 West Little Creek Road
Norfolk, VA 23505
757-423-3900

Bayview Veterinary Clinic
7930 Chesapeake Boulevard #B
Norfolk, VA 23518
757-588-1909

Boulevard Veterinary Hospital
6636 East Virginia Beach Boulevard
Norfolk, VA 23502
757-461-4416

Carpenter-Pope Veterinary Hospital
879 East Little Creek Road
Norfolk, VA 23518
757-588-8755

Cat Hospital of Tidewater
6048 East Virginia Beach Boulevard
Norfolk, VA 23502
757-466-9151

Little Creek Veterinary
2456 East Little Creek Road
Norfolk, VA 23518
757-583-2619

Tidewater Animal Hospital
7445 Tidewater Drive
Norfolk, VA 23505
757-588-0608

West Animal Clinic
830 West 21st Street
Norfolk, VA 23517
757-622-4551

Noah's Ark Veterinary Hospital
7297 Richmond Road
Norge, VA 23127
757-564-9815

O

Orange Veterinary Clinic
13421 James Madison Highway
Orange, VA 22960
540-672-1600

P

Petersburg Animal Hospital
2901 South Crater Road
Petersburg, VA 23805
804-732-4905

Poquoson Veterinary Hospital
43 Wythe Creek Road
Poquoson, VA 23662
757-868-8532

Actin Animal Hospital
4020 Portsmouth Boulevard
Portsmouth, VA 23701
757-488-8606

Airline Boulevard Veterinary
615 Airline Boulevard
Portsmouth, VA 23707
757-393-1011

Casey Animal Hospital
2607 Airline Boulevard
Portsmouth, VA 23701
757-465-5332

Scarr Animal Hospital
4205 Faigle Road
Portsmouth, VA 23703
757-397-6241

Pound Veterinary Hospital
8005 B South Mountain Road
Pound, VA 24279
540-796-4861

Powhatan Animal Hospital
2540 Anderson Highway
Powhatan, VA 23139
804-598-3168

Prince George Animal Hospital
4815 Mount Sinai Road
Prince George, VA 23875
804-458-0601

New Kent Animal Hospital
5230 Pocahontas Trail
Providence Forge, VA 23140
804-966-5097

Pulaski Animal Clinic
168 East Main Street
Pulaski, VA 24301
540-980-2180

Tipton Ridge Veterinary Center
1858 Bob White Boulevard
Pulaski, VA 24301
540-980-0186

Loundoun Veterinary Service
1043 East Main Street
Purcellville, VA 22132
540-338-7118

Loundoun Veterinary Service
150 North Hatcher Avenue
Purcellville, VA 22132
540-338-4118

R

West End Animal Clinic
829 Second Street
Radford, VA 24141
540-731-1111

Animal Clinic of Tall Oak
12004 North Shore Drive
Reston, VA 20190
703-437-5600

Reston Animal Hospital
2403 Reston Parkway
Reston, VA 20191
703-620-2566

Allied Animal Hospital
7209 West Broad Street
Richmond, VA 23294
804-672-7200

Ambassador Animal Hospital
6506 West Broad Street
Richmond, VA 23230
804-282-4215

Battlefield Veterinary Clinic
2779 Charles City Road
Richmond, VA 23231
804-222-1370

Boulevard Animal Hospital
1 East Belt Boulevard
Richmond, VA 23224
804-232-8951

Broad Street Veterinary
3320 West Broad Street
Richmond, VA 23230
804-353-4491

Brook Run Animal Clinic
7412 Brook Road
Richmond, VA 23227
804-262-8621

Cary Street Veterinary Hospital
3210 West Cary Street
Richmond, VA 23221
804-355-9144

Oxbridge Veterinary Clinic
10005 Hull Street Road
Richmond, VA 23236
804-745-4243

Patterson Veterinary Hospital
12491 Patterson Avenue
Richmond, VA 23233
804-784-5758

Pets First Animal Hospital
9201 Staples Mill Road
Richmond, VA 23228
804-672-3576

Pocoshock Animal Hospital
2801 Turner Road
Richmond, VA 23224
804-745-3276

Quioccasin Veterinary Hospital
9218 Quioccasin Road
Richmond, VA 23229
804-741-3200

Stonehenge Veterinary Hospital
906 Southlake Boulevard
Richmond, VA 23236
804-794-4713

Stony Point Animal Clinic
3068 Stony Point Road
Richmond, VA 23235
804-320-5991

Three Chopt Animal Clinic
9912 Three Chopt Road
Richmond, VA 23229
804-270-1080

Tuckahoe Veterinary Hospital
9001 Quioccasin Road
Richmond, VA 23229
804-740-7600

Varina Veterinary Clinic
6415 Osborne Turnpike
Richmond, VA 23231
804-226-0771

Veterinary Emergency Center
3312 West Cary Street
Richmond, VA 23221
804-353-9000

Bonsack Veterinary Hospital
1620 Blue Ridge Boulevard
Roanoke, VA 24012
540-977-5520

Brandon Animal Hospital
3403 Brandon Avenue
 Southwest
Roanoke, VA 24018
540-345-8486

Cave Spring Veterinary Clinic
4538 Old Cave Spring Road
Roanoke, VA 24018
540-989-8582

North Roanoke Veterinary Hospital
5200 Peters Creek Road
 Northwest
Roanoke, VA 24019
540-563-8041

Roanoke Animal Hospital
2814 Franklin Road
 Southwest
Roanoke, VA 24014
540-343-8021

Southern Hills Animal Hospital
3500 Avenham Avenue
 Southwest
Roanoke, VA 24014
540-343-4155

Valley Animal Hospital
5146 Hildebrand Road
 Northwest
Roanoke, VA 24012
540-366-3433

Varina Veterinary Clinic
6415 Osborne Turnpike

Veterinarians to Cats
2214 Electric Road
Roanoke, VA 24018
540-989-1400

Pell Animal Clinic
1021 Pell Avenue
Rocky Mount, VA 24151
540-483-7444

Animal Clinic of Caroline
21539 Jefferson Davis
 Highway
Ruther Glen, VA 22546
804-448-1905

S

Salem Animal Hospital
3153 West Main Street
Salem, VA 24153
540-380-4638

Oaks Veterinary Clinic
14202 Benns Church
 Boulevard
Smithfield, VA 23430
757-357-2324

Rogers Veterinary Hospital
1500 South Church Street
Smithfield, VA 23430
757-357-3251

Smithfield Animal Hospital
938 South Church Street
Smithfield, VA 23430
757-357-9308

Spotsylvania Animal Hospital
9133 Courthouse Road
Spotsylvania, VA 22553
540-582-6370

Burke Forest Veterinary Clinic
6214 Rolling Road
Springfield, VA 22152
703-569-8181

Saratoga Animal Hospital
8054 Rolling Road
Springfield, VA 22153
703-455-1188

Springfield Animal Hospital
6580 Backlick Road
Springfield, VA 22150
703-451-1995

Aquia-Garrisonville Hospital
878 Garrisonville Road
Stafford, VA 22554
540-659-8140

Stafford Animal Hospital
3454 Jefferson Davis
 Highway
Stafford, VA 22554
540-659-3811

Augusta Veterinary Hospital
1003 Greenville Avenue
Staunton, VA 24401
540-885-8169

Valley Animal Hospital
555 Richmond Avenue
Staunton, VA 24401
540-885-8985

Newtown Veterinary Clinic
5005 Barley Drive
Stephens City, VA 22655
540-869-1616

Stephens City Animal Hospital
101 Highlander Road
Stephens City, VA 22655
540-869-2100

Animal Hospital of Stuarts Draft
201 North Main Street
Stuarts Draft, VA 24477
540-337-5005

Alliance Animal Hospital
1510 Holland Road
Suffolk, VA 23434
757-539-5200

Nansemond Veterinary Hospital
110 Kensington Boulevard
Suffolk, VA 23434
757-539-6371

Suffolk Animal Hospital
1232 Holland Road
Suffolk, VA 23434
757-539-1385

T

Toano Animal Clinic
100 Depot Street
Toana, VA 23168
757-566-1100

Old Dominion Veterinary Clinic
65 Boone Drive
Troutville, VA 24175
540-992-4877

V

Animal Clinic of Verona
5027 Lee Highway
Verona, VA 24482
540-248-6310

Middle River Veterinary
336 Rolla Mill Road
Verona, VA 24482
540-248-7203

Oakton-Vienna Veterinary Hospital
320 Maples Avenue East #A
Vienna, VA 22180
703-938-2800

Vienna Animal Hospital
531 Maples Avenue West
Vienna, VA 22180
703-938-2121

Vinton Veterinary Hospital
1309 East Washington Avenue
Vinton, VA 24179
540-342-7821

Acredale Animal Hospital
1200 Lake James Drive
Virginia Beach, VA 23464
757-523-6100

Aloro Pet Clinic
2212 Laskin Road
Virginia Beach, VA 23454
757-340-5040

Animal Emergency Care
1060 Lynnhaven Parkway
Virginia Beach, VA 23452
757-468-0071

Animal Medical Center of Virginia Beach
1556 Mill Dam Road
Virginia Beach, VA 23454
757-481-5213

Bay-Beach Veterinary Medical Center
4340 Virginia Beach Boulevard
Virginia Beach, VA 23452
757-340-3913

Beach Pet Hospital
237 First Colonial Road
Virginia Beach, VA 23454
757-428-3251

Birdneck Animal Hospital
508 North Birdneck Road #C
Virginia Beach, VA 23451
757-425-9426

Little Neck Animal Hospital
3259 Virginia Beach Boulevard
Virginia Beach, VA 23452
757-340-0923

Pembroke Veterinary Clinic
4548 Wishart Road
Virginia Beach, VA 23455
757-464-0169

Pet Care Veterinary Hospital
5201 Virginia Beach Boulevard #A
Virginia Beach, VA 23462
757-473-0111

Princess Anne Veterinary Hospital
2492 Holland Road
Virginia Beach, VA 23456
757-427-5201

Pungo Veterinary Clinic
1776 Prince Anne Road #I
Virginia Beach, VA 23456
757-426-6174

Owl Creek Veterinary Hospital
587 South Birdneck Road #A
Virginia Beach, VA 23451
757-428-4344

River Shores Animal Hospital
700 South Military Highway
Virginia Beach, VA 23464
757-420-3691

Sajo Farm Veterinary Hospital
1094 Diamond Springs Road
Virginia Beach, VA 23455
757-464-6009

Strawbridge Animal Hospital
2129 General Booth Boulevard #102
Virginia Beach, VA 23454
757-427-6120

Tidewater Veterinary Emergency
5425 Virginia Beach Boulevard
Virginia Beach, VA 23462
757-499-5463

Timberlake Veterinary Hospital
712 Timberlake Shopping Center
Virginia Beach, VA 23462
757-467-5090

Virginia Beach Veterinary
1700 Pleasure House Road #102
Virginia Beach, VA 23455
757-460-3308

W

Animal Care Clinic
657 Falmouth Street
Warrenton, VA 22186
540-347-7788

New Baltimore Animal Hospital
5296 Lee Highway
Warrenton, VA 22186
540-347-0964

Old Dominion Animal Clinic
236 West Lee Highway
Warrenton, VA 22186
540-347-1225

Old Waterloo Equine Clinic
7355 South Run Lane
Warrenton, VA 22186
540-347-0807

Village Veterinary Clinic
278 Broadview Avenue #A
Warrenton, VA 22186
540-347-6611

Animal Health Care Center
250 Market Avenue
Waynesboro, VA 22980
540-943-2273

Animal Hospital of Waynesboro
1009 West Main Street
Waynesboro, VA 22980
540-943-3081

Agape Animal Care
102 Tewning Road
Williamsburg, VA 23188
757-253-0656

Animal Clinic
7316 Merrimac Trail
Williamsburg, VA 23185
757-253-0812

Tidewater Equine Clinic
3516 Mott Lane #A
Williamsburg, VA 23185
757-253-8048

Apple Valley Animal Hospital
1207 Cedar Creek Grade
Winchester, VA 22602
540-678-0202

Berryville Avenue Animal Clinic
844 Berryville Avenue
Winchester, VA 22601
540-722-2665

Linden Heights Animal Hospital
274 Linden Drive
Winchester, VA 22601
540-667-4290

Plaza Pet Clinic
1855 Senseny Road
Winchester, VA 22602
540-722-3200

Professional Veterinary Service
227 Sunnyside Plaza Circle
Winchester, VA 22603
540-662-2340

Silver Spring Veterinary Hospital
241 Garber Lane
Winchester, VA 22602
540-662-2301

Winchester Animal Hospital
901 North Loudoun Street
Winchester, VA 22601
540-667-0260

Wise County Animal Hospital
404 Hurricane Road
  Northeast
Wise, VA 24293
540-328-5034

Minnieville Animal Hospital
14005 Minnieville Road
Woodbridge, VA 22193
703-680-4000

Old Bridge Veterinary Hospital
3604 Old Bridge Road
Woodbridge, VA 22192
703-494-0094

Occoquan Animal Hospital
14234 Jefferson Davis
  Highway
Woodbridge, VA 22191
703-491-1400

Ridge Lake Animal Hospital
1400 Old Bridge Road
Woodbridge, VA 22192
703-690-4949

Tacketts Mill Veterinary Hospital
12793 Harbor Drive
Woodbridge, VA 22192
703-494-8293

Woodbridge Animal Hospital
13312 Jefferson Davis
  Highway
Woodbridge, VA 22191
703-494-5191

Seven Bends Veterinary Hospital
1205 South Main Street
Woodstock, VA 22664
540-459-8387

Blue Ridge Veterinarian Service
850 Chapman Road
Wytheville, VA 24382
540-223-1000

Y

Magruder Tabb Animal Clinic
3440 Hampton Highway
Yorktown, VA 23693
757-865-6510

Yorktown Animal Hospital
2400 Fort Eustis Boulevard
Yorktown, VA 23692
757-898-3932

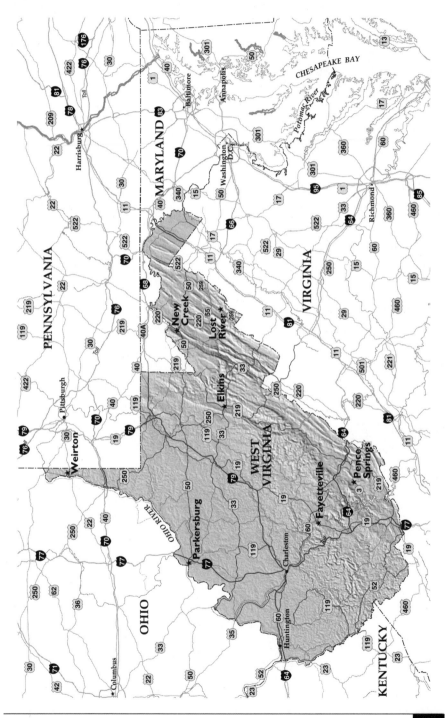

West Virginia

Cheat River Lodge

Cheat River Lodge
Route 1, Box 115
Faulkner Road
Elkins, West Virginia 26241
304-636-2301

Room Rates:	$58–$63.
Pet Charges or Deposits:	$10 per stay. Sorry, no cats.
Rated: 4 Paws 🐾🐾🐾🐾	6 guest rooms and 6 cabins on 4 miles of riverfront property. Kitchens, fireplaces and hot tubs.

T he lodge, made from cedar and fieldstone, is located on a country lane overlooking the river, with large picture windows. Rocking chairs, wicker groupings and picnic tables on the screened porches provide casual areas for lounging.

Six individual log-and-stone homes, each with its own private, 7-foot outdoor hot tub, comprise the rest of the property. Inside, you will delight in the exposed log walls and cathedral ceilings, stone hearths with glass-fronted wood stoves and fully equipped kitchens. The accommodations are well appointed and fully equipped. You will be greeted with freshly made beds and the hot tub warm and ready.

The Cheat River Lodge is located on the Cheat River in the Monongahela National Forest, six miles east of Elkins, West Virginia. Here you will find excellent hiking, biking, birding, rock climbing and cross-country and downhill ski areas. The river provides the ideal place for canoeing, tubing and fishing.

Morris Harvey House

Morris Harvey House
201 West Maple Avenue
Fayetteville, West Virginia 25840
304-574-1902

Room Rates:	$85, including full breakfast.
Pet Charges or Deposits:	Small pets only. Manager's prior approval required.
Rated: 3 Paws 🐾🐾🐾	4 guest rooms

A gentle blend of antique charm and elegance takes you back in time in this three-story historic Victorian home. Relax in the heart of the Fayetteville historic district with well-appointed guest rooms, each with its own fireplace and private bath.

A delicious, home-cooked breakfast is included in your room rate. Stroll through the garden, planted in the spectacular fleur-de-lis pattern, and notice the corresponding design on the stained glass windows located throughout the historic Morris Harvey House.

Inn at Lost River

Inn at Lost River
Mailing Address: HC 83, Box 8A2
Physical Address: Route 259 and Mill Gap Road
Lost River, West Virginia
304-897-6788
E-mail: innatlr@hardynet.com

Room Rates:	$75–$90; some rates include breakfast.
Pet Charges or Deposits:	Manager's prior approval required.
Rated: 3 Paws 🐾🐾🐾	3 guest rooms, 2 cottages and cabins.

O riginally built in the late 1800s, the Inn retains features of a turn-of-the-century farmhouse in rural West Virginia but provides all the comforts of modern life. Located just 2½ hours southwest of Washington, D.C, the Inn offers a close and comfortable retreat from the city.

The Lost River area offers many recreational opportunities for those who enjoy the outdoors including Lost River State Park and George Washington National Forest.

Thorn Run Inn

Thorn Run Inn
HC 75, Box 125
New Creek, West Virginia 26743
304-749-7733
E-mail: narope@aol.com

Room Rates:	$55–$75, including full breakfast.
Pet Charges or Deposits:	None.
Rated: 3 Paws 🐾🐾🐾	5 guest rooms on 20 acres that abuts on a Nature Conservancy preserve. Pool and outdoor hot tub and fish pond.

Thorn Run Inn is a 14-room Georgian-style brick farmhouse built in 1871. The Inn features large, colorful guest rooms, all with hardwood floors and valley views.

Situated on 20 hilly acres overlooking a mosaic of farmland and forest in the Northern Potomac Highlands, this little piece of heaven is about 18 miles northwest of Petersburg, WV. Here, people are scarce and the deer are plentiful.

A hearty, full country breakfast with gourmet coffee and baked goods made from scratch is served each morning in the dining room, on the side porch, or in the orchard. With advanced notice dinner of freshly baked breads, soups or salads, main course and freshly made seasonal desserts can be prepared for you by the owner, Robin. House specialties include her walnut and spinach lasagna and a number of African dishes.

Blennerhassett Hotel

Blennerhassett Hotel
320 Market Street
Parkersburg, West Virginia 26101
800-262-2536 ▪ 304-422-3131

Room Rates:	$69–$129, including full breakfast and complimentary newspaper. AAA, AARP, AKC and ABA discounts.
Pet Charges or Deposits:	$25 refundable deposit. Manager's prior approval required. Sorry, no cats.
Rated: 3 Paws 🐾🐾🐾	104 guest rooms and 4 suites. Use of local fitness facility. Restaurants and lounge.

Built before the turn of the century, this hotel exudes the captivating atmosphere of the gaslight era. Registered as a National Historic Landmark, the style of the hotel is seen in its rich crown moldings, authentic English doors, brass and leaded-glass chandeliers and antiques hand-carried from England.

Fine continental and regional American cuisine is enjoyed in the renowned Harman's Restaurant. For the past five consecutive years Harman's has had the distinction of being awarded AAA's 4-Diamond rating.

Pence Springs Hotel

Pence Springs Hotel
P.O. Box 90
Pence Springs, West Virginia 24962
800-826-1829 ▪ 304-445-2606
Web Site: www.wvweb.com/www/Pence_Springs_Hotel

Room Rates:	$70–$100, including full breakfast. AAA and AARP discounts.
Pet Charges or Deposits:	$15 per stay. Manager's prior approval required.
Rated: 3 Paws ❀❀❀	24 guest rooms and 9 suites on a 400-acre plantation. Restaurant.

Known as The Grand Hotel, this National Registry inn is one of the historic mineral spas of the Virginias. A premier retreat from 1897 until the Great Depression, Pence Springs was the most popular and expensive hotel in West Virginia. Now a fine country inn on a 400-acre plantation, Pence Springs Hotel has attracted national attention.

Guest rooms accommodate every need and are furnished in the style of the 1920s, all with private baths. Room rates include a full breakfast.

You can be as active or inactive as you want to be—relax on the porch with a good book, play croquet and horseshoes on the lawn, ride a bike through the surrounding countryside, ride on horseback on 15,000-year-old buffalo trails, hike along the many trails on the property, take a canoe trip on the Greenbrier River or go smallmouth bass fishing on the hotel's riverfront.

Best Western Inn at Weirton

Best Western Inn at Weirton
350 Three Springs Drive
Weirton, West Virginia 26062
800-528-1234 ▪ 304-723-5522

Room Rates:	$68–$76, including free coffee. AAA and AARP discounts.
Pet Charges or Deposits:	$10 per day. $50 refundable deposit. Small pets only.
Rated: 3 Paws 🐾🐾🐾	111 guest rooms and 4 suites. Pool and Jacuzzi. Lounge and restaurant.

When it comes to relaxation and affordable accommodations with all the amenities of home, look no further than this Best Western. Poolside service and a large pool with plenty of space to romp make soaking up the sun a favorite pastime for visitors.

Annie's Lounge provides a good backdrop for enjoying the giant screen TV, entertainment and free happy-hour hors d'oeuvres. The dining room highlights prime rib, veal and fresh seafood.

Guest rooms feature remote control TVs with HBO and ESPN channels, AM/FM radios, and computer and FAX hook-ups. The Executive Suites offer king-sized beds, TVs in both sitting rooms and bedrooms and interface capabilities for both FAX and computers.

West Virginia

Please Note: *Pets must be on a leash at all times and may be restricted to certain areas. For directions, use fees, pet charges and general information, contact the numbers listed below.*

National Forest

U.S. Forest Service
200 Sycamore Street
Elkins, West Virginia 26241-3962
800-280-2267 • 304-636-1800

Division of Tourism and Parks
State Capitol Complex
Charleston, West Virginia 25305
800-225-5982

Monogahela National Forest, located in eastern West Virginia, is a 901,000-acre park with camping, picnic areas, hiking trails, boating, a boat ramp, boat rentals, fishing, swimming, winter sports and a visitors' center. For more information, call 304-636-1800.

National River

New River Gorge, between Fayetteville and Hinton, consists of 62,000 acres of parkland with picnic areas, hiking trails, boating, fishing, swimming and a visitors' center. For more information, call 304-465-0508.

Army Corps of Engineers

BURNSVILLE

Burnsville Lake is a 970-acre park located just off Interstate 79 at the Burnsville exit. The park offers water-skiing, camping, picnic areas, boating, a boat ramp, boat rentals, fishing, swimming, hiking trails and a visitors' center.

HUNTINGTON

Beech Fork Lake is a 720-acre park located about 15 miles southeast of Huntington on State Route 152. The park offers camping, picnic areas, hiking trails, boating, a boat ramp, boat rentals, fishing, swimming and a visitors' center.

SUTTON

Sutton Lake is a 1,440-acre park 5 miles northeast of Sutton. Visitors to the park will enjoy water-skiing, camping, picnic areas, hiking trails, boating, a boat ramp, boat rentals, fishing and swimming.

WAYNE

East Lynn Lake encompasses 1,005 acres of parkland and is located 10 miles south of Wayne on State Route 37. Visitors to the park will find water-skiing, camping, picnic areas, hiking trails, boating, a boat ramp, boat rentals, fishing, swimming and a visitors' center.

WILLIAMSON

R. D. Bailey Lake is a 630-acre park 30 miles east of Williamson. It offers water-skiing, camping, picnic areas, boating, a boat ramp, boat rentals, fishing, swimming and a visitors' center.

State Parks

Division of Tourism and Parks
State Capitol Complex
Charleston, West Virginia 25305
800-225-5982

GRAFTON

Tygart Lake State Park is a 2,134-acre park located 2 miles south of Grafton on County Road 44 along the eastern bank of the Tygart River Reservoir, offering scuba diving, water-skiing, camping, picnic areas, hiking trails, boating, a boat ramp, boat rentals, fishing, swimming and a visitors' center. For more information, call 304-265-3383 or 800-225-5982.

HINTON

Bluestone Lake State Park, 15 miles southeast of Hinton on State Route 20, consists of 2,155 acres of parkland with water-skiing, camping, picnic areas, hiking trails, boating, a boat ramp, boat rentals, fishing, swimming and a visitors' center. For more information, call 304-466-0156 or 304-466-1234.

HUNTINGTON

Beech Fork State Park is a 3,981-acre park located 15 miles southeast of Huntington on State Route 152. The park offers a playground, camping, picnic areas, hiking trails, boating, a boat ramp, boat rentals, fishing and a visitors' center.

LOGAN

Chief Logan State Park is a 3,305-acre park 3 miles north of Logan off State Route 10, with outdoor drama, camping, picnic areas, fishing, swimming and hiking trails.

NEW MANCHESTER

Tomlinson Run State Park, located 2 miles north of New Manchester off State Route 8, is a 1,398-acre park. It has camping, picnic areas, hiking trails, boating, boat rentals, fishing and swimming.

WESTON

Stonewall Jackson Lake State Park, 2 miles east of Interstate 79 near Weston, offers camping, picnic areas, hiking trails, boating, a boat ramp, boat rentals, fishing and a visitors' center. For more information, call 304-296-0523.

Other Recreation Areas

Division of Tourism and Parks
State Capitol Complex
Charleston, West Virginia 25305
800-225-5982

BECKLEY

Lake Stephens is a 2,500-acre park located 9 miles west of Beckley on State Route 3. Visitors to the park will find camping, picnic areas, hiking trails, boating, a boat ramp, fishing and swimming.

BUCKHANNON

Pringle Tree, 2 miles north of Buckhannon off U.S. Highway 119 and State Route 20, consists of 4.5 acres of parkland with picnic areas, boating, a boat ramp and fishing.

MOUNT HOPE

Plum Orchard Lake, located off U.S. Highway 19 between Mount Hope and Oak Hill, offers camping, picnic areas, hiking trails, boating and fishing.

NEOLA

Lake Sherwood, 11 miles northeast of Neola on State Route 14, has camping, picnic areas, hiking trails, boating, a boat ramp, boat rentals, fishing and swimming.

OAK HILL

Plum Orchard Lake, located off U.S. Highway 19 between Mount Hope and Oak Hill, offers camping, picnic areas, hiking trails, boating and fishing.

WELLSBURG

Brook Hills Park encompasses 700 acres of parkland, 4 miles east of Wellsburg on State Route 27. Visitors will find golf, swimming, tennis, picnic areas, swimming and winter sports.

WHEELING

Oglebay Park consists of 1,500 acres, with horse rentals, picnic areas, hiking trails, boating, fishing, swimming, winter sports and a visitors' center. For more information, call 304-243-4000 or 800-624-6988.

Wheeling Park is a 406-acre park that has picnic areas, boating, swimming, winter sports and a visitors' center. For more information, call 304-242-3770.

Veterinary Care In West Virginia

A

Alderson Veterinary Service
700 Alta Drive
Alderson, WV 24910
304-445-2856

Augusta Animal Hospital
Ford Hill Road
Augusta, WV 26704
304-496-7746

B

Barboursville Veterinary Clinic
6310 Farmdale Road
Barboursville, WV 25504
304-736-8939

Olson Animal Hospital
5980 US Route 60 East
Barboursville, WV 25504
304-736-1677

Beckley Veterinary Hospital
215 Dry Hill Road
Beckley, WV 25801
304-255-4159

Raleigh County Animal Hospital
198 Ragland Road
Beckley, WV 25801
304-253-4787

Perry's Animal Hospital
112 East Dupont Avenue
Belle, WV 25015
304-949-2744

Animalia Veterinary Care
Route 522 South
Berkeley Springs, WV 25411
304-258-5819

Berkeley Springs Animal Clinic
Rural Route 4, Box 277
Berkeley Springs, WV 24511
304-258-4123

Audobon Animal Clinic
17 Chenoweth Drive
Bridgeport, WV 26330
304-842-4836

Buckhannon Animal Clinic
6 Vicksburg Road
Buckhannon, WV 26201
304-472-0323

Upshur Veterinary Hospital
Route 33 West
Buckhannon, WV 26201
304-472-6575

C

Ceredo Kenova Animal Clinic
750 C Street
Ceredo, WV 25507
304-453-6384

Hillside Veterinary Hospital
Rural Route 1, Box 331
Charles Town, WV 25414
304-728-2203

Jefferson Animal Hospital
231 North Samuel Street
Charles Town, WV 25414
304-725-0428

Animal Care Associates
840 Oakwood Road
Charleston, WV 25314
304-344-2244

Kanawha City Veterinary Hospital
5405 Maccorkle Avenue
  Southeast
Charleston, WV 25304
304-925-4974

Phillips Animal Hospital
100 Virginia Street East
Charleston, WV 25301
304-342-3330

Valley West Veterinary Hospital
210 Virginia Street West
Charleston, WV 25302
304-343-6783

Chester Veterinary Clinic
Old Route 30
Chester, WV 26034
304-387-2030

All Pets Animal Clinic
408 First Avenue
Clarksburg, WV 26301
304-624-5311

Clarksburg Veterinary Hospital
403 Milford Street
Clarksburg, WV 26301
304-623-3545

Harrison Central Veterinary
Old Bridgeport Hill Road
Clarksburg, WV 26301
304-624-9305

Mountaineer Animal Clinic
323 South Monticello Avenue
Clarksburg, WV 26301
304-622-0672

Crab Orchard Veterinary Hospital
Route 16 South
Crab Orchard, WV 25827
304-252-0110

Cross Lanes Veterinary Hospital
524 Old Goff Mountain Road
Cross Lanes, WV 25313
304-776-4501

D

Daniels Veterinary Hospital
1340 Ritter Drive
Daniels, WV 25832
304-252-4330

Dunbar Animal Hospital
217 Tenth Street
Dunbar, WV 25064
304-766-6407

E

Beverly Pike Veterinary Clinic
Chenoweth Creek Road
Elkins, WV 26241
304-636-7886

Elk Valley Veterinary Hospital
113 Frame Road
Elkview, WV 25071
304-965-7675

F

Deerfield Animal Clinic
Route 250
Fairmont, WV 26554
304-367-0784

Fairmont Veterinary Hospital
619 Gaston Avenue
Fairmont, WV 26554
304-363-0930

Mannington Animal Hospital
US Route 250
Farmington, WV 26571
304-825-1145

Faithful Friends Animal Clinic
Main Street
Franklin, WV 26807
304-358-2360

G

Central West Virginia Animal Hospital
783 State Street
Gassaway, WV 26624
304-364-5252

Grafton Animal Hospital
Route 50
Grafton, WV 26354
304-265-4850

H

Animal Care Center
1009 Chestnut Street
Henderson, WV 25106
304-675-1659

Animal Care Clinic
313 Third Avenue
Huntington, WV 25701
304-525-7629

Ayers Animal Hospital
1514 Norway Avenue
Huntington, WV 25705
304-529-6049

Cabell Veterinary Clinic
2429 Eighth Avenue
Huntington, WV 25703
304-529-3075

Guyan Animal Hospital
5602 US Route 60 East
Huntington, WV 25705
304-736-3456

Huntington Dog and Cat Hospital
200 Fifth Street West
Huntington, WV 25701
304-525-5121

Stonecrest Animal Medical Center
1 Stonecrest Drive, #1
Huntington, WV 25701
304-525-1800

Godfrey's Animal Clinic
3842 Teays Valley Rd
Hurricane, WV 25526
304-757-8781

Hurricane Animal Hospital
1 Davis Court
Hurricane, WV 25526
304-562-3321

Valley Veterinarians
3763 Teays Valley Road
Hurricane, WV 25526
304-757-8902

K

Mountain Land Animal Hospital
Route 7 West
Kingwood, WV 26537
304-329-1586

L

Fairlea Animal Hospital
Davis Stuart Road
Lewisburg, WV 24901
304-645-3550

Greenbrier Veterinary Hospital
HC 37, Box 74
Lewisburg, WV 24901
304-645-1476

Lewisburg Veterinary Hospital
US Route 60 West
Lewisburg, WV 24901
304-645-1434

Knowles Animal Hospital
615 Stratton Street
Logan, WV 25601
304-752-8387

M

Madison Animal Hospital
178 State Street
Madison, WV 25130
304-369-5100

Big Spring Animal Hospital
1530 Winchester Avenue
Martinsburg, WV 25401
304-267-2909

Martinsburg Animal Hospital
246 Warm Springs Avenue
Martinsburg, WV 25401
304-267-7468

Shenandoah Veterinary Hospital
East Moler Avenue Exit
Martinsburg, WV 25401
304-263-2112

Milton Animal Hospital
302 East Main Street
Milton, WV 25541
304-743-4039

Mineral Wells Veterinary Clinic
State Route 14
Mineral Wells, WV 26150
304-489-2799

Moorefield Animal Hospital
110 Beans Lane
Moorefield, WV 26836
304-538-7795

Animal Medical Center
460 Hartman Run Road
Morgantown, WV 26505
304-292-0126

Cheat Lake Animal Hospital
7 Mariners Plaza
Morgantown, WV 26508
304-594-1124

Easton-Avery Animal Hospital
3 Stockett Road
Morgantown, WV 26508
304-594-1283

Hillcrest Veterinary Clinic
3083 Point Marion Road
Morgantown, WV 26505
304-292-6933

Morgantown Veterinary Hospital
149 North Main Street
Morgantown, WV 26505
304-599-3111

Mountaineer Veterinary Clinic
239 Greenbag Road
Morgantown, WV 26501
304-296-1667

Paw Prints Veterinary Clinic
1745 Mileground Road
Morgantown, WV 26505
304-296-7387

Companion Animal Clinic
Route 250
Moundsville, WV 26041
304-845-7815

Ohio Valley Animal Care Center
901 Lockwood Avenue
Moundsville, WV 26041
304-845-7007

Crossroads Small Animal Clinic
124 American Camper Road
Mount Hope, WV 25880
304-877-6270

N

Riverside Animal Clinic
1004 North State Route 2
New Martinsville, WV 26155
304-455-3990

Valley Animal Clinic
State Route 2
New Martinsville, WV 26155
304-455-3511

New River Animal Hospital
Route 87, Box 2A
Nimitz, WV 25978
304-466-0251

O

Oak Hill Animal Hospital
Lochgelly Road
Oak Hill, WV 25901
304-465-8267

Oceana Animal Clinic
Main Street
Oceana, WV 24870
304-682-4677

P

**Animal House Small
Animal Clinic**
1217 Murdoch Avenue
Parkersburg, WV 26101
304-422-3352

Kincaid Animal Hospital
1602 Blizzard Drive
Parkersburg, WV 26101
304-422-6981

**Parkersburg Veterinary
Hospital**
1504 36th Street
Parkersburg, WV 26104
304-422-6971

**Valley Mills Animal
Hospital**
8426 Emerson Avenue
Parkersburg, WV 26101
304-464-4018

**Mill Creek Animal
Hospital**
North Mill Creek Road
Petersburg, WV 26847
304-257-4291

**Town and Country
Veterinary Center**
3305 Jackson Avenue
Point Pleasant, WV 25550
304-675-2441

Animal Care Hospital
1 Grand Veterinary Place
Princeton, WV 24740
304-425-7387

R

**Apple Tree Animal
Clinic**
900 North Mildred Street
Ranson, WV 25438
304-725-8840

**Valley Veterinary
Service**
515 East Fifth Avenue
Ranson, WV 25438
304-725-1471

**Mountain Spring
Veterinary Service**
52 Potomac Street South
Ridgeley, WV 26753
304-728-0093

**Town and Country
Veterinary Center**
Rural Route 1, Box 139
Ripley, WV 25271
304-372-5709

**Augusta Animal
Hospital**
75 West Gravel Lane
Romney, WV 26757
304-822-3751

S

**Academy Animal
Hospital**
2374 Cleveland Avenue
Saint Albans, WV 25177
304-727-2442

**Gateway Animal
Veterinary Hospital**
55 Maccorkle Avenue
Saint Albans, WV 25177
304-727-4331

**Buckeye Run Veterinary
Clinic**
Buckeye Run
Salem, WV 26426
304-782-4011

**Pocatalico Animal
Hospital**
6440 Starlight Drive
Sissonville, WV 25320
304-984-0064

**Avalon Dog and Cat
Hospital**
712 Maccorkle Avenue
Southwest
South Charleston, WV 25303
304-744-4721

Cain Veterinary Clinic
638 Arnoldsburg Road
Spencer, WV 25276
304-927-3528

**Nicholas Animal
Hospital**
325 Fairview Heights Road
Summersville, WV 26651
304-872-5030

U

**Seven Springs
Veterinary Clinic**
Shanklin Avenue
Union, WV 24983
304-772-5727

W

**Brooke Hills Animal
Hospital**
1230 Washington Pike
Wellsburg, WV 26070
304-737-2528

**Wellsburg Animal
Hospital**
98 Seventh Street
Wellsburg, WV 26070
304-737-2673

**Doddridge Animal
Hospital**
206 Cheuvront Avenue
West Union, WV 26456
304-873-2250

**Weston Veterinary
Hospital**
Sunset Acres
Weston, WV 26452
304-269-3288

**Ohio Valley Animal Care
Center**
86 27th Street
Wheeling, WV 26003
304-233-7007

**Town and Country
Animal Hospital**
831 Old Fairmont Pike
Wheeling, WV 26003
304-242-9575

**Tug Valley Veterinary
Clinic**
102 West Third Avenue
Williamson, WV 25661
304-235-2838

**Williamson Animal
Hospital**
202 East Fourth Avenue
Williamson, WV 25661
304-235-3500

**Country Roads
Veterinary Hospital**
3240 Winfield Road
Winfield, WV 25213
304-586-0700

Index

About the Author...
From a Dog's Point of View

Dreamer Dawg, office manager and "cover girl" for Bon Vivant Press, is an eleven-year-young Labrador Retriever. When not exploring the food and lodging for each regional book, you can find Dreamer relaxing onboard her boat in the Monterey harbor or running with the horses in Pebble Beach.

Owners Kathleen & Robert Fish, authors of the popular "Secrets" series, have researched and written twenty-six award-winning cookbooks and travel books, and are always on the lookout for lodgings with style and character.

Other titles in the Pets Welcome™ series are *Pets Welcome™ California, Pets Welcome™ America's South, Pets Welcome™ New England and New York, Pets Welcome™ Pacific Northwest, Pets Welcome™ Southwest* and *Pets Welcome™ National Edition.*

Bon Vivant Press

A division of The Millennium Publishing Group
PO Box 1994
Monterey, CA 93942
800-524-6826 • 831-373-0592 • 831-373-3567 FAX • Website: http://www.millpub.com

Send _____ copies of **Pets Welcome America's South** at $15.95 each.

Send _____ copies of **Pets Welcome California** at $15.95 each.

Send _____ copies of **Pets Welcome Mid-Atlantic and Chesapeake** at $15.95 each.

Send _____ copies of **Pets Welcome New England and New York** at $15.95 each.

Send _____ copies of **Pets Welcome Pacific Northwest** at $15.95 each.

Send _____ copies of **Pets Welcome Southwest** at $15.95 each.

Send _____ copies of **Pets Welcome National Edition** at $19.95 each.

Add $4.50 postage and handling for the first book ordered and $1.50 for each additional book.
Please add 7.25% sales tax per book, for those books shipped to California addresses.

Please charge my ☐ Visa   # _____
                          ☐ MasterCard

Expiration date _____ Signature_____

Enclosed is my check for _____

Name_____

Address _____

City_____ State _____ ZIP_____

☐ This is a gift. Send directly to:

Name_____

Address _____

City_____ State _____ ZIP_____

☐ Autographed by the author

Autographed to_____

Notes

Bon Vivant Press

A division of The Millennium Publishing Group
PO Box 1994 • Monterey, CA 93942
800-524-6826 • 831-373-0592 • 831-373-3567 FAX • Website: http://www.millpub.com

Send _____ copies of **Cooking With the Masters of Food & Wine** at $34.95 each.
Send _____ copies of **The Elegant Martini** at $17.95 each.
Send _____ copies of **Cooking Secrets from Mid-Atlantic and Chesapeake** at $19.95 each.
Send _____ copies of **Vegetarian Pleasures** at $19.95 each.
Send _____ copies of **California Wine Country Cooking Secrets** at $14.95 each.
Send _____ copies of **Cape Cod's Cooking Secrets** at $14.95 each.
Send _____ copies of **Cooking Secrets for Healthy Living** at $15.95 each.
Send _____ copies of **Cooking Secrets From America's South** at $15.95 each.
Send _____ copies of **Cooking Secrets From Around the World** at $15.95 each.
Send _____ copies of **Florida's Cooking Secrets** at $15.95 each.
Send _____ copies of **Jewish Cooking Secrets From Here and Far** at $14.95 each.
Send _____ copies of **Louisiana's Cooking Secrets** at $15.95 each.
Send _____ copies of **Monterey's Cooking Secrets** at $13.95 each.
Send _____ copies of **New England's Cooking Secrets** at $14.95 each.
Send _____ copies of **Pacific Northwest Cooking Secrets** at $15.95 each.
Send _____ copies of **San Francisco's Cooking Secrets** at $13.95 each.
Send _____ copies of **The Gardener's Cookbook** at $15.95 each.
Send _____ copies of **The Great California Cookbook** at $14.95 each.
Send _____ copies of **The Great Vegetarian Cookbook** at $15.95 each.

Add $4.50 postage and handling for the first book ordered and $1.50 for each additional book. Please add 7.25% sales tax per book, for those books shipped to California addresses.

Please charge my ☐ Visa   ☐ MasterCard   # _____

Expiration date _____ Signature _____

Enclosed is my check for _____

Name _____

Address _____

City _____ State _____ ZIP _____

☐ **This is a gift. Send directly to:**

Name _____

Address _____

City _____ State _____ ZIP _____

☐ **Autographed by the author**
Autographed to _____

Notes

Reader's Response Card

Please return to:
   Bon Vivant Press
   P.O. Box 1994
   Monterey, CA 93942
   Fax your information to: (831) 373-3567

Please assist us in updating our next edition. If you have discovered an interesting or charming inn, hotel, guest ranch or spa in the Mid-Atlantic or Chesapeake area that allows pets, or any special neighborhood parks that allow pets, please let us hear from you and include the following information:

Type of lodging (check one):
   ☐ Bed and Breakfast   ☐ Hotel   ☐ Inn   ☐ Guest Ranch   ☐ Spa

Lodging Name _____

Lodging Address _____

City _____ State _____ ZIP _____

Phone (_____) _____

Comments _____

_____

_____

Park Name _____

Address or Cross Streets _____

City _____ State _____ ZIP _____

Phone: (if known) (_____) _____ Leashes required? Yes | No

Comments _____

_____

We appreciate your assistance. It is wonderful to discover new and interesting places to take your pets. If you have discovered an interesting or charming inns, hotels, guest ranches, or spas in other states that allows pets, and any special neighborhood parks, please let us hear know for future editions.

Notes